MW01008301

BEING
AS
COMMUNION

Studies in Personhood and the Church

CONTEMPORARY GREEK THEOLOGIANS

NUMBER FOUR

EDITORIAL COMMITTEE
Professor Christos Yannaras
Bishop Kallistos of Diokleia
Costa Carras

JOHN D. ZIZIOULAS

BEING AS COMMUNION

Studies in Personhood and the Church

with a Foreword by

JOHN MEYENDORFF

ST VLADIMIR'S SEMINARY PRESS
CRESTWOOD, NEW YORK

Library of Congress Cataloging-in-Publication Data

Zizioulas, Jean, 1931–
    Being as communion
    (Contemporary Greek theologians; no. 4)
    Bibliography: p.
    Includes index.
        1. Church—Addresses, essays, lectures.   2. Orthodox
    Eastern Church—Doctrines—Addresses, essays, lectures.   I.
    Title.   II. Series
    BX323.Z59   1985   262   85-2134
    ISBN 0-88141-029-2

BEING AS COMMUNION

Copyright © 1985 by
St Vladimir's Seminary Press
575 Scarsdale Road, Crestwood, NY 10707
1-800-204-2665   www.svspress.com

All Rights Reserved

ISBN 978-0-88141-029-7

PRINTED IN THE UNITED STATES OF AMERICA

For Costa and Lydia Carras

Contents

Foreword

One of the major and permanent goals of a theologian, who wants to express the Christian faith, as it is held by the Orthodox Catholic Tradition, is to be able to do justice to history as well as to "systematic" thought addressed to contemporaries. In most cases, however, historians limit themselves to history establishing the facts of the past and leaving open the issue of objective truth. Systematic theologians, on the contrary, neglect the rigorous demands of historical criticism, and use the past merely as a source of proof-texts, selected by them to support their own, so often arbitrary interpretation of the truth.

This dichotomy is particularly dangerous for Orthodox theology, which simply ceases to be Orthodox if it either neglects Tradition, uncovered in history, or forgets the truth, which is its *raison d'être*.

The present work by John Zizioulas should, I believe, be seen as important not only because it obviously transcends the dichotomy referred to above, but also because it succeeds brilliantly in showing that the Orthodox doctrines of man and of the Church cannot be compartmentalized in neatly separate sections of theological science—"theology," "anthropology," "ecclesiology"—but are simply meaningless if approached separately. Only together do they reflect the true "mind of Christ" of which St Paul wrote, the "true gnosis" defended by St Irenaeus, and the authentic experience of God, called for by the Fathers of later centuries.

Abundant in the various languages of the Balkans and Eastern Europe, Orthodox theological literature has become, in the last two decades, much more accessible in English as well. It includes general introductions to Orthodox history and doctrine, some important specialized studies and monographs, and a great abundance of texts related to spirituality. In *Being As Communion*, attentive readers will discover how all these dispersed elements of Tradition are linked to the Gospel itself, as it was lived by the early Christian community and expressed by the great Fathers. They will also see that it transcends historical limitations and is immediately relevant to today's problems.

The book is not always easy reading. It presupposes some awareness of contemporary theological trends. Zizioulas' disciplined and critical mind finds itself in constant dialogue with others, either giving them credit, or critizing them—mostly on grounds of onesidedness, i.e. on the ground that they lack an authentically "catholic" grasp of ecclesial reality. His thought is, in many ways, close to that of the late Father Nicholas Afanasiev—well known exponent of "eucharistic ecclesiology"—but how sharp (and in my opinion, how justified) is also Zizioulas' criticism of Afanasiev! Was not Afanasiev somehow overlooking the trinitarian and anthropological dimension of ecclesiology, focusing his thought on the "local" nature of the eucharistic community and, somewhat, excluding the problems of truth and of the universal presuppositions of unity?

I hope that readers will not be set back by the technical character of this book. John Zizioulas is actually dealing with the most contemporary, the most urgent, the most existential issues facing the Orthodox Church today. Unless the visible reality of our Church life becomes consistent with that communion which is revealed to us in the Eucharist, unless our ecclesiastical structures—especially here in the West—conform themselves to that which the Church truly is, unless the eucharistic nature of the Church is freed from under the facade of anachronism, and ethnic politics, which hide it today, no ecumenical witness, no authentic mission to the world is possible.

Born in Greece in 1931, John Zizioulas is a graduate of the Theological Faculty of the University of Athens, where he also later received a degree of Doctor of Theology, with a thesis on *The Unity of the Church in the Eucharist and the Bishop during the First Three Centuries* (Athens, 1965). He also studied Patristics at Harvard and was a Fellow at Dumbarton Oaks Center for Byzantine Studies. For several years, he served on the staff of the Commission on Faith and Order, World Council of Churches, in Geneva and was gradually recognized as one of the most influential Orthodox theologians of the younger generation. As a representative of the ecumenical patriarchate, he is a member of the International Commission for dialogue with Roman Catholicism. His ecumenical involvement has led him to publish a number of articles and studies in various periodicals. Some of these articles appeared in the French volume *L'Etre ecclésial* (Paris, Labor et Fides, 1981). These same articles, with important additions are included in this volume.

At present, John Zizioulas is professor of theology at the University of Glasgow. He was also recently appointed to a part-time position at the University of Thessalonica.

— *John Meyendorff*

Preface

Certain parts of this book have already appeared in French in my *L'être ecclésial* (Labor et Fides, Geneva, 1981). The rest are published for the first time here in English. In both cases the text has undergone special revision in view of the present English edition.

I should like to express warmest thanks to my friends, the Reverend John Clarke and Mrs Elizabeth Templeton for their invaluable help in translating from the French the Introduction of this book, and to Father Norman Russell for translating so brilliantly chapter I from the original Greek. My special gratitude is due to Dr Peter J. Bussey, of the Department of Natural Philosophy of the University of Glasgow, for the interest he has shown in chapter II of this book both as a scientist and as Christian. I am indebted to him for kindly taking the initiative to translate himself this chapter from French into English.

Finally, I wish to thank most warmly Mr Costa Carras for the great amount of time and work he contributed in arranging for the publication of this book. To him and to his wife Lydia I dedicate this book with gratitude for their unfailing friendship over the last years.

J.D.Z.

Introduction

The Church is not simply an institution. She is a "mode of existence," *a way of being*. The mystery of the Church, even in its institutional dimension, is deeply bound to the being of man, to the being of the world and to the very being of God. In virtue of this bond, so characteristic of patristic thought, ecclesiology assumes a marked importance, not only for all aspects of theology, but also for the existential needs of man in every age.

In the first place, ecclesial being is bound to the very being of God. From the fact that a human being is a member of the Church, he becomes an "image of God," he exists as God Himself exists, he takes on God's "way of being." This way of being is not a moral attainment, something that man *accomplishes*. It is a way of *relationship* with the world, with other people and with God, an event of *communion,* and that is why it cannot be realized as the achievement of an *individual,* but only as an *ecclesial* fact.

However, for the Church to present this way of existence, she must herself be an image of the way in which God exists. Her entire structure, her ministries etc. must express this way of existence. And that means, above all else, that the Church must have a right faith, a correct vision with respect to the being of God. Orthodoxy concerning the being of God is not a luxury for the Church and for man: it is an existential necessity.

* * *

During the patristic period, there was scarcely mention of the being of the Church, whilst much was made of the being of God. The question that preoccupied the Fathers was not to know if God existed or not—the existence of God was a "given" for nearly all men of this period, Christians or pagans. The question which tormented entire generations was rather: *how* he existed. And such a question had direct consequences as much for the Church as for man, since both were considered as "images of God."

To answer the question about the being of God, during the patristic period, was not easy. The greatest difficulty stemmed from ancient Greek ontology which was fundamentally monistic: the being of the world and the being of God formed, for the ancient Greeks, an unbreakable unity. That linked together the being of God and the being of the world, while biblical faith proclaimed God to be absolutely free with regard to the world. The Platonic conception of the creator God did not satisfy the Fathers of the Church, and this, precisely because the doctrine of creation from pre-existing matter limited divine freedom. So it was necessary to find an ontology that avoided the monistic Greek philosophy as much as the "gulf" between God and the world taught by the gnostic systems— the other great danger of this period. The creation of this ontology was perhaps the greatest philosophical achievement of patristic thought.

The *ecclesial* experience of the Fathers played a decisive role in breaking ontological monism and avoiding the gnostic "gulf" between God and the world. The fact that neither the apologists, such as Justin Martyr, nor the Alexandrian catechetical theologians, such as the celebrated Clement and Origen, could completely avoid the trap of the ontological monism of Greek thought is not accidental: they were above all "doctors," academic theologians interested principally in Christianity as "revelation." By contrast, the bishops of this period, pastoral theologians such as St Ignatius of Antioch and above all St Irenaeus and later St Athanasius, approached the being of God through the experience of the ecclesial community, of *ecclesial being*. This experience revealed something very important: the being of God could be known only through personal relationships and personal love. Being means life, and life means *communion*.

This ontology, which came out of the eucharistic experience of the Church, guided the Fathers in working out their doctrine of the being of God, a doctrine formulated above all by Athanasius of Alexandria and the Cappadocian Fathers, Basil the Great, Gregory of Nazianzus and Gregory of Nyssa. Below, in brief, is the result of this important philosophical development which would never have been possible without the experience of ecclsial being, and without which ecclesiology would lose its deep existential meaning.

The being of God is a relational being: without the concept of communion it would not be possible to speak of the being of God. The tautology "God is God" says nothing about ontology, just as the logical affirmation A = A is a dead logic and consequently a denial of being which is life. It would be unthinkable to speak of the "one God" before speaking of the God who is "communion," that is to say, of the Holy Trinity. The Holy Trinity is a *primordial* ontological concept and not a notion which is added to the divine substance or rather which follows it, as is the case in the dogmatic manuals of the West and, alas, in those of the East in modern times. The substance of God, "God," has no ontological content, no true being, apart from communion.

In this way, communion becomes an ontological concept in patristic thought. Nothing in existence is conceivable in itself, as an individual, such as the τόδε τί of Aristotle, since even God exists thanks to an event of communion. In this manner the ancient world heard for the first time that it is communion which makes beings "be": nothing exists without it, not even God.

But this communion is not a relationship understood for its own sake, an existential structure which supplants "nature" or "substance" in its primordial ontological role—something reminiscent of the structure of existence met in the thought of Martin Buber. Just like "substance," "communion" does not exist by itself: it is the *Father* who is the "cause" of it. This thesis of the Cappadocians that introduced the concept of "cause" into the being of God assumed an incalculable importance. For it meant that the ultimate ontological category which makes something really *be,* is neither an impersonal

and incommunicable "substance," nor a structure of communion existing by itself or imposed by necessity, but rather
the *person*. The fact that God owes His existence to the Father,
that is to a person, means (a) that His "substance," His
being, does not constrain Him (God does not exist because He
cannot but exist), and (b) that communion is not a constraining structure for His existence (God is not in communion,
does not love, because He cannot but be in communion and
love). The fact that God exists because of the Father shows
that His existence, His being is the consequence of a free
person; which means, in the last analysis, that not only communion but also *freedom*, the free person, constitutes true
being. True being comes only from the free person, from the
person who loves freely—that is, who freely affirms his being,
his identity, by means of an event of communion with other
persons.

In this way the discussion of the being of God leads patristic thought to the following theses, which are fundamentally
bound up with ecclesiology as well as ontology:

(a) There is no true being without communion. Nothing
exists as an "individual," conceivable in itself. Communion
is an ontological category.

(b) Communion which does not come from a "hypostasis,"
that is, a concrete and free person, and which does not lead
to "hypostases," that is concrete and free persons, is not an
"image" of the being of God. The person cannot exist without
communion; but every form of communion which denies or
suppresses the person, is inadmissible.

This theology of the person, which appeared for the first
time in history through the patristic vision of the being of God,
could never have become a live experience for man without
the mystery of the Church. Humanism or sociology could
struggle as much as they wished to affirm the importance of
man. The existentialist philosophers, however, have shown
in our day—with an intellectual honesty that makes them
worthy of the name of philosopher—that, humanly speaking,
the person as an absolute ontological freedom remains a quest
without fulfilment. Between the being of God and that of
man remains the gulf of creaturehood, and creaturehood means

precisely this: the being of each human person is *given* to him; consequently, the human person is not able to free himself absolutely from his "nature" or from his "substance," from what biological laws dictate to him, without bringing about his annihilation. And even when he lives the event of communion either in the form of love or of social and political life, he is obliged in the last analysis, if he wants to survive, to relativize his freedom, to submit to certain natural and social "givens." The demand of the person for absolute freedom involves a "new birth," a birth "from on high," a *baptism*. And it is precisely the ecclesial being which "hypostasizes" the person according to God's way of being. That is what makes the Church the image of the Triune God.

* * *

But patristic theology insisted from its origins on something very significant: man can approach God only through the Son and in the Holy Spirit. Ecclesiology which uses the notion of the "image of God" cannot be founded simply on triadology. The fact that man in the Church is the "image of God" is due to the *economy* of the Holy Trinity, that is, the work of Christ and the Spirit in *history*. This economy is the *basis* of ecclesiology, without being the *goal* of it. The Church is built by the historical work of the divine economy but leads finally to the vision of God "as He is," to the vision of the Triune God in his eternal existence.

This meta-historical, eschatological and iconological dimension of the Church is characteristic of the Eastern tradition, which lives and teaches its theology liturgically; it contemplates the being of God and the being of the Church with the eyes of worship, principally of eucharistic worship, image of the *"eschata"* par excellence. It is for that reason that Orthodoxy is often thought of, or presented by its spokesmen, as a sort of Christian Platonism, as a vision of future or heavenly things without an interest in history and its problems. By contrast, Western theology tends to limit ecclesiology (and actually even the whole of theology) to the historical content of the faith—to the economy—and to project realities belonging to history and time into the eternal existence of God. In this way the dialectic of God and the world, the uncreated and the created, history and the *eschata* is lost. The Church ends by being completely "historicized"; it ceases to be the manifestation of the *eschata* and becomes the image of this world and of historical realities. Ecclesial being and the being of God are no longer organically bound; ecclesiology no longer has need of "theo-logy" to function. Orthodox theology runs the danger of historically disincarnating the Church; by contrast, the West risks tying it primarily to history, either in the form of an extreme Christocentrism—an *imitatio Christi*—lacking the essential influence of pneumatology or in the form of a social activism or moralism which tries to play in the Church the role of the image of God. Consequently, the two theologies, Eastern and Western, need to meet in depth, to recover the authentic patristic synthesis which will protect them from the above dangers. Ecclesial being must never separate itself from the absolute demands of the being of God—that is, its eschatological nature—nor from history. The institutional dimension of the Church must always incarnate its eschatological nature without annulling the dialectic of this age and the age to come, the uncreated and the created, the being of God and that of man and the world.

*   *   *

But how can we draw together ecclesial being and the being of God, history and eschatology, without destroying their dialectical relationship? To achieve this we need to find again the lost consciousness of the primitive Church concerning the decisive importance of the *eucharist* in ecclesiology.

The rediscovery of this consciousness, lost in the tortuous paths of medieval scholasticism and the "Babylonian captivity" of modern Orthodoxy, presupposes that we give up envisaging the eucharist as one sacrament among many, as an objective act or a "means of grace" "used" or "administered" by the Church. The ancient understanding of the eucharist—common in its general lines until about the twelfth century to both East and West—was very different. The celebration of the eucharist by the primitive Church was, above all, the gathering of the people of God ἐπὶ τὸ αὐτό, that is, both the manifestation and the realization of the Church. Its celebration on Sunday—the day of the *eschata*—as well as all its liturgical content testified that during the eucharist, the Church did not live only by the memory of a historical fact—the Last Supper and the earthly life of Christ, including the cross and the resurrection—but it accomplished an *eschatological* act. It was in the eucharist that the Church would contemplate her eschatological nature, would taste the very life of the Holy Trinity; in other words she would realize man's true being as image of God's own being. All the fundamental elements which constituted her historical existence and structure had, by necessity, to pass through the eucharistic community to be "sure" (according to Ignatius of Antioch) or "valid" and "canonical" (according to the terminology of contemporary canon law), that is, to be ecclesiologically *true*. No ordination to fundamental and structural ministries of the Church took place outside the eucharistic community. It was there, in the presence of all the people of God and of all the orders, in an event of free communion, that the Holy Spirit distributed gifts "by constituting the whole structure of the Church." Thus the eucharist was not the act of a pre-existing Church; it was an event *constitutive* of the being of the Church, enabling the Church to *be*. The eucharist *constituted* the Church's being.

Consequently, the eucharist had the unique privilege of reuniting in one whole, in one unique experience, the work of Christ and that of the Holy Spirit. It expressed the eschatological vision through historical realities by combining in the ecclesial life the institutional with the charismatic elements. For it was only in the eucharist that the dialectical relationship between God and the world, between the *eschata* and history, was preserved without creating dangerous polarizations and dichotomies. This is because:

(a) The eucharist manifests the *historical* form of the divine economy, all that which was "transmitted" (cf. I Cor. 10:23: eucharist = "tradition") through the life, the death and the resurrection of the Lord, as well as through the "form" of bread and wine and a "structure" practically unchanged since the night of the Last Supper. The eucharist realizes in the course of history the continuity that links each Church to the first apostolic communities and to the historical Christ: in short, all that was *instituted* and is *transmitted.* The eucharist is thus the affirmation *par excellence* of history, the sanctification of time, by manifesting the Church as historical reality, as an *institution.*

(b) But a eucharist founded uniquely on history and manifesting the Church as simply "institution" is not the true eucharist. It might be said, by paraphrasing the biblical sentence, that "history kills, it is the Spirit who gives life." The epiclesis and the presence of the Holy Spirit mean that in the eucharist the being of the Church is not founded simply on its historical and institutional base, but that it dilates history and time to the infinite dimensions of the *eschata,* and it is that which forms the specific work of the Holy Spirit. The eucharistic community makes the Church eschatological. It frees it from the causality of natural and historical events, from limitations which are the result of the individualism implied in our natural biological existence. It gives it the taste of eternal life as love and communion, as the image of the being of God. The eucharist, as distinct from other expressions of ecclesial life, is unthinkable without the gathering of the whole Church in one place, that is, without an event of *communion;* consequently, it manifests the Church not simply as something instituted, that is, historically *given,* but also as something *con-stituted,* that is constantly realized as an event of free communion, prefiguring the divine life and the Kingdom to come. In ecclesiology, the polarization between "institution" and "event" is avoided thanks to a correct understanding of the eucharist: Christ and history give to the Church her being, which becomes *true being* each time that the Spirit con-stitutes the eucharistic community as Church. In this way, the eucharist is not a "sacrament," something parallel to the divine word: it is the eschatologization of the historical word, the voice of the historical Christ, the voice of the Holy Scripture which comes to us, no longer simply as "doctrine" through history, but as life and *being* through the *eschata.* It is not the sacrament completing the word, but rather the word becoming flesh, the risen Body of the Logos.

* * *

Through the studies of this volume, the reader will easily recognize the fundamental presuppositions of "eucharistic ecclesiology." Since the late Fr Nicholas Afanasiev, a modern Orthodox theologian, published his well known thesis, many Western theologians know Orthodoxy in the form of this "eucharistic ecclesiology." However the reader who wants to study the present texts with attention and to place them in the light of the history of theology will certainly discover some fundamental differences from this "eucharistic ecclesiology." It is therefore necessary to be aware in what important respects the author of these studies wishes to go further than Afanasiev, or to disassociate his own opinions from the latter, without either underestimating or minimizing the importance of this Russian theologian and those who have faithfully followed him.

First of all, the preceding pages have made clear the desire of the author of this book to enlarge, as much as possible, the horizon of ecclesiology in order to relate the theology of the Church to its philosophical and ontological implications as well as to the rest of theology. It is certain that such a project, to be properly carried out, demands a work of synthesis rather than a collection of studies as is the case in this present volume. However, in the first two chapters the efforts of the author seek to show that the mystery of the Church, and more especially its eucharistic realization and expression, are very deeply bound to the entirety of theology with its existential implications. That must be stated so as to distance the present studies from the opinion that eucharistic ecclesiology is founded simply on the concept or on the celebration of a sacramental act. For the opinion frequently recurs among a great many Western Christians as well as among Orthodox, in referring to eucharistic ecclesiology, that Orthodox ecclesiology is only a projection of the mystery of the Church into sacramental categories: a sacramentalization of theology. And

in effect, such an impression appears inevitable if we do not
go beyond what eucharistic ecclesiology has said up until now,
if we do not try to widen both our theological and philosophical horizons.

Furthermore, eucharistic ecclesiology such as has been developed by Fr Afanasiev and his followers raises serious
problems, and because of this it is in need of fundamental
correction. The principle "wherever the eucharist is, there is
the Church" on which this ecclesiology is built, tends to lead
towards two basic errors that Fr Afanasiev did not avoid, any
more than those who have faithfully followed him.

The first of these errors consists in considering even the
parish where the eucharist takes place as a complete and
"catholic" Church. Several Orthodox, following Afanasiev,
have come to this conclusion without recognizing that they are
raising in a very acute manner the entire problem of the
structure of the Church. The reason is the following: if a
local Church comprises only a single eucharistic parish-com-
munity, as must have been the case in the primitive Church,
it is then possible to speak of a complete and "catholic"
Church, given that it fulfils all the conditions of catholicity: a
gathering of *all the members* of the Church of one place (so
an overcoming of all kinds of division: natural, social, cultural etc.) in the presence of *all the ministers,* including the
college of presbyters with the *bishop* at its head. But when a
eucharistic community does not meet these conditions, how
can it be called a complete and "catholic" Church? The parish,
as it has been formed in the course of history, does *not* include
all the faithful of a place, nor all the presbyterium with the
bishop at its head. Consequently, in spite of the fact that the
eucharist is celebrated there, the parish is not a complete and
"catholic" Church. But then, does the principle of eucharistic
ecclesiology "wherever the eucharist is, there is the Church"
find itself weakened? Not necessarily, but it needs a new inter-
pertation so as to manifest the correct relationship between the
parish and the diocese, between the eucharist and the Church.

The other great problem created by "eucharistic ecclesiology" as Fr Afanasiev has developed it concerns the relationship between the local Church and the Church "universal."

The eucharistic community envisaged in its parochial or even episcopal form is necessarily *local*. The principle "wherever the eucharist is, there is the Church" risks suggesting the idea that each Church could, *independently of other local Churches,* be the "one, holy, catholic and apostolic Church." Here there is a need for special attention and creative theological work to keep an adequate balance between the "local Church" and the "universal Church." Roman Catholic ecclesiology before Vatican II (which drew attention to the importance of the local Church) tended to identify the "catholic Church" with the "universal Church" (an identification which had already begun in the West with Augustine), thus considering the local Church as simply a "part" of the Church. This tendency has begun to fade a little, at least among certain groups of Roman Catholic theologians, but it remains an open question. On the other hand, in certain Protestant churches, the local Church (whose meaning is not always clear) retains priority and almost exhausts the concept of Church. Several Orthodox theologians faithful to the doctrine of eucharistic ecclesiology —Afanasiev had already given such an interpretation—have an equal tendency to give priority to the local Church. Others, by contrast, basically following Roman Catholic ecclesiology before Vatican II, refuse to accept both the catholicity of the local Church and eucharistic ecclesiology, which they regard as responsible for an inadmissible "localism" in ecclesiology.

It is clear that we must steer towards a third solution, which would justify eucharistic ecclesiology without carrying with it the risk of "localism." And it is the eucharist itself which will guide us in this, for, by its nature, it expresses simultaneously both the "localization" and the "universalization" of the mystery of the Church, that is the transcending of both "localism" and "universalism." It is in this direction that the studies of this volume would wish to point the reader.

* * *

These studies are not intended to be simply a contribution to the theological dialogue between Orthodox. Written in the West on the occasion of different international and ecumenical theological conferences, they presuppose a certain knowledge of the theological problems which today preoccupy the Western world. Situated in the context of Western theological problematic, they are motivated by two basic concerns: the first consists in detaching Western theology from the confessional mentality with which it habitually approaches Orthodoxy, by considering it as something "exotic," different, "worth the trouble" of being known. If Orthodoxy is only this sort of "interesting" subject, provoking the curiosity and enriching merely the knowledge of Western theologians, it would be better that it stop being presented: it has played this role enough up until now and accomplished this "task." These studies are addressed to the reader who seeks in Orthodox theology the dimension of the faith of the Greek Fathers, a dimension necessary to the *catholicity* of the faith of the Church and to the *existential* implications of Christian doctrine and of the ecclesial institution. They are addressed to the Western Christian who feels, as it were, "amputated" since the East and the West followed their different and autonomous paths.

As for the second concern of these texts, it is a result and a consequence of the first: it provokes and invites contemporary theology to work with a view to a synthesis between the two theologies, Eastern and Western. It is of course true that, in some respects, these two theologies seem incompatible. That is due, among other things, to the independent historical roads followed by East and West since the great schism or perhaps even earlier. However, this was not the case during the early patristic period. As the late Fr Georges Florovsky liked to repeat, the authentic catholicity of the Church must include both the West and the East.

It may be said in conclusion that these studies are intended to offer their contribution to a "neopatristic synthesis" capable of leading the West and the East nearer to their common roots, in the context of the existential quest of modern man. This object may perhaps justify their appearance in the shape of this volume.

1.

Personhood and Being

Respect for man's "personal identity" is perhaps the most important ideal of our time. The attempt of contemporary humanism to supplant Christianity in whatever concerns the dignity of man has succeeded in detaching the concept of the person from theology and uniting it with the idea of an autonomous morality or with an existential philosophy which is purely humanistic. Thus, although the person and "personal identity" are widely discussed nowadays as a supreme ideal, nobody seems to recognize that *historically* as well as *existentially* the concept of the person is indissolubly bound up with theology. Within the very narrow limits of this study an attempt will be made to show how deep and indestructible is the bond that unites the concept of the person with patristic theology and ecclesiology. The person both as a concept and as a living reality is purely the product of patristic thought. Without this, the deepest meaning of personhood can neither be grasped nor justified.

I. *From Mask to Person:*
    The Birth of an Ontology of Personhood

1. Many writers have represented ancient Greek thought as essentially "non-personal."[1] In its Platonic variation, every-

[1]The most categorical, though undoubtedly somewhat one-sided and exaggerated statement of this view, is to be found in the following words of the modern Russian scholar, A. Th. Losev, based on the study of Platonism and inspired by Hegel's interpretation of classical Greek culture through ancient

thing concrete and "individual" is ultimately referred to the
abstract idea which constitutes its ground and final justification. Aristotelian philosophy, with its emphasis on the concrete and the individual, offers the basis of a certain concept
of the person, but the inability of this philosophy to provide
permanence, some kind of continuity and "eternal life," for
the total psychosomatic entity of man renders impossible the
union of the person with the "substance" (οὐσία) of man,
that is, with a true ontology. In Platonic thought the person
is a concept which is ontologically impossible, because the
soul, which ensures man's continuity, is not united permanently with the concrete, "individual" man: it lives eternally
but it can be united with another concrete body and can constitute another "individuality," e.g. by reincarnation.[2] With
Aristotle, on the other hand, the person proves to be a logically
impossible concept precisely because the soul is indissolubly
united with the concrete and "individual": a man is a concrete
individuality; he endures, however, only for as long as his
psychosomatic union endures—death dissolves the concrete
"individuality" completely and definitively.[3]

sculpture: "Against a dark background, as a result of an interplay of light
and shadow, there stands out a blind, colorless, cold marble and divinely beautiful, proud and majestic body, a statue. And the world is such a statue, and
gods are statues; the city-state also, and the heroes, and the myths, and ideas
all conceal underneath them this original sculptural intuition . . . There is
no personality, no eyes, no spiritual individuality. There is a "something,"
but not a "someone," an individualized "it," but no living person with his
proper name . . . There is no one at all. There are bodies, and there are
ideas. The spiritual character of the ideas is killed by the body, but the warmth
of the body is restrained by the abstract idea. There are here beautiful, but cold
and blissfully indifferent statues." Quoted by G. Florovsky, "Eschatology in
the Patristic Age: An Introduction," in Studia Patristica, ed. F.L. Cross, II
(1957), pp. 235-50, at p. 248.
    [2]According to Plato's Timaeus (41 D f.) the souls were all created alike;
they become "different" only when they acquire bodies. This could be taken
to imply (see e.g. E. Rohde, Psyche [1925], p. 472) that there is some kind
of distinct "personality" in an incarnate soul. However Plato seems to. allow
for many reincarnations of one and the same soul, even in the bodies of animals (see Phaedo 249B; Repub. 618A; Tim. 42 BC etc.). This makes it
impossible for a particular soul to acquire a distinct "personality" of its own
on the basis of a particular body.
    [3]According to Aristotle (e.g. De Anima 2, 4. 415 A, 28-67), the concrete
individual cannot be everlasting, since it cannot share in the ἀεὶ καὶ θεῖον.
Death dissolves the individual thing (the αὐτό), and what survives is only

The reasons for this inability of ancient Greek philosophy to endow human "individuality" with permanence and thus to create a true ontology of the person as an absolute concept are deeply rooted in Greek thought. Ancient Greek thought remained tied to the basic principle which it had set itself, the principle that being constitutes in the final analysis a unity in spite of the multiplicity of existent things[4] because concrete existent things finally trace their being back to their necessary relationship and "kinship" with the "one" being, and because consequently every "differentiation" or "accidence" must be somehow regarded as a tendency towards "non-being," a deterioration of or "fall" from being.[5]

This ontological monism which characterizes Greek philosophy from its inception[6] leads Greek thought to the concept of the *cosmos,* that is, of the harmonious relationship of existent things among themselves. Not even God can escape from this ontological unity and stand freely before the world, "face to face" in dialogue with it.[7] He too is bound by

the οἷον αὐτό, i.e. the species (εἶδος). Cf. E. Rohde, *op. cit.,* p. 511. Originally Aristotle seems to have held the view that the "mind" (νοῦς), as the intelligent part of the soul, survives after death (cf. *Metaph.* 13, 9. 1070 a, 24-26; *De Anima* 3, 5. 436a, 23). But he abandoned this view later on in life in favor of the position stated above in this note. Cf. H.A. Wolfson, "Immortality and Resurrection in the Philosophy of the Church Fathers," in K. Stendhal, ed., *Immortality and Resurrection* (1965), pp. 54-96, esp. 96.

[4]From the Presocratics to the Neoplatonists this principle is invariably maintained in Greek thought. Whatever exists is essentially one and its "reason" is "common" (ξυνὸς λόγος) for all those who are "awake" (Heraclitus, *Frs.* 89, 73 etc.). "Being" and "knowing" (νοεῖν) also form a unity (Parmenides, *Fr.* 5d. 7. Cf. Plato, *Parm.* 128b). The creation of the world takes place on the basis of this principle of necessary unity, and it is for this reason that the creator does not simply choose to but *must* make the world spherical, since the spherical shape is that of unity and thus of perfection (Plato, *Tim.* 32d-34b. Cf. G. Vlastos, *Plato's Universe* [1975], p. 29). For the Neoplatonics also there is a basic unity between the intelligible world, the mind and being (Plotinus, *En.* V, 1, 8. Cf. K. Kremer, *Die neuplatonische Seinsphilosophie und ihre Wirkung auf Thomas von Aquin* [1966, new ed. 1971], pp. 79ff.).

[5]This was particularly present in Neoplatonism, which for this reason regarded as outrageous the Christian view that the world is contigent and not eternal. Cf. E. von Ivanka, *Plato Christianus* (1960), pp. 152f. and 128f.

[6]For the view that there is consistent monism in Greek thought, see C.J. de Vogel, *Philosophia* I, *Studies in Greek Philosophy* (Philosophical Texts and Studies 19, I, 1970), pp. 397-416.

[7]The gods could always make extraordinary interventions in nature through

ontological necessity to the world and the world to him,
either through the creation of Plato's *Timaeus*[8] or through the
Logos of the Stoics[9] or through the "emanations" of Plotinus'
Enneads.[10] In this way Greek thought creates a wonderful
concept of "cosmos," that is, of unity and harmony, a world
full of interior dynamism and aesthetic plentitude, a world
truly "beautiful" and "divine." However, in such a world it is
impossible for the unforeseen to happen or for freedom to
operate as an absolute and unrestricted claim to existence:[11]

miracles as well as in men's lives, causing them even to suffer madness (ἀτή).
Cf. E.R. Dodds, *The Greeks and the Irrational* (1956), p. 49 and passim.
This view, however, undergoes a radical transformation in the hands of the
classical philosophers and the tragedians, who clearly deny the gods the right
to transgress the laws of justice or "measure," i.e. the κόσμος (= just
behavior) which holds the world together in one necessary unity. "If the
gods do anything that is ugly, they are not the gods" (Euripides, *Fr.* 292
acc. to Bellerophon). Cf. M. Eliade, *A History of Religious Ideas*, I (1979),
p. 261. This transformation takes place together with the idea that Zeus is at
the same time "nature's inflexible law and mind dwelling in mortal men," he
who leads "*according to justice* all that happens here below" (Euripides,
Troad. 884ff.).

[8]Unlike Heracleitus and the physiologists, Plato attributes the existence of
the world to God, the creator νοῦς or πατήρ. But Plato's creator is not
absolutely free in relation to the world he creates. He is subject to necessity
(ἀνάγκη) in that he has to use matter (ὕλη) and space (χώρα), which
not only pre-exist but also impose on him their own laws and limitations
(*Tim.* 48a; 51 a-b). Furthermore, Plato's creator *has to* take into account the
ideas of symmetry, justice etc. (cf. above note 4), which *pre-exist* and serve
as *paradeigmata* for creation. The fact that, in one passage in the *Republic*
Plato appears to identify God with the idea of the *Good* which is ἐπέκεινα
τῆς οὐσίας, does not seem to have convinced the majority of specialists
that Plato's God is above and independent of the world of ideas. See D. Ross,
Plato's Theory of Ideas (1951), pp. 43-44, 78-79. In fact, it is open to discussion whether the idea of Good is identical with God. See P. Shorey, *What
Plato Said* (1943), p. 231, and for the opposite view C. Ritter, *The Essence
of Plato's Philosophy* (1933), p. 374.

[9]For the Stoics God is inseparably linked with the world. He is "spirit
penetrating everything," even the most material and base things (J. ab Arnim,
Stoicorum veterum fragmenta, II [1923] 306/1027, 307/1035. Cf. E. Zeller,
Grundriss der Geschichte der griechischen Philosophie [1928], p. 142).

[10]See notes 4-6 above.

[11]Hegel speaks of ancient Greece as the place where the concept of "free
individuality" appeared for the first time in connection with sculpture. However, as he puts it himself, this was "substantive individuality" in which "the
accent is only put on the general and the permanent . . . while the transitory
and the fortuitous are rejected." (*Vorlesungen über die Ästhetik, Sämtliche
Werke*, X, pp. 353f. and 377).

whatever threatens cosmic harmony and is not explained by "reason" (*logos*), which draws all things together and leads them to this harmony and unity,[12] is rejected and condemned. This also holds true for man.

The place of man in this unified world of harmony and reason is the theme of ancient Greek tragedy. And it is precisely here that (by coincidence?) the term "person" (πρόσωπον) appears in ancient Greek usage. Of course the term is not absent from the vocabulary of ancient Greek outside the life of the theater. It seems originally to have meant specifically the part of the head that is "below the cranium."[13] This is its "anatomical" meaning.[14] But how and why did this meaning come to be identified so quickly with the mask (προσωπεῖον) which was used in the theater?[15] What connection does the actor's mask have with the human person? Is it simply that the mask in some way recalls the real person?[16] Or is there perhaps some deeper consideration linking these two uses of the term "person"?

The theater, and tragedy in particular, is the setting in which

[12]The original concept and root of the term *logos*, as analyzed by M. Heidegger, *Einführung in die Metaphysik* (1953), p. 96 ff., is characteristic. The growth of *logos* into a cosmological principle, as may be observed in a developed form in Stoicism, is a natural consequence of the original identification of *logos* with "being" (e.g. in Heracleitus) and of the whole outlook of ancient Hellenism.

[13]See Aristotle, *History of Animals* I. VIII, 491b; Homer, *Ilied* E24, H212, etc.

[14]A concept of the person as one of reference or relationship could perhaps reasonably be put forward as the original concept of the term on the basis of some kind of etymological analysis of it. But there is no evidence for such a concept in the ancient Greek texts. Consequently an attempt has been made to trace the etymology of the word on the basis of a strict anatomical analysis: e.g. the part defined by the eyes (τὸ πρὸς τοῖς ὠψὶ μέρος). See H. Stephanus, *Thesaurus Graecae Linguae* VI, col. 2048.

[15]This use of the term πρόσωπον is already found in Aristotle (τὰ τραγικὰ πρόσωπα, *Problems* XXXI, 7, 958a, 17). See also Plato Comicus, *fragm.* 142. This leads to the use of the term not only for the physical mask but also for the theatrical role of the actor: "there being three leading πρόσωπα as in the comedies—the slanderer, the one slandered, and the one who hears the slander' (Lucian, *Slander* 6). Thus the term πρόσωπον comes to be identified fully with the term προσωπεῖον as a synonym. (See Josephus, *Jewish War* IV, 156; cf. Theophrasetus, *Characters* VI, 3).

[16]For this interpretation see, for example, S. Schlossmann, *Persona und Prosopon im Recht und im christlichen Dogma* (1906), p. 37.

the conflicts between human freedom and the rational necessity of a unified and harmonious world, as they were understood by the ancient Greeks, are worked out in dramatic form. It is precisely in the theater that man strives to become a "person," to rise up against this harmonious unity which oppresses him as rational and moral necessity.[17] It is there that he fights with the gods and with his fate; it is there that he sins and transgresses; but it is there too that he constantly learns—according to the stereotyped principle of ancient tragedy —that he can neither escape fate ultimately, nor continue to show *hubris* to the gods without punishment, nor sin without suffering the consequences. Thus he confirms tragically the view, expressed so typically in Plato's *Laws*, that *the world does not exist for the sake of man, but man exists for its sake.*[17a] His freedom is circumscribed, or rather there is no freedom for him—since a "circumscribed freedom" would be a contradiction in terms—and consequently his "person" is nothing but a "mask," something which has no bearing on his true "hypostasis," something without ontological content.

This is one aspect, one concept, of the term "prosopon." But together with this there is also another, namely, that as a result of this mask man—the actor, but properly also the spectator—has acquired a certain taste of freedom, a certain

[17]Tragedy in art is precisely "man's answer to this universe that crushes him so pitilessly. Destiny scowls upon him; his answer is to sit down and paint her as she stands." F. L. Lucas, *Tragedy* (1957), p. 78.

[17a]"But thou failest to perceive that *all partial generation is for the sake of the whole* in order that for the life of the whole blissful existence may be secured. For *it (the whole) is not brought into being for thy sake, but thou art for its sake*" (Plato, *Laws*, X, 903 c-d)." This contrasts sharply with the Biblical and Patristic view that man was created *after* the world was brought into being and indeed *for his sake.* There is an intrinsic relationship between, on the one hand, the principle that it is wholeness and totality that ultimately matter in ontology (the partial exists for the sake of the total—hence man exists for the sake of the cosmos), and on the other hand the *necessity* which is built into ontology by Greek thought through the ideas of "logos" and nature, to which we have been referring here. "No particular thing, not even the least, can be otherwise than according to common nature and reason (*logos*)" writes Plutarch in quoting and commenting on the Stoic Chrysippus (J. ab Armin, *op. cit. II,* 937). It is noteworthy that Plutarch himself understands this as meaning "fate" (*Ibid*). Nature, logos and fate are interrelated; by being based on these ontological principles existence is inevitably determined by necessity.

specific "hypostasis," a certain identity, which the rational and moral harmony of the world in which he lives denies him. Of course, the same man, thanks to the same mask, has also acquired the bitter taste of the consequences of his rebellion. But as a result of the mask he has become a person, albeit for a brief period, and has learned what it is to exist as a free, unique and unrepeatable entity. The mask is not unrelated to the person, but their relationship is tragic.[18] In the ancient Greek world for someone to be a person means that he has something added to his being; the "person" is not his true "hypostasis." "Hypostasis" still means basically "nature" or "substance."[19] Many centuries would have to elapse before Greek thought would reach the historic identification of "hypostasis" with "person."

Similar conclusions can be drawn from a consideration of the idea of "person" in ancient Roman thought. Specialists have debated the degree of influence which the Greek use of πρόσωπον has exercised on the Roman *persona* and whether the term *persona* is derived from a Greek or from some other source.[20] However, leaving aside the etymological problem, the reality seems to be that at least in the beginning the Roman use of the term did not differ essentially from the Greek. In its anthropological connotation the Roman *persona* leaned perhaps more heavily than its Greek equivalent towards the idea of

---

[18]Cf. the statement of this great problem by the Metropolitan Meliton of Chalcedon, "A Sermon delivered in the Cathedral of Athens (8 March 1970)," *Stachys* 19-26 (1969-71), p. 49ff.: "The phenomenon of the profound and anxious demand of the human soul to be liberated from its daily hypocrisy by the assumption of an anonymous, dionysiac, new hypocrisy is most ancient. The carnival clown is a tragic figure. He seeks to be liberated from hypocrisy by pretence. He seeks to dissolve all the various masks which he wears every day by a new, more fantastic mask. He seeks to expel what has been thrust down into his subconscious and be liberated, but there is no liberation; the tragedy of the carnival clown remains unresolved. His deepest demand is to be transformed."

[19]See note 23.

[20]See M. Nédoncelle, "Prosopon et persona dans l'antiquité classique," *Revue des sciences religieuses* 22 (1948), pp. 277-99. The origin of *persona* is probably to be traced back to the Etruscan word *phersu,* which would connect it with the ritual or theatrical mask (cf. the Greek προσωπεῖον) and perhaps with the Greek mythological figure of *Persephone.* Cf. *ibid.,* pp. 284 ff.

concrete individuality,[21] but in its sociological and later on[22] in its legal usage it never ceased to express the ancient Greek πρόσωπον or προσωπεῖον in its theatrical nuance of *rôle*: *persona* is the role which one plays in one's social or legal relationships, the moral or "legal" person which either collectively or individually has nothing to do with the *ontology* of the person.

This understanding of the person is tied to the concept of man in Roman antiquity in a very basic way. Roman thought, which is fundamentally organizational and social, concerns itself not with ontology, with the *being* of man, but with his *relationship* with others, with his ability to form associations, to enter into contracts, to set up *collegia,* to organize human life in a *state.* Thus personhood, once again, does not have any ontological content. It is an adjunct to concrete ontological being, something which permits—without this disturbing the Roman mentality in the least—the same man to enact more than one *prosopa,* to play many different roles. In this situation freedom and the unexpected are again alien to the concept of the person. Freedom is exercized by the group, or ultimately by the state, the organized totality of human relationships, which also defines its boundaries. But exactly as we observed in the case of the Greek πρόσωπον or προσωπεῖον the Roman *persona* expresses simultaneously both the denial and the affirmation of human freedom: as *persona* man subordinates his freedom to the organized whole, but also assures himself simultaneously of a means, a possibility, of tasting freedom, or affirming his identity. This *identity*—that vital component of the concept of man, that which makes one man differ from another, which makes him *he who is*—is guaranteed and *provided* by the state or by some organized whole. Even when the authority of the state is called into question and man rebels against it, even then, if he succeeds in escaping punishment for this *hubris* of his, he will look to some

---

[21]The nuance of concrete individuality is first found in Cicero (*De amicit.* I, 4; *Ad Att. VIII,* 12; *De or.* II, 145 etc.). This author, however, uses *persona* also in the sense of *role* (theatrical, social etc).

[22]Or rather, after the 2nd century A.D. See S. Schlossmann, *op. cit.,* p. 119 ff. For the collective sense of *persona* see already Cicero, *Off.* I, 124: "est . . . proprium munus magistratus intelligere se gerere personam civitatis."

legal and political power, to some concept of the state, to give him his new identity, a confirmation of his selfhood. The politicization of contemporary man and the rise of sociology in our age cannot be understood without reference to the Roman *persona*. The point at issue is the overwhelmingly *Western* mentality of our civilization, the coalescence of *persona* with the προσωπεῖον of the ancient Greeks.

This is as far as the ancient Graeco-Roman world takes the idea of personhood. The glory of this world consists in its having shown man a dimension of existence which may be called *personal*. Its weakness lies in the fact that its cosmological framework did not allow this dimension to be justified ontologically. Προσωπεῖον and *persona* remained pointers towards the person. But they *consciously*—and this is precisely what was demanded by the cosmological framework of a self-authenticating cosmic or state harmony—constituted a reminder that this personal dimension is not and *ought* never to be identical with the essence of things, with the true being of man. Other powers, not the quality of personhood, laid claim to the ontological content of human existence.

How, then, could we have arrived at an identification of the person with the being of man? How could freedom have become identical with the "world," the identity of the concrete man a product of freedom, and man in his very being identical with the person? For these things to have come about, two basic presuppositions were necessary: (a) a radical change in cosmology which would free the world and man from ontological necessity; and (b) an ontological view of man which would unite the person with the *being* of man, with his permanent and enduring existence, with his genuine and absolute identity.

The first of these could only be offered by Christianity with its biblical outlook. The second could only be attained by Greek thought with its interest in ontology. The Greek Fathers were precisely those who could unite the two. With a rare creativity worthy of the Greek spirit they gave history the concept of the person with an absoluteness which still moves modern man even though he has fundamentally abandoned their spirit.

2. The concept of the person with its absolute and ontological content was born historically from the endeavor of the Church to give ontological expression to its faith in the Triune God. This faith was primitive—it goes back to the very first years of the Church—and was handed down from generation to generation with the practice of baptism. The constant and profound contact, however, between Christianity and Greek philosophy sharpened the problem of the interpretation of this faith in a manner which would satisfy Greek thought. What does it mean to say that God is Father, Son and Spirit without ceasing to be *one* God? The history of the disputes which broke out on this great theme do not interest us here in detail. What is significant is that this history includes a philosophical landmark, a revolution in Greek philosophy. This revolution is expressed historically through an identification: *the identification of the "hypostasis" with the "person."* How was this unforeseen revolution accomplished? What kind of consequences did it have for the concept of the person? These are questions that must occupy us briefly.

The term "hypostasis" never had any connection with the term "person" in Greek philosophy. As we have seen, "person" would have been regarded by the Greeks as expressive of anything but the essence of man, whereas the term "hypostasis" was already closely linked with the term "substance" and finally was identified fully with it.[23] It is precisely this identification of substance with hypostasis, diffused so widely in the Greek thought of the first Christian centuries, that created all the difficulties and disputes concerning the Holy Trinity in the fourth century. It is relevant to our theme that the term "person," which had already been used in the West from the time of Tertullian for the doctrine of the Holy

---

[23]St Athanasius, *Letter to the bishops of Egypt and Libya* (PG. 26, 1036 B,) clearly identifies the two: "*hypostasis* is *ousia* and has no other meaning apart from being (τὸ ὄν) itself . . . For *hypostasis* and *ousia* are existence (ὕπαρξις): it is and it exists (ἔστι καὶ ὑπάρχει)." On the basis of this identification the Synodical letter of Alexandria 362 AD refers to Nicaea as having anathematized those who profess that the Son is "of another hypostasis *or* ousia," allowing, however, for the use of the expression "three hypostases" on condition that this would not imply separation between these hypostases. It was the merit of the Cappadocian Fathers to show how this could be worked out philosophically. Cf. below.

Trinity (*una substantia, tres personae*),[24] did not meet with acceptance in the East *precisely because the term "person" lacked an ontological content* and led towards Sabellianism (the manifestation of God in three "roles").[25] That is how foreign the term "person" was to ontology! Instead of this term the East was already in the time of Origen[26] using the term "hypostases" for the Holy Trinity. But this term also had its dangers. It could have been interpreted in a Neoplatonic fashion—Plotinus already speaks of the hypostases of the divine—with all the dangers which a union of God and the world in the Neoplatonic manner would have held for Christian theology.[27] Moreover, it could have been interpreted tritheistically if the then current identification of hypostasis with substance had been taken into consideration.[28] A mode of expression thus had to be found which would give theology the ability to avoid Sabellianism, that is, which would give an ontological content to each person of the Holy Trinity, without endangering its biblical principles: monotheism and the absolute ontological independence of God in relation to the world. From this endeavour came the identification of hypostasis with person.

The historical aspect of this development is very obscure and does not interest us here directly.[29] I believe myself that

[24]See Tertullian, *Against Praxeas* 11-12 (PL 2, 1670D).

[25]See for example, St Basil, *Ep.* 236, 6: "those who say that ousia and hypostasis are the same (note the *radical* departure from the philosophical terminology of St Athanasius and his time—note 23 above) are compelled to confess only different *prosopa* and by avoiding the use of the words *treis hypostaseis* do not succeed in escaping the Sabellian evil." We are clearly confronted with a change in terminology dictated by the concern, prompted by Sabellianism, to give to *prosopon* full ontological content.

[26]Origen, *Com. on St John's Gospel*, II, 6 (PG 14, 12B).

[27]Plotinus (*Enn V*, I) defines the "primary hypostases" as the supreme good, intelligence and the world soul. This is yet another case of ontological monism (cf. above), linking God with the world in a single unity, which endangers the Biblical understanding of the relation between God and the world. For the contribution of Plotinus to the philosophical use of the term "hypostasis," see K. Oehler, *Antike Philosophie und byzantinisches Mittelalter* (1969), p. 23 ff.

[28]See note 23 above.

[29]A detailed study of this problem is badly needed. On the notion of "Substance" see the work of C. Stead, *Divine Substance* (1977). A rather general but very careful discussion of the developments in philosophical terminology

the key to this development must be sought in the western
Greek writer, Hippolytus, who is perhaps the first to use the
Greek term πρόσωπον—in imitation of Tertullian?—in trinitarian theology. It would be of historical interest to investigate
the nuances of the term "hypostasis" which occasioned its
divergence from the term "substance."[30] However, none of
this can explain the momentous step of the identification of
"hypostasis" with the term "person," without an examination

with regard to this subject is to be found in the now old but still very useful
work of C. C. J. Webb, *God and Personality* (1918).

[30]The history of the terms "substance" (οὐσία) and "hypostasis" is
extremely complicated. In particular there exists the opinion with regard to
the use of these terms in the trinitarian theology of the Greek Fathers that
the distinction between substance and hypostasis had been made possible on
the basis of the logical distinction of Aristotle between "primary substance"
and "secondary substance" (*Categories* 5, 2a, 11-16; *Metaphysics* VII, 11,
1037a .5). According to this opinion the Cappadocian Fathers in their trinitarian theology identified the term "hypostasis" with the "primary substance"
(the individual and concrete), and the term "substance" with the "secondary
substance" (the general and common) of Aristotle. See, for example, G.L.
Prestige, *God in Patristic Thought* (1936), p. 245 ff., J.N.D. Kelly, *Early
Christian Creeds* (1950), p. 243 ff. and K. Oehler, *op. cit.* p. 23 ff. But this
opinion appears very debatable upon a close study of the Greek Fathers (e.g.
for Athanasius see note 23 above), from whose thought the Aristotelian distinction between primary and secondary substance seems to be entirely absent.
It is also doubtful whether this distinction represents even Aristotle's thought
correctly, as an outstanding specialist observes. See D.M. Mackinnon, "Substance in Christology—A Cross-bench View," *Christ, Faith and History:
Cambridge Studies in Christology*, ed. S.W. Sykes and J.P. Clayton (1972),
pp. 279-300. A relationship between the development of these terms and the
history of the philosophical sense of the term ὑποκείμενον in the period
after Aristotle appears probable. Because of the double meaning which Aristotle
seems to accord this term (ὑποκείμενον is [a] matter and [b] concrete and
independent being; see *Metaphysics* VII, 3, 1029a), in the period after Aristotle
the term "hypostasis" displaces the term ὑποκείμενον because of the ma-
terialistic sense of the latter and itself assumes the meaning of concrete and
independent being. Thus in the first centuries of the Christian era the term
"hypostasis" gradually acquired the meaning of real and concrete being in
opposition to that which is merely apparent and evanescent. This evolution
seems to have been brought about mainly by the Stoics (cf. E. Zeller, *Philosophie der Griechen* III [1881], p. 644 ff.). Cf. on this C.C.J. Webb, *op. cit.*
Granted that the influence of Stoicism in the Philosophy of the patristic period
is strong, it is probable that the use of the term "hypostasis" for the expression
of concrete (as opposed to general) being should have had the ground prepared for it in this way. It remains a fact, however, that the theological
thought of the Cappadocians brought about a *radical* change in the philosophical use of these terms.

of the broader philosophical changes which were effected in the patristic age in relation to Greek thought.

The deeper significance of the identification of "hypostasis" with "person"—a significance the revolutionary nature of which in the development of Greek thought seems to have escaped the attention of the history of philosophy—consists in a twofold thesis: (a) The person is no longer an adjunct to a being, a category which we *add* to a concrete entity once we have first verified its ontological hypostasis. *It is itself the hypostasis of the being.* (b) Entities no longer trace their being to being itself—that is, being is not an absolute category in itself—but to the person, to precisely that which *constitutes* being, that is, enables entities to be entities. In other words from an adjunct to a being (a kind of mask) the person becomes the being itself and is simultaneously—a most significant point—*the constitutive element* (the "principle" or "cause") of beings.

For Greek thought to have arrived at such a radical re-appraisal of its ontology, two basic "leavenings" had previously taken place in the field of patristic theology. The first concerns that which I have just named the ontological absoluteness of cosmological necessity. In accordance with biblical theology, of which the Fathers cannot have been ignorant, the world is not ontologically necessary. Although the ancient Greeks assumed with regard to the ontology of the world that it was something necessary of itself, the biblical doctrine of creation *ex nihilo* obliged the Fathers to introduce a radical difference into ontology, to trace the world back to an ontology outside the world, that is, to God.[31] They thus broke the circle of the closed ontology of the Greeks, and at the same time did something much more important, which is of direct interest to us here: they made being—the existence of the world, existent things—*a product of freedom.* That is how the first "leavening" was accomplished: with the doctrine of creation *ex nihilo* the "principle" of Greek ontology, the "ἀρχή" of the world, was transposed to the sphere of

[31]Cf. G. Florovsky, "The Concept of Creation in Saint Athanasius," *Studia Patristica* VI (1962), pp. 36-67.

freedom. That which exists was liberated from itself; the being of the world became free from necessity.

But there was also a second "leavening" which led to an even further reappraisal of Greek ontology. Not only was the being of the world traced back to personal freedom, but *the being of God Himself* was identified with the person. This "leavening" was effected through the disputes on the Holy Trinity, mainly through the theology of the Cappadocian Fathers and above all by St Basil.[32] This theology does not concern us here except for one basic point, which unfortunately is usually overlooked. As is known, the final formulation of the doctrine of the Holy Trinity speaks of "one substance, three persons" (μία οὐσία, τρία πρόσωπα). One would therefore have said that the unity of God, the "ontology" of God, consists in the *substance* of God. This would bring us back to the ancient Greek ontology: God first *is* God (His substance or nature, His being), and then[33] exists as Trinity, that is, as persons. This interpretation in fact prevailed in Western theology and unfortunately entered into modern Orthodox dogmatics with the arrangement in the dogmatic handbooks of the headings "On the One God" followed by "On the Trinity."[34] The significance of this interpretation lies in the assumption that the ontological "principle" of God is not found in the person but in the substance, that is, in the "being" itself of God. Indeed the idea took shape in Western theology that that which constitutes the unity of God is the one divine substance, the one divinity; this is, as it were, the ontological "principle" of God.

But this interpretation represents a misinterpretation of the Patristic theology of the Trinity. Among the Greek Fathers the unity of God, the one God, and the ontological "principle" or "cause" of the being and life of God does not consist in the one substance of God but in the *hypostasis*, that is, *the person of the Father*. The one God is not the one sub-

---

[32]See below ch. 2, II 2-3.

[33]The words "first" and "then" refer here of course to a priority which is not temporal but logical and ontological.

[34]Cf. K. Rahner's critique of this typically Western approach to the doctrine of God in his work, *The Trinity* (1970), *passim* and esp. p. 58 ff.

stance but the Father, who is the "cause" both of the generation of the Son and of the procession of the Spirit.[35] Consequently, the ontological "principle" of God is traced back,
once again, to the person. Thus when we say that God "is,"
we do not bind the personal freedom of God—the being of
God is not an ontological "necessity" or a simple "reality"
for God—but we ascribe the being of God to His personal
freedom. In a more analytical way this means that God, as
Father and not as substance, perpetually confirms through
"being" His *free* will to exist. And it is precisely His trinitarian existence that constitutes this confirmation: the Father out
of love—that is, freely—begets the Son and brings forth the
Spirit. If God exists, He exists because the Father exists, that is,
He who out of love freely begets the Son and brings forth the
Spirit. Thus God as person—as the hypostasis of the Father
—makes the one divine substance to be that which it is: the one
God. This point is absolutely crucial. For it is precisely with
this point that the new philosophical position of the Cappadocian Fathers, and of St Basil in particular, is directly connected. That is to say, the substance never exists in a "naked"
state, that is, without hypostasis, without "a mode of existence."[36] And the one divine substance is consequently the
being of God only because it has these three modes of existence, which it owes not to the substance but to one person,
the Father. Outside the Trinity there is no God, that is, no
divine substance, because the ontological "principle" of God
is the Father. The personal existence of God (the Father)
constitutes His substance, makes it hypostases. The being of
God is identified with the person.[37]

[35]The problem of the *Filioque* is linked directly with this theme. The West,
as the study of the trinitarian theology of Augustine and Thomas Aquinas
witnesses, had no difficulty in maintaining the *Filioque* precisely because it
identified the being, the ontological principle, of God with His substance
rather than with the person of the Father.

[36]See St Basil, *Letter* 38, 2, PG 32:325 ff. Cf. G.L. Prestige, *op. cit.*, pp.
245 and 279. This important thesis is used later by St Maximus the Confessor,
who distinguishes between λόγος φύσεως and τρόπος ὑπάρξεως, and
stresses that the various λόγοι never exist in a "naked" state but as "modes
of existence" (see, for example, *Ambigua* 42, PG 91:1341D ff.). Cf. Gregory
of Nyssa, *Against Eunomius* 1, PG 45:337.

[37]The basic ontological position of the theology of the Greek Fathers might

3. What therefore is important in trinitarian theology is that God "exists" on account of a person, the Father, and not on account of a substance. Because its significance is not simply theoretical or academic but profoundly existential, let us attempt a brief analysis of it.

(a) The ultimate challenge to the freedom of the person is the "necessity" of existence. The moral sense of freedom, to which Western philosophy has accustomed us, is satisfied with the simple power of choice: a man is free who is able to choose one of the possibilities set before him. But this "freedom" is already bound by the "necessity" of these possibilities, and the ultimate and most binding of these "necessities" for man is his existence itself: how can a man be considered absolutely free when he cannot do other than accept his existence? Dostoevsky poses this great problem in a startling manner in *The Possessed*. There Kirilov says: "Every man who desires to attain total freedom must be bold enough to put an end to his life. . . . This is the ultimate limit of freedom; this is all; there is nothing beyond this. Whoever dares to commit suicide becomes God. Everyone can do this and so bring the existence of God to an end, and then there will be absolutely nothing. . . ."

These words of Kirilov express the most tragic side of the person's quest: the transcendence of the "necessity" of existence, the possibility of affirming his existence not as a recognition of a given fact, of a "reality," but as the product of his free consent and self-affirmation. This and nothing less than this is what man seeks in being a person.[38] But in man's

be set out briefly as follows. No substance or nature exists without person or hypostasis or mode of existence. No person exists without substance or nature, *but* the ontological "principle" or "cause" of being—i.e. that which makes a thing to exist—is not the substance or nature but the *person* or hypostasis. Therefore being is traced back not to substance but to person.

[38]This is especially apparent in art. Art as genuine creation, and not as a representational rendering of reality, is nothing other than an attempt by man to affirm his presence in a manner free from the "necessity" of existence. Genuine art is not simply creation on the basis of something which already exists, but a tendency towards creation *ex nihilo*. This explains the tendency of modern art (which, it may be noted, is linked historically with an emphasis on freedom and on the person) to ignore or even to abolish and shatter the form or nature of beings (their natural or verbal shapes etc. cf. Michael-

case this quest comes into conflict with his createdness: as a creature he cannot escape the "necessity" of his existence. The person, consequently, cannot be realized as an intramundal or fully human reality. Philosophy can arrive at the confirmation of the reality of the person, but only theology can treat of the genuine, the authentic person, because the authentic person, as absolute ontological freedom, must be "uncreated," that is, unbounded by any "necessity," including its own existence. If such a person does not exist in reality, the concept of the person is a presumptious daydream. If God does not exist, the person does not exist.

(b) But what is this freedom of self-affirmation of existence? How is it expressed? How is it realized? The disturbing words which Dostoevsky puts in Kirilov's mouth sound an alarm: if the only way of exercising absolute ontological freedom for man is suicide, then freedom leads to nihilism; the person is shown to be the negator of ontology. This existential alarm, the fear of nihilism, is so serious that in the last analysis it must itself be regarded as responsible for the relativization of the concept of the person. Indeed every claim to absolute freedom is always countered by the argument that its realization would lead to chaos. The concept of "law," as much in its ethical as in its juridical sense, always presupposes some limitation to personal freedom in the name of "order" and "harmony," the need for symbiosis with others. Thus "the other" becomes a threat to the person, its "hell" and its "fall," to recall the words of Sartre. Once again the concept of the person leads human existence to an impasse: humanism proves unable to affirm personhood.

At this point theology (literally, "speech or thought about God") unavoidably intervenes yet again if the concept of the person is to receive a positive content. But, to repeat once more, only a correct (ὀρθή) theology, as formulated by the Greek Fathers, can give the answer. (Orthodoxy here is not an

angelo's words: when shall I finish with this marble to get on with my works?). What is apparent in all this is the tendency of the person to liberate itself in its self-affirmation from the "necessity" of existence, that is, to become God. The vital point is that this tendency is linked intrinsically with the concept of the person.

optimal extra for human existence.) How does God affirm his ontological freedom?

I have said earlier that man cannot exercise his ontological freedom absolutely, because he is tied by his createdness, by the "necessity" of his existence, whereas God as "uncreated" does not experience this limitation. If the ground of God's ontological freedom lies simply in His "nature," that is, in His being uncreated by nature, whereas we are by nature created, then there is no hope, no possibility, that man might become a person in the sense that God is one, that is, an authentic person. But no, the ground of God's ontological freedom lies not in His nature but in His personal existence, that is, in the "mode of existence" by which He subsists as divine nature.[39] And it is precisely this that gives man, in spite of his different nature, his hope of becoming an authentic person.

The manner in which God exercises His ontological freedom, that precisely which makes Him ontologically free, is the way in which He transcends and abolishes the ontological necessity of the substance by being God as *Father*, that is, as He who "begets" the Son and "brings forth" the Spirit. This ecstatic character of God, the fact that His being is identical with an act of communion, ensures the transcendence of the ontological necessity which His substance would have demanded—if the substance were the primary ontological predicate of God—and replaces this necessity with the free self-affirmation of divine existence. For this communion is a product of freedom as a result not of the substance of God but of a person, the Father—observe why this doctrinal detail is so important—who is Trinity not because the divine *nature* is ecstatic but because the Father as a *person* freely wills this communion.[40]

[39]God's nature does not exist "naked" i.e. without hypostases (cf. note 36 above). It is this that makes it free. "Naked" nature or *ousia* by indicating being *qua* being points not to freedom but to ontological necessity.

[40]The concept of *ekstasis* as an ontological category is found in the mystical Greek Fathers (particularly in the so-called Areopagitical writings and in Maximus the Confessor) and also totally independently in the philosophy of M. Heidegger. Chr. Yannaras, in his important work, Τὸ ὀντολογικὸν Περιεχόμενον τῆς Θεολογικῆς Ἐννοίας τοῦ Προσώπου

(1970), attempts a use of Heidegger for the philosophical justification and understanding of Greek patristic theology. It is generally acknowledged that Heidegger represents an important stage in the progress of Western thought, especially in the liberation of ontology from an absolute "ontism" and from philosophical rationalism, though not in fact from the concept of consciousness and of the subject. (See the critique of Heidegger by the important contemporary philosopher, E. Levinas, in his brilliant work, *Totalité et Infini. Essai sur l'Extériorité* [1971⁴], p. 15: *"Sein und Zeit* n'a peut-être soutenu qu'une seule thèse: l'être est inséparable de la compréhension de l'être [que se déroule comme temps], l'être est déjà appel à la subjectivité.") However, the use of Heidegger in the interpretation of patristic theology runs into fundamental difficulties. As pointers to these one would have to pose among others the following questions: (a) Is it possible to conceive of an ontology outside time in Heidegger, or of an ontology within time predicated of God in the Greek Fathers? (b) Is it possible for death to be an ontological concept in the Fathers, who regard it as the last enemy of being? (c) Is it possible to regard the concept of truth (ἀ-λήθεια), in the sense of a manifestation of or outgrowth from oblivion (λήθη), as an inevitable attribute of the ontology predicated of God? These questions prove to be crucial when one takes into consideration that those contemporary Western theologians who have attempted to utilize Heidegger in their theology have not succeeded in avoiding either the introduction of the concept of time in God (K. Barth), or the view that the concept of revelation is an essential ontological category of the being of God, so that the "economy," the mode of God's revelation to man, constitutes the basis, the starting-point and the *ontological structure* of the theology of the Holy Trinity (K. Rahner). Yannaras, in a new edition of his book (under the title, *To Prosopo kai o Eros* [1976], p. 60 ff.), attempts to advance beyond Heidegger by identifying ecstasy not "simply with the *mode* by which whatever exists *appears* to emerge on the horizon of time," but "with the experience of personal catholicity, that is, of ecstatic, erotic self-transcendence." The difficulty, however, in utilizing Heidegger in the interpretation of patristic theology remains insurmountable when one also takes into consideration, apart from the three crucial questions which I have just posed, the general problem of the relationship between philosophy and theology as it manifests itself in the case of Heidegger. With our insistence here on the thesis that God is ecstatic, that is, that He exists on account of being the *Father,* we deny simultaneously not only the ontological priority of the substance over the person, but also a "panoramic" ontology (the term belongs to the crtitique of Heidegger by E. Levinas, *op. cit.* p. 270 ff.; cf. p. 16 ff.), which would view the Trinity as a parallel co-existence of the three persons, a kind of multiple manifestation of the being of God. The insistence on the "monarchy" of the Father by Greek patristic thought excludes completely a differentiation of the persons justified ontologically by the "horizon" of their manifestation. In God such a horizon is non-existent and inconceivable, and consequently ontology as manifestation is (perhaps?) possible for the "economic" theology which is accomplished "in time" but not also for an ontology of the trinitarian existence of God who is outside time. This means that a theological ontology which is based on the concept of the monarchy of the Father and excludes equally the priority of the substance over the person and the parallel co-existence of the three persons of the Trinity in a common "horizon" of manifestation, liberates ontology from gnosiology.

It thus becomes evident that the only exercise of freedom in an ontological manner is *love*. The expression "God is love" (I John 4:16) signifies that God "subsists" as Trinity, that is, as person and not as substance. Love is not an emanation or "property" of the substance of God—this detail is significant in the light of what I have said so far—but is *constitutive* of His substance, i.e. it is that which makes God what He is, the one God. Thus love ceases to be a qualifying —i.e. secondary—property of being and becomes *the supreme ontological predicate*. Love as God's mode of existence "hypostasizes" God, *constitutes* His being. Therefore, as a result of love, the ontology of God is not subject to the necessity of the substance. Love is identified with ontological freedom.[41]

All this means that personhood creates for human existence the following dilemma: either freedom as love, or freedom as negation. The choice of the latter certainly constitutes an expression of personhood—only the person can seek negative freedom—but it is a negation nevertheless of its ontological content. For nothingness has no ontological content when the person is seen in the light of trinitarian theology.

(c) The person does not simply want to be, to exist "eternally," that is, to possess an ontological content. It wants something more: to exist as a *concrete, unique* and *unrepeatable* entity. The person cannot be understood simply as the "ecstasy" of the substance; it must necessarily be regarded

This is not the case in Heidegger, but perhaps neither in any philosophical ontology which is always tied to gnosiology. Consequently, a more general problem comes into being: is a philosophical justification of patristic theology possible? Or does patristic theology in its essence constitute the converse, that is, a *theological justification of philosophy*, a proclamation that philosophy and the world can acquire a true ontology only if they accept the presupposition of God as the *only* existent whose being is truly identified with the person and with freedom?

[41]However, it must again be added at once that this love which "hypostasizes" God is not something "common" to the three persons, something, that is, like the common nature of God, but is identified with the *Father*. When we say that "God is love," we refer to the Father, that is, to that person which "hypostasizes" God, which makes God to be three persons. A careful study of I John reveals that there too the phrase "God is love" refers to the *Father*: the word "God" is identified with Him who "sent His only-begotten Son," etc. (I John 4:7-17).

also as a *hypostasis* of the substance, as a concrete and unique identity.

Uniqueness is something absolute for the person. The person is so absolute in its uniqueness that it does not permit itself to be regarded as an arithmetical concept, to be set alongside other beings, to be combined with other objects, or to be used as a means, even for the most sacred goal. The goal is the person itself; personhood is the total fulfilment of being, the catholic expression of its nature. This tendency of the person, like freedom, is the "two-edged sword" of existence. For applied to man it leads to the denial of others, to egocentrism, to the total destruction of social life. As in the case of freedom, so with the unique and hypostatic nature of the person, a relativisation appears to be indispensible if chaos is to be avoided. Thus uniqueness is relativised in social life, and man becomes—in a greater or lesser degree but nevertheless assuredly so—a useful "object," a "combination," a *persona*. But it is precisely this which constitutes the tragic aspect of the person. Diffused today throughout all forms of social life is the intense search for personal identity. The person is not relativized without provoking a reaction.

Man's inability to ensure his absolute identity in the world culminates in death. Death becomes tragic and unacceptable only when man is regarded as person, and above all as hypostasis and unique identity. As a biological event death is something natural and welcome, because only in this way is life perpetuated. In the natural world "personal" identity is ensured by childbearing, by the "survival" of the parents in the faces of their children. But this is not a survival of persons; it is a survival of the species, which may be observed equally in the whole animal kingdom and is directed by the harsh laws of natural selection. The survival of the person as a unique identity is not ensured by marriage and childbearing, which in the last analysis are shown only to supply matter for death. For if through all this being survives finally as the "substance" or as the 'species" of a man, what does not survive is the concrete and unique identity, the person.

The survival of the uniqueness, the hypostasis, of a person cannot be ensured by any property of the substance or nature.

The attempt of ancient Greek philosophy—and also under its influence of various forms of Christianity—to place the survival of man on a natural or "substantial" basis, such as the immortality of the soul, does not lead to a personal survival. If the soul is immortal by nature, then personal survival is necessary—and we return again to the ancient classical ontology. Even God is then immortal through His nature, that is, of necessity, and man is related substantially—necessarily—to God. All this, which was so natural for the ancient Greek, who had no full concept of the person, creates enormous existential problems when applied to the person in its Christian sense. For an inescapable immortality is not conceivable for the free God and constitutes a challenge to the person. How then is the absolute and unique identity of the person ensured, seeing that the substance cannot do it?

Humanistic existential philosophy tends to give the answer through an ontologizing of death, through an indissoluble union of being with non-being, of existence with death. This is not the place for a critique of this "ontology." Such a philosophy is absolutely consequent upon itself because it refuses from the beginning, exactly like ancient philosophy, to discuss whether the hypothesis of an ontology outside this world is tenable. It is those theologians who accept this "ontology" of death while speaking at the same time about God that are inconsistent. For God constitutes the affirmation of being as life "eternal life," and is not "God of the dead, but of the living" (Matt. 22:32). And this means that theology, unlike philosophy, teaches an ontology which transcends the tragic aspect of death without in the least accepting death as an ontological reality, death being the "last enemy" of existence (I Cor. 15:26).

The survival of a personal identity is possible for God not on account of His substance but on account of His trinitarian existence. If God the Father is immortal, it is because His unique and unrepeatable identity as Father is distinguished eternally from that of the Son and of the Spirit, who call Him "Father." If the Son is immortal, He owes this primarily not to His substance but to His being the "only-begotten" (note here the concept of uniqueness) and His being the one in whom the Father is "well pleased."[42] Likewise the Spirit is "life-giving" because He is "communion" (II Cor. 13:14). The life of God is eternal because it is personal, that is to say, it is realized as an expression of free communion, as love. Life and love are identified in the person: the person does not die only because it is loved and loves; outside the communion of love the person loses its uniqueness and becomes a being like other beings,[43] a "thing" without absolute "identity" and "name," without a face. Death for a person means ceasing to love and to be loved, ceasing to be unique and unrepeatable, whereas life for the person means the survival of the uniqueness of its hypostasis, which is affirmed and maintained by love.[44]

II. *From Biological to Ecclesial Existence: The Ecclesiological Significance of the Person*

The eternal survival of the person as a unique, unrepeatable and free "hypostasis," as loving and being loved, constitutes the quintessence of salvation, the bringing of the Gospel to man. In the language of the Fathers this is called "divinization"

[42]The word "only-begotten" in the Johannine writings means not only the unique mode of generation of the Son by the Father, but also "Him who is beloved in a unique manner" (S. Agourides, *Hypomnima eis tas A', B' kai C' Epistolas tou Apo: tolou Ioa' nou*, 1973, p. 158). It is precisely this identification of ontology with love in God that signifies that eternity and immortality do not belong to His "nature" but to the personal relationship which is initiated by the Father.

[43]Anyone interested in the ontology of love should take the trouble to read *The Little Prince* by Antoine de St-Exupéry. In its simplicity it is a deeply theological book.

[44]The mystery of the person as an ontological "principle" and "cause" consists in the fact that love can endow something with uniqueness, with absolute identity and name. It is precisely this which is revealed by the term "eternal life," which for this very reason signifies that the person is able to raise up to personal value and life even inanimate objects, provided that they constitute an organic part of a loving relationship (for example, all creation can be saved thanks to its "recapitulation" in the loving relationship between the Father and the Son). Conversely, condemnation to eternal death is nothing other than a person's being allowed to decline into a "thing," into absolute anonymity, to hear the terrifying words, "I do not know you" (Matt. 25:12). (It is precisely against this that the Church reacts when it commemorates the "names" at the eucharist.)

(*theosis*), which means participation not in the nature or
substance of God, but in His personal existence. The goal of
salvation is that the personal life which is realised in God
should also be realized on the level of human existence.
Consequently salvation is identified with the realization of
personhood in man. But is not "man" a person even without
salvation? Is it not sufficient for him to be a "man" in order
to be also a person?

Patristic theology considers the person to be an "image
and likeness of God." It is not satisfied with a humanistic
interpretation of the person. From this standpoint patristic
theology sees man in the light of two "modes of existence."
One may be called the *hypostasis of biological existence*, the
other the *hypostasis of ecclesial existence*. A brief analysis
and comparison of these two modes of human existence will
explain why the concept of the person is inextricably bound
up with theology.

1. The *hypostasis of biological* existence is "constituted" by
a man's conception and birth. Every man who comes into
the world bears his "hypostasis," which is not entirely unrelated to love: he is the product of a communion between
two people. Erotic love, even when expressed coldly without
emotional involvement, is an astounding mystery of existence,
concealing in the deepest act of communion a tendency
towards an ecstatic transcendence of individuality through
creation. But this biological constitution of man's hypostasis
suffers radically from two "passions" which destroy precisely
that towards which the human hypostasis is thrusting, namely
the person. The first "passion" is what we may call "ontological necessity." Constitutionally the hypostasis is inevitably
tied to the natural instinct, to an impulse which is "necessary"
and not subject to the control of freedom. Thus the person
as a being "subsists" not as freedom but as necessity. As a
result it does not have the power to affirm its hypostasis with
absolute ontological freedom as I have described it above: if
it attempts to raise freedom to the level of its ontological

absoluteness, it will be confronted with the dilemma of nihilism.[45]

The second "passion" is a natural consequence of the first. At its earliest stage it may be called the "passion" of *individualism*, of the *separation* of the hypostases. Finally, however, it is identified with the last and greatest passion of man, with the disintegration of the hypostasis, which is death. The biological constitution of the human hypostasis, fundamentally tied as it is to the necessity of its "nature," ends in the perpetuation of this "nature" through the creation of bodies, that is, of hypostatic unities which affirm their identity as *separation* from other unities or "hypostases." The body, which is born as a biological hypostasis, behaves like the fortress of an ego, like a new "mask" which hinders the hypostasis from becoming a person, that is, from affirming itself as love and freedom. The body tends towards the person but leads finally to the individual. The result of this situation is that for a man to take the affirmation of his hypostasis further he has no need of a relationship (an ontological relationship, not simply a psychological one) with his parents. On the contrary, the breaking of this relationship constitutes the *precondition* of his self-affirmation.

Death is the "natural" development of the biological hypostasis, the cession of "space" and "time" to other individual hypostases, the sealing of hypostasis as individuality. At the same time it is also the definitely tragic "self-negation" of its own hypostasis (dissolution and annihilation of the body and of individuality), which in its attempt to affirm itself as hypostasis discovers that finally its "nature" has led it along a false path towards death. This "failure" of nature, as it is expressed in the biological identity of man, reveals two things simultaneously. The first is that, contrary to the "assurance" of its biological drive, for the "hypostasis" to survive it must express itself as "ecstasy"—not sequentially but simultaneously, not first as being and then as person.

[45]Cf. the reference made earlier to Dostoevsky. The youth in adolescence, in the very period in which he becomes conscious of his freedom, asks: "and who consulted me when I was brought into the world?" Unconsciously he articulates the great theme of the ontological necessity which exists in the biological hypostasis.

The second is that this "failure" of the survival of the biological hypostasis is not the result of some acquired fault of
a moral kind (a transgression), but of the very *constitutional
make-up* of the hypostasis, that is, of the biological act of the
perpetuation of the species.[46]

All this means that man as a biological hypostasis is intrinsically a tragic figure. He is born as a result of an *ecstatic*
fact—erotic love—but this fact is interwoven with a natural
necessity and therefore lacks ontological freedom. He is born
as a *hypostatic* fact, as a body, but this fact is interwoven
with individuality and with death. By the same erotic act with
which he tries to attain ecstasy he is led to individualism. His
body is the tragic instrument which leads to communion with
others, stretching out a hand, creating language, speech, con-
versation, art, kissing. But at the same time it is the "mask"
of hypocrisy, the fortress of individualism, the vehicle of the
final separation, death. "Wretched man that I am! Who will
deliver me from this body of death?" (Rom. 7:24). The
tragedy of the biological constitution of man's hypostasis
does not lie in his not being a person because of it; it lies in
his tending towards becoming a person through it and failing.
Sin is precisely this failure. And sin is the tragic prerogative
of the person alone.

Consequently, for salvation to become possible, for the un-
successful hypostasis to succeed, it is necessary that eros
and the body, as expression of ecstasy and of the hypostasis

---

[46]St Maximus the Confessor, following Gregory of Nyssa (*On the Creation
of Man* 16-18, PG 44:177 ff.), comes to the very root of the problem of
human existence when he regards the biological mode of procreation as a
result of the Fall (*Ambigua* 41, 42, PG 81:1309A, 1340C ff.; cf. *To
Thalassius: On Various Questions* 61, PG 90:6363). Those who attribute
this view of Maximus to a monastic or ascetic bias ignore the fact that he is
not an ordinary thinker but perhaps one of the greatest and most creative
geniuses in history, and that it is therefore impossible for him to say something without this being an organic and integral part of his whole thought.
Maximus's position on this question is inspired by Matt. 22:30, that is, by
the basic presupposition that the true "being" of man is found only in his
eschatological state (see below). Victory over death, the survival of the person, is incomprehensible without a change in the constitutive mode of the
human hypostasis, without a transcendence of the biological hypostasis. This
does not imply Manichaeism: the biological and the eschatological hypostases
are not mutually exclusive (see below at note 61).

of the person, should cease to be the bearers of death. Two things therefore appear to be indispensible: (a) that the two basic components of the biological hypostasis, eros and the body, should *not* be destroyed (a flight from these elements would entail for man a privation of those means by which he expresses himself equally as ecstasy and as hypostasis, that is, as person[47]); and (b) that the *constitutional make-up of the hypostasis* should be changed—not that a moral change or improvement should be found but a kind of new birth for man. This means that although neither eros nor the body are abandoned, they nevertheless change their activity, adapt themselves to the new "mode of existence" of the hypostasis, reject from this activity of theirs which is constitutive of the human hypostasis whatever creates the tragic element in man, and retain whatever makes the person to be love, freedom and life. This is precisely what constitutes that which I have called the "hypostasis of ecclesial existence."

2. The *hypostasis of ecclesial existence* is constituted by the new birth of man, by baptism. Baptism as new birth is precisely an act constitutive of hypostasis. As the conception and birth of a man constitute his biological hypostasis, so baptism leads to a new mode of existence, to a regeneration (I Pet. 1:3,23), and consequently to a new "hypostasis." What is the basis of this new hypostasis? How is man hypostasized by baptism and what does he become?

We have seen that the fundamental problem of the biological hypostasis of man lies in the fact that the ecstatic activity which leads to his birth is bound up with the "passion" of ontological necessity, in the fact that ontologically nature precedes the person and dictates its laws (by "instinct"), thus destroying freedom at its ontological base. This "passion" is closely connected with createdness, that is, with the fact that

[47]Soteriologies which are not inspired by genuine patristic theology have created the following dilemma: either hypostasis without ecstasy (a kind of individualist pietism), or ecstasy without hypostasis (a form of mystical escape from the body, an ecstasy of the type of the Hellenistic mysteries). The key to the soteriological problem lies in the safeguarding of both the ecstatic and the hypostatic dimensions of the person equally, without the "passions" of ontological necessity, individualism and death.

man as a person confronts, as we have already seen, the necessity of existence. Consequently it is impossible for created existence to escape ontological necessity in the constitution of the biological hypostasis: without "necessary" natural laws, that is, without ontological necessity, the biological hypostasis of man cannot exist.[48]

Consequently, if, in order to avoid the consequences of the tragic aspect of man which we have discussed, the person as absolute ontological freedom needs a hypostatic constitution without ontological necessity, his hypostasis must inevitably be rooted, or constituted, in an ontological reality which does not suffer from createdness. This is the meaning of the phrase in Scripture about being born "anew" or "from above." (John 3:3,7). It is precisely this possibility that patristic Christology strives to proclaim, to announce to man as the good news.

Christology, in the definitive form which the Fathers gave it, looks towards a single goal of purely existential significance, the goal of giving man the assurance that the quest for the person, not as a "mask" or as a "tragic figure," but as the authentic person, is not mythical or nostalgic but is a *historical reality*. Jesus Christ does not justify the title of Savior because he brings the world a beautiful revelation, a sublime teaching about the person, but because He realizes in history *the very reality of the person* and makes it the basis and "hypostasis" of the person for every man. Patristic theology therefore regarded the following points as the indispensible elements of Christology:

a) The identification of the person of Christ with the hypostasis of the Son of the Holy Trinity. The long dispute with Nestorianism was not an exercise of academic theology but a hard struggle with the existential question: how is it possible for Christ to be the Savior of man if His hypostasis is what I have called here the "hypostasis of biological existence"? If Christ as a person "subsists" not in freedom but according to the necessity of nature, then He too finally, that

[48]The artificial conception of a human being, if it is ever achieved, will by no means imply freedom as regards the constitutive mode of the human hypostasis. Instead it will imply the henceforth unfree replacement of nature and its laws with the laws of human reason.

is, definitively, fails to escape the tragic aspect of the human person.[49] The meaning of the virgin birth of Jesus is the negative expression of this existential concern of patristic theology. The positive expression of the same concern consists in the Chalcedonian doctrine that the person of Christ is *one* and is identified with the *hypostasis of the Son of the Trinity*.

b) The *hypostatic* union of the two natures—divine and human—in Christ. At this point it is important that a difference of emphasis should be stressed between the Greek and the Western Fathers which is parallel to that which was noted earlier in relation to the doctrine of the Holy Trinity. In the West, as is apparent in the *Tome* of Pope Leo I, the starting-point of Christology is found in the concept of the "natures" or "substances," whereas in the Greek Fathers, for example in Cyril of Alexandria, the starting-point of Christology is the hypostasis, the person. However much this might seem at first sight a mere detail, it is of the greatest significance. For it stresses not only, as we have seen, with regard to God but now also with regard to man that the basis of ontology is the person: just as God "is" what He is in His nature, "perfect God," only as person, so too man in Christ is "perfect man" only as hypostasis, as person, that is, as freedom and love. The perfect man is consequently only he who is authentically a person, that is, he who subsists, who possesses a "mode of existence" which is constituted as being, *in precisely the manner in which God also subsists as being—*

---

[49]I stress the word "finally" because this is of vital importance in Christology. All things in Christology are judged in the light of the resurrection. The incarnation in itself does not constitute a guarantee of salvation. The fact that *finally* death is conquered gives us the right to believe that the conqueror of death was also *originally* God. This is the way in which Christology in the New Testament has developed—from the resurrection to the incarnation, not the other way round—and patristic theology has never lost this eschatological approach to Christology. Consequently, when we say that Christ escaped the necessity and the "passions" of nature, we do not imply that He remained a stranger to the conditions of biological existence (for example, He suffered the supreme passion of the biological hypostasis, the passion of death). But the fact that He rose from the dead rendered this passion "without hypostasis": the real hypostasis of Christ was proved to be not the biological one, but the eschatological or trinitarian hypostasis.

in the language of human existence this is what a "hypostatic union" signifies.

Christology consequently is the proclamation to man that his nature can be "assumed" and hypostasized in a manner free from the ontological necessity of his biological hypostasis, which, as we have seen, leads to the tragedy of individualism and death. Thanks to Christ man can henceforth himself "subsist," can affirm his existence as personal not on the basis of the immutable laws of his nature, but on the basis of a relationship with God which is identified with what Christ in freedom and love possesses as Son of God with the Father. This adoption of man by God, the identification of his hypostasis with the hypostasis of the Son of God, is the essence of baptism.[50]

I have called this hypostasis which baptism gives to man "ecclesial" because, in fact, if one should ask, "How do we see this new biological hypostasis of man realised in history?" the reply would be, "In the Church." In early patristic literature the image of the Church as mother is often employed. The spirit of this image is precisely that in the Church a birth is brought about; man is born as "hypostasis," as person. This new hypostasis of man has all the basic characteristics of what I have called authentic peronhood, characteristics which distinguish the ecclesial hypostasis from the first hypostasis, the biological one. In what do these characteristics consist?

The first and most important characteristic of the Church is that she brings man into a kind of relationship with the world which is not determined by the laws of biology. The Christians of the early centuries, when their consciousness of what the Church is was lucid and clear, expressed this transcendence over the relationships created by the biological hypostasis by transferring *to the Church* the terminology which is used of

[50]The structure of the sacrament of baptism was identified at the outset with the structure of the evangelical narrative of the baptism of Jesus. The words, "this is my beloved [or: only-begotten] Son in whom I am well pleased," uttered by the Father with reference to the Son of the Trinity in the presence of the Spirit, are pronounced at baptism with reference to the person being baptized. In this way the structure of the Trinity is made the structure of the hypostasis of the person being baptized, a fact which makes Paul summarize the sense of baptism with the phrase, "Spirit of adoption, in which we cry Abba, Father" (Rom. 8:15).

the family.[51] Thus for the new ecclesial hypostasis "father" was not the physical progenitor but He "who is in heaven," and "brothers" were the members of the Church, not of the family. That this signified not a parallel co-existence of the ecclesial with the biological hypostasis but a transcendence of the latter by the former is apparent from the harshness of sayings like those which demand of Christians the abandonment—even the "hatred"—of their own relations.[52] These sayings do not signify a simple denial. They conceal an affirmation: the Christian through baptism stands over against the world, he exists as a relationship with the world, as a person, in a manner free from the relationship created by his biological identity. This means that henceforth he can love not because the laws of biology oblige him to do so—something which inevitably colors the love of one's own relations—but *unconstrained* by the natural laws. As an ecclesial hypostasis man thus proves that what is valid for God can also be valid for man: the nature does not determine the person; the person enables the nature to exist; freedom is identified with the being of man.

The result of this freedom of the person from the nature, of the hypostasis from biology, is that in the Church man transcends exclusivism. When man loves as a biological hypostasis, he inevitably excludes others: the family has priority in love over "strangers," the husband lays exclusive claim to the love of his wife—facts altogether understandable and "natural" for the biological hypostasis. For a man to love someone who is not a member of his family *more* than his own relations constitutes a transcendence of the exclusiveness which is present in the biological hypostasis. Thus a characteristic of the ecclesial hypostasis is the capacity of the person to love without exclusiveness, and to do this not out of conformity with a moral commandment ("Love thy neighbor,"

---

[51]"And I take it to mean Christ and the Church" (Eph. 5:32).

[52]"You are all brethren; and call no man your father on earth, for you have one Father, who is in heaven" (Matt. 23:8,9). Cf. Matt, 4:21; 10:25,27; 19:29 and parallel texts, especially Luke 14:26: "If anyone comes to me and does not hate his own father and mother and wife and children and brothers and sisters, yes, and even his own life . . ." that is, the whole network of relations that constitutes the biological hypostasis.

etc.), but out of his "hypostatic constitution," out of the fact
that his new birth from the womb of the Church has made
him part of a network of relationships which transcends every
exclusiveness.[53] This means that only in the Church has man
the power to express himself as a catholic person. Catholicity,
as a characteristic of the Church, permits the person to become
a hypostasis without falling into individuality, because in the
Church two things are realized simultaneously: the world
is presented to man not as mutually exclusive portions which
he is called upon to unite *a posteriori,* but as a single whole,
which is expressed in a catholic manner without division in
every concrete being; simultaneously the same man, while
relating to the world precisely through this catholic mode
of existence that he has, comes to express and realize a catholic presence in the world, a hypostasis which is not an individual but an authentic person. Thus the Church becomes
Christ Himself in human existence, but also every member of
the Church becomes Christ[54] and Church.[55] The ecclesial
hypostasis exists historically in this manner as a confirmation
of man's capacity not to be reduced to his tendency to become
a bearer of individuality, separation and death. The ecclesial
hypostasis is the *faith* of man in his capacity to become a
person and his *hope* that he will indeed become an authentic
person. In other words it is faith and hope in the immortality
of man as a person.

    This last sentence leads us to a most important point, to
which we must address ourselves at once. For all that I have
said so far leaves a question unanswered: what happens to
the biological hypostasis of man when that which I have
called the ecclesial hypostasis is brought into being? Experience tells us that in spite of the existence of baptism and the
ecclesial hypostasis, man does not cease at the same time to

---

[53]Thus the Church proves (a) that salvation is not a matter of moral
perfection, an improvement of nature, but a new hypostasis of nature, a new
creation, and (b) that this new hypostasis is not something theoretical, but
a historical *experience,* even though it is not permanent.

[54]It is characteristic that according to the Fathers every baptized person
becomes "Christ."

[55]St Maximus the Confessor in his *Mystagogy* (4, PG 91:672 BC) applies
the catholicity of the Church to the existential make-up of each believer.

be born and to die in accordance with his biological hypostasis. What kind of experience of authentic personhood is it that the ecclesial hypostasis offers?

In order to reply to this question we really need a new ontological category—not to destroy the distinction which I have made between biological and ecclesial hypostases, but to express the relationship of these two to each other. In fact the encounter between the ecclesial and the biological hypostases creates a paradoxical relationship in human existence. Man appears to exist in his ecclesial identity not as that which he is but as that which he *will* be; the ecclesial identity is linked with eschatology, that is, with the final outcome of his existence.

This consideration of the human person from the point of view of a *telos* must not be interpreted with the help of an Aristotelian entelechy, that is, with the help of a potentiality existing in man's nature which enables him to become something better and more perfect than that which he is now.[56] Through all that I have said in this study, I have excluded every possibility of regarding the person as an expression or emanation of the substance or nature of man (or even of God Himself as "nature"). Consequently there is no question of the ecclesial hypostasis, the authentic person, emerging as a result of an evolution of the human race, whether biological or historical.[57] The situation created by the expectation and hope of the ecclesial identity, by this paradoxical hypostasis which has its roots in the future and its branches in the present,[58] could perhaps have been expressed by another ontological category, which I would call here a *sacramental* or *eucharistic hypostasis.*

3. All that I have said above to describe the ecclesial hypostasis as something different from the biological corresponds

---

[56]Teilhard de Chardin's understanding of man bears no relation to patriatic theology.

[57]Herein also lies a fundamental distinction between Christianity and Marxism.

[58]The Epistle to the Hebrews (11:1) uses the term "hypostasis" precisely with the meaning which I am endeavoring to describe here, that is, as an ontology which has its roots in the future, in eschatology.

historically and experientially only to the holy eucharist. The transcendence of the ontological necessity and exclusiveness entailed by the biological hypostasis constitutes an experience which is offered by the eucharist. When it is understood in its correct and primitive sense—and not how it has come to be regarded even in Orthodoxy under the influence of Western scholasticism—the eucharist is first of all an assembly (*synaxis*),[59] a community, a network of relations, in which man "subsists" in a manner different from the biological as a member of a body which transcends every exclusiveness of a biological or social kind. The eucharist is the only historical context of human existence where the terms "father," "brother," etc., lose their biological exclusiveness and reveal, as we have seen, relationships of free and universal love.[60] Patristic theology saw in the eucharist the historical realization of the philosophical principle which governs the concept of the person, the principle that the hypostasis expresses the whole of its nature and not just a part. There Christ is "parted but not divided" and every communicant is

[59]The term ἐκκλησία is not unrelated in its original Christian usage to the fact of the eucharistic community. For the relevant sources see my work, *The Unity of the Church in the Holy Eucharist and the Bishop during the First Three Centuries* (in Greek—1965), pp. 29-59.

[60]If the Lord's prayer was indeed, as it appears, a eucharistic prayer from the beginning, there is special significance in the fact that the expression, "Our Father, who are in heaven," appears there evidently in contradistinction to the relation of every believer with his earthly father. Also illuminating is the history of the use of the term "father" for the clergy. Originally it was used only of the bishop, precisely because only he was seated "in the place of God" (Ignatius) and offered the eucharist. Then it was transferred to the presbyter when he finally assumed a role of leadership in the eucharistic community with the creation of parishes. With regard to the catholicity of the eucharistic community, that is, the transcendence of natural and social divisions, let us note the strict ancient canonical requirement that only one eucharist should be celebrated in the same place on the same day. This prescription (which today among the Orthodox is circumvented "intelligently" by the erection of a new altar and the services of another priest in the same church on the same day) had as its aim precisely the practical safeguarding of the possibility for all the faithful of the same locality to participate in the same eucharistic community. I leave aside the other new custom of celebrating the eucharist only for certain groups of Christians, whether social (for students, scholars, etc.) or natural (for small children, etc.), or even specially for members of organizations. What we have here is the establishment of a heresy in the midst of Orthodoxy, the denial of the catholicity of the eucharistic community.

the whole Christ and the whole Church. The ecclesial identity, consequently, in its historical realization is eucharistic. This explains why the Church has bound every one of her acts to the eucharist, which has as its object man's transcendence of his biological hypostasis and his becoming an authentic person, like those acts which we call "sacraments." The sacraments when not united with the eucharist are a blessing and confirmation which is given to nature as biological hypostasis. United, however, with the eucharist, they become not a blessing and confirmation of the biological hypostasis, but a rendering of it transcendent and eschatological.[61]

It is precisely this eschatological character of the eucharist that helps us to reply to the question, "What is the relationship of the ecclesial with the biological hypostasis?" The eucharist is not only an assembly in one place, that is, a historical realization and manifestation of the eschatological existence of man; it is at the same time also *movement,* a progress towards this realization. Assembly and movement are the two fundamental characteristics of the eucharist, which unfortunately have lost their vigor in the modern teaching of dogma, even in the Orthodox Church. However, they constitute the vital core of patristic eucharistic theology.[62] Besides this, they make the eucharist *liturgy.* This liturgical, progressive movement of the eucharist, its eschatological orientation, proves that in its eucharistic expression the ecclesial hypostasis is not of this world—it belongs to the eschatological

[61]On the fact that the sacraments were all formerly linked with the eucharist see P. Trembelas, 'I Theia Efcharietia kata tin synarthrosin aftis pros ta alla mystiria kai mystirioeideis teletas', *Efcharistirion,* essays in honour of H. Alivisatos, 1958, pp. 462-72. The theological significance of this liturgical fact is immense. For example, it would be a mistake to regard marriage as a simple confirmation and blessing of a biological fact. Linked with the eucharist it becomes a reminder that although the newly married couple have been blessed in order to create their own family, nevertheless the ultimate and essential network of relationships which constitutes their hypostasis is not the family but the Church as expressed in the eucharistic assembly. This eschatological transcendence of the biological hypostasis is also conveyed by the "crowning" of the bride and groom, but is lost essentially and existentially from the moment the rite of marriage is separate from the eucharist.

[62]In St Maximus's *Mystagogy* the holy eucharist is understood as movement, as progress towards the goal (τὸ πέρας). This dimension of the eucharist is weakened in the interpretations of the eucharist towards the end of the Byzantine age, and is lost entirely in the modern dogmatic handbooks.

transcendence of history and not simply to history. The ecclesial hypostasis reveals man as a person, which, however, has its roots in the future and is perpetually inspired, or rather maintained and nourished, by the future. *The truth and the ontology of the person belong to the future, are images of the future.*[63]

What exactly does this hypostasis mean for the existence of man, this hypostasis which is "the assurance (ὑπόστασις) of things hoped for, the conviction of things not seen" (Heb. 11:1)? Does not this siutation bring us back to the tragic aspect of the person?

This eschatological character of the ecclesial hypostasis contains, of course, a kind of dialectic, the dialectic of "already but not yet." This dialectic pervades the eucharist.[64] It makes man as a person always sense that his true home is not in this world, a perception which is expressed by his refusal to locate the confirmation of the hypostasis of the person in this world, in the goods and values of this world.[65] The ecclesial hypostasis, as a transcendence of the biological, draws its being from the being of God and from that which it *will* itself be at the end of the age. It is precisely this which makes the ecclesial hypostasis ascetic.[66]

[63]Maximus gives a philosophical summary of the authentic patristic (and one would also say "biblical") ontology when he identifies the true nature of beings with the future, with the last things: "For 'shadow' refers to the things of the Old Testament, 'image' to the things of the New Testament, and 'truth' to the future state" (Scholion on the *Ecclesiastical Hierarchy* 3, 3, 2, PG 4:137D). Cf. below ch. II.

[64]See, for example the Revelation of St John: although nothing is more certain there than the presence of Christ in the eucharist, and yet the cry, "Come, Lord," and the assurance, "I am coming soon" (22:8-17) change Him who is already present into Him who is expected, or rather, make Him present precisely as the expected one. Cf. *Didaohe* 9, 10.

[65]It is therefore better understood for example why "the root of all evils is avarice" (1 Tim 6:10) and wealth excludes from the Kingdom of God (Luke 6:24 etc.). This has to do not with a moral fault but with the location of the hypostasis of being, of its security, in this world, in the substance and not in the person. (Is it simply a coincidence that the term οὐσία came also to mean "property" or "possessions" very early on? See Luke 15:12. Cf. Euripides. *Madness of Herakles* 337; Aristophanes, *Ekklesiazousai* 729.)

[66]The meaning of asceticism consists in the fact that the less one makes one's hypostasis rely on nature, on the substance, the more one is hypostasized as a person. In this way asceticism does not deny "nature" but frees it from

The ascetic character of the ecclesial hypostasis does not come from a denial of the world or of the biological *nature* of existence itself.[67] It implies a denial of the biological *hypostasis*. It accepts the biological nature but wishes to hypostasize it in a non-biological way, to endow it with real being, to give it a true ontology, that is, eternal life. It is for this reason that I stated previously that neither eros nor the body must be abandoned but must be hypostasized according to the "mode of existence" of the ecclesial hypostasis. The ascetic character of the person, derived as it is from the eucharistic form of the ecclesial hypostasis, expresses the authentic person precisely when it does not deny eros and the body but hypostasizes them in an ecclesial manner. In accordance with what I have said so far, in practice this means basically that eros as *ecstatic* movement of the human person drawing its hypostasis from the future, as it is expressed in the eucharist (or from God through the eucharist, as it is expressed in the Trinity), is freed from ontological necessity and does not lead any more to the exclusiveness which is dictated by nature. It becomes a movement of free love with a universal character, that is, of love which, while it can concentrate on one person as the expression of the whole of nature, sees in this person the hypostasis through which all men and all things are loved and in relation to which they are hypostasized.[68] The body, for

the ontological necessity of the biological hypostasis; it enables it to *be* in an authentic manner. It is superfluous to stress that this does not suffice to bring about the transcendence of the biological hypostasis if nature is not "hypostasized" simultaneously in the eucharistic community. Other, non-Christian soteriological systems also exhibit asceticism as a transcendence of the biological hypostasis. But only the Church offers the positive side of this transcendence in the way I have just described with reference to the eucharist. (From the point of view of the historical phenomenology of religions it must some day be understood that only the eucharist in its correct sense is the specific differentiating factor of Christianity.) Without the ascetic dimension, the person is inconceivable. But in the end the context of the manifestation of the person is not the monastery: it is the eucharist.

[67]The λόγος φύσεως has no need of transformation; the τρόπος φύσεως demands it. Maximus, *Ambigua* 42, PG 91:1340BC, 1341C.

[68]The great existential significance of patristic Christology consists in the fact that the capacity of the person to love in one person alone all things and all men is an attribute of God, who as *Father,* although He hypostasizes and loves one Son alone (the "only-begotten"), can "through the Son" love and

its part, as the hypostatic expression of the human person, is liberated from individualism and egocentricity and becomes a supreme expression of *community*—the Body of Christ, the body of the Church, the body of the eucharist. Thus it is proved experientially that the body is not in itself a negative or exclusive concept, but the reverse: a concept of communion and love. In this hypostasis which it has, the body transcends together with its individualism and separation from other beings even its own dissolution, which is death. Since it has been shown as a body of communion to be free from the laws of its biological nature with regard to individualism and exclusiveness, why should it not also be shown finally to be free even from the very laws relating to death, which are only the other side of the same coin? The ecclesial existence of man, his hypostasization in a eucharistic manner, thus constitutes a pledge, an "earnest," of the final victory of man over death. This victory will be a victory not of nature but of the person, and consequently not a victory of man in his self-sufficiency but of man in his hypostatic union with God, that is, a victory of Christ as the man of patristic Christology.

It is precisely on this point that the eucharistic hypostasis differs from the tragic person of humanism, that is, on the fact that in spite of living the tragic aspect of the biological hypostasis intensely and absolutely—from which christian asceticism also comes[69]—it does not draw its being from what it is now but is rooted ontologically in the future, the pledge and earnest of which is the resurrection of Christ. As often as he tastes and experiences this hypostasis in the eucharist, man is confirmed in his certitude that the person which is hypostasized by love freed from biological necessity and exclusiveness will not finally die. When the eucharistic community keeps alive the memory of our loved ones—living as well as dead—it does not just preserve a psychological recol-

---

bestow hypostasis on all creation ("all things were created through Him and for Him." Col. 1:16).

[69]The similarities which appear at first sight to exist between the understanding of man in the works of the ascetic Fathers and the insights of contemporary existentialism arise from this. But the ascetic Fathers do not exhaust the concept of the person in the reality of the biological hypostasis; they also recognize its echatological transcendence.

lection; it proceeds to an act of ontology, to the assurance that the person has the final word over nature, in the same way that God the Creator as person and not as nature had the very first word. Belief in creation *ex nihilo*—biblical faith—thus encounters belief in ontology—Greek faith—to give to human existence and thought its most dear and precious good, the concept of the person. This and nothing less than this is what the world owes to Greek patristic theology.

2.

Truth and Communion

I. Introduction: The Problem of Truth in the Patristic Era

Christology is the sole starting point for a Christian understanding of truth. Christ's claim to be the truth (John 14:6) constitutes a fundamental presupposition for Christian theology. On this point, both East and West have always been in agreement. It would serve no purpose to make reference to concrete examples from the history of Christian thought to demonstrate this common presupposition to all the Christian traditions. Nevertheless, this presupposition is by no means easy to interpret. How should one understand Christ to be the truth? "What is truth?" (John 18:38) Christ left Pontius Pilate's question unanswered, and throughout the ages the Church has not answered it with one voice. Our problems today concerning truth appear to stem directly from these different understandings of truth in the course of the Church's history.

The fundamental distinctions which are made in connection with this subject appear to date back to the first encounter of Christianity with Greek thought. Even though we must always keep in mind the fact that in the Bible itself Greek thought is very often mixed up with what is customarily termed Semitic thought, or the Jewish mentality,[1] we should nevertheless be aware of the existence of a particular thought-form which could be called "Hellenic" and which tends to assert

[1] See J. Barr, *The Semantics of Biblical Language* (1961), and recently the massive study by M. Hengel, *Judaism and Hellenism*, I-II (1974).

67

its own characteristics in its encounter with the Gospel. This being said, it would be wrong to deduce too easily, as many scholars have done, that biblical thinking, particularly in its New Testament form, is to be identified with what one would call Hebrew or Jewish thought-forms. When St Paul presents the cross of Christ as the content of his preaching, he stands against the Greek and Jewish mentalities simultaneously. The Christian message may be confused neither with the "wisdom" of the Greeks nor with the Jewish preoccupation with "signs" (I Cor. 1:22).

This confrontation between the Christological content of the Gospel message on one hand, and on the other the Jewish as well as the Greek mentality, is directly connected with the problem of truth. It is usually felt that the principal characteristic of Hebrew thinking as opposed to that of the Greeks resides in the Jews' interest in history. The "signs" which the Jews seek, says St Paul, are precisely the manifestations of God's presence and His activity in history. By and in these "signs," truth makes itself known historically as God's faithfulness towards His people. When in the Old Testament the *'emeth* of God is proffered, it follows that the Word of God is sound, certain and consistent.[2] Truth thus becomes identical with the "oath" of God who goes back on nothing (Ps. 132:11) and for this reason offers security.[3] All this takes place within the field of a history which is created by God's promises to His People. Consequently, the people's response itself forms part of this definition of truth. Loyalty to God, the carrying out of His will or the fulfilling of His Law amount to "doing the truth."[4] According to this way of understanding truth, it is God's promises which may be considered as ultimate truth, and these promises coincide with the goal or fulfilment of history. It is in short an eschatological truth which orients the human spirit towards the future.

The Greek mind, for its part, seeks truth in a way which transcends history. Starting from the observation of the world, Greek thought raises the question of being in a way which

2E.g. II Sam. 7:28; Ps. 119:160, cf. Deut. 7:9; Is. 49:7, etc.
3Ps. 40:12, 61:8, etc.
4I Kings 2:4; II Kings 20:3; Is. 38:3; Ps. 86:11, etc.

is organically and inseparably connected with the observing and perceiving mind. In the presocratic period Greek thought concentrated on the basic link between *being* (εἶναι) and thought (νοεῖν).[5] Despite later developments, and many variations throughout its history,[6] Greek thought never abandoned the unity existing between the intelligible world (νοητά), the thinking mind (νοῦς) and being (εἶναι).[7] Thanks to the unity between these three elements, the Greek mind achieved a wonderful sense of κόσμος, a term which signifies harmony and beauty. It is precisely in this unity that truth is to be found. Truth is essentially identical with virtue (ἀρετή) and beauty (τὸ καλόν).[8] This is why truth for the Greeks is primarily a *cosmological* question.

As a consequence of this way of thinking, the place of *history* is problematical in Greek ontology. Historical events either have to be explained by some λόγος, that is, they must be attributed to some cause which accounts for them,[9] or else explained away, i.e. dismissed as having no meaning in existence.[10] To explain history or to explain it away are not as different as might appear at first sight. The Neoplatonism which explains away history and matter was as Greek in mentality as the great historians and artists of the classical

[5]E.g. Parmenides, *Fragments* 5d, 7: "Thought and being are one and the same. Thought and that for which thought exists are one and the same." Cf. Plato, *Parmenides* 128b. Cf. Clement of Alexandria, *Strom.* VI.

[6]On the nuances of the relationship between εἶναι and λόγος, see M. Heidegger's observations in his *Einführung in die Metaphysik* (1953), esp. p. 88f.

[7]This is found as late in the history of Greek thought as the Neoplatonic period. See e.g. Plotinus, *En.* V, 1, 8, etc. C.f. K. Kremer, *Die neuplatonische Seinsphilosophie und ihre Wirkung auf Thomas von Aquin* (1966 [1971]), p. 79ff. Concerning the fact that we have here a survival of the original monism of Greek thought, see C.J. De Vogel, *Philosophia I, Studies in Greek Philosophy* (Philosophical Texts and Studies, 19) I (1970), pp. 397-416. C.f. on these problems Chapter I of this book.

[8]The idea of the good appears also to be identical with truth, and it is the λόγος which creates this identity so that ἀρετή and γνῶσις become one and the same (e.g. throughout the *Meno* and in the *Republic* of Plato).

[9]Greek classical historiography used this method. See C.N. Cochrane, *Christianity and Classical Culture* (1944), p. 457ff.

[10]Neoplatonic thought betrays this attitude. According to his biographer Porphyry, Plotinus was ashamed of his body and refused to speak of his ancestors or to pose for a sculptor or painter (Porphyry, *Vita Plot.* I).

period. Both sides shared the same ontological presupposition which assumed that existence constituted a *unity,* a *closed circle*[11] which is formed by the λόγος and the νοῦς. History and matter either had to conform to this unity or else fall from existence. History insomuch as it is the domain of *freedom,* where the person—divine or human—seems so often to be operating "irrationally" and arbitrarily, thus contradicting the closed ontological unity created by the conjunction of being and λόγος, could not be the basis for and approach towards truth.[12]

This "closed ontology" or monism of the Greek mind constitutes in our opinion the crucial point of conflict between Greek thought and biblical thought in the period of the Greek Fathers. It is this point which, with the inseparably linked problem of history and matter, illustrates the challenge hurled at the Bible by Greek thought concerning truth, not just in the period of the Greek Fathers but also in the Middle Ages and in modern times, including our own era. The problem may thus be presented as follows: How can a Christian hold to the idea that truth operates in history and creation when the ultimate character of truth, and its uniqueness, seem irreconcilable with the change and decay to which history and creation are subject?

The New Testament way of understanding truth, with its christological character, seems to contradict both the Jewish and Greek ideas of truth such as have been presented here. By referring to Christ as the Alpha and Omega of history, the New Testament has transformed radically the linear histori-

[11]Cf. E. L. Mascall, *The Openness of Being* (1971), p. 246f, who refers to classical Greek thought, Platonic and Aristotelian alike, as holding a doctrine of "closed" natures. For all pagan Greeks "everything had a nicely rounded-off nature which contained implicitly everything that the being could ever become . . . What Greek thought could not have tolerated . . . would have been the idea that a being could become more perfect in its kind by acquiring some characteristic which was not implicit in its nature before."

[12]It is noteworthy that, whatever notion of history one encounters in Middle Platonism, one is always faced with 'the conviction that the original truth suffers a sort of deprivation or "fall" when it passes through history. See, for example, concerning Celsus, C. Andresen, *Logos und Nomos: Die Polemik des Kelsus wider das Christentum* (1955), pp. 146ff., or concerning Nemesius, J. H. Waszink, *Timaeus a Calcidio Translatus* (1962), pp. XLIIff.

cism of Hebrew thought, since in a certain way the end of
history in Christ becomes *already* present here and now. Likewise, in affirming that Christ, i.e. a historical being, is the
truth, the New Testament hurls a challenge to Greek thought,
since it is in the flow of history and through it, through its
changes and ambiguities, that man is called to discover the
meaning of existence.[13] If, therefore, we want to be faithful to
the christological character of truth, we must affirm the historical character of truth and not despise it for the sake of its
"meaning." In this connection, the reactions in our time
against cetrain "demythologizing" approaches to the New
Testament are clearly justified.[14] Nevertheless, it must be
affirmed that if by this "historicity" of the truth we understand
a linear, Jewish historicism, for which the future constitutes
a reality still to come, as though it had not at all arrived in
history, then we are departing radically from the conception
of the truth found in the New Testament. Thus, the problem
which the christological character of truth has presented to
the Church from its earliest days may be summarized in the
following question: How can we hold at one and the same
time to the historical nature of truth and the presence of
ultimate truth here and now? *How, in other words, can
truth be considered simultaneously from the point of view
of the "nature" of being (Greek preoccupation)[15] from the
view of the goal or end of history (preoccupation of the*

[13]For a Greek life Plato, for example, truth is not only one but also stable
and unchanging. As such it belongs to the world of ideas and not to history
or the world of sensible reality: to the latter belongs only opinion (δόξα).

[14]See e.g. W. Pannenberg, *Grundzüge der Christologie* (1964), p. 97; also
his "Die Aufnahme des philosophischen Gottesbegriffs als dogmatisches Problem der früchrist. Theologie," in *Zeitschrift für Kirchengeschichte* 70 (1950),
pp. 1-45.

[15]The association of truth with the "nature" of being (φύσις) in the
Christian tradition arises out of the Greek concept of truth. C.f. T. F. Torrance,
"Truth and Authority: Theses on Truth," in *The Irish Theological Quarterly*
39 (1972), p. 222. This is established principally through Aristotle, whose
metaphysics "is not torn between ontology and theology, as is often still
asserted, following Jaeger, but find its centre of gravity in ousiology," substance
being for Aristotle the foundation for all ontology:" H. Barreau *Aristotle et
l'analyse du savoir* (Philosophie de tous les temps 81) I (1972), p. 113. The
problem thus made out, and the way that the Greek Fathers overcame it, will
be discussed in part II, 3 of this chapter.

Jews), and from the viewpoint of Christ, who is both a historical person and the permanent ground (the λόγος*) of being (the Christian claim)—and all while preserving God's "otherness" in relation to creation?*

The intention of this study is to try to give an answer to this question, with the aid of Greek patristic thought. We believe that the question and also the answer worked out by the Greek Fathers for their age are extremely meaningful for ourselves today. We also think that the idea of "communion" has been the decisive tool in the hands of the Greek Fathers to allow them to answer this question, and that it continues to be the key to our own answer to the problem today. And so we shall try first to understand the efforts of the Greek Fathers, their failures and their successes, in arriving at an understanding of truth which might have meaning for a person of Greek mentality, without betraying or distorting the message of the Bible. From there we shall pass on to apply this understanding of truth to the essential requirements of the Christian faith, that is, to the relationship between truth and salvation. Finally, we shall try to see the importance of all this for ecclesiology, in both its theoretical and its practical implications for the structure and ministry of the Church.

II.   *Truth, Being and History: The Greek Patristic Synthesis*

1.   *The "Logos" Approach*

One of the most dramatic attempts to reconcile the Greek idea of truth with the Christian claim, that Christ is the truth, was that made in the first three centuries with the help of the idea of *logos*. This attempt seems to have originated with the Greek apologists, particularly Justin, but found its most audacious representatives among the Alexandrian theologians: Clement and above all Origen.

It is well known that the concept of *logos* became in the hands of Philo an instrument for harmonizing Greek cosmology with the Old Testament (Gen. 1: the world was created by the *logos* of God). By applying this idea to Christ, on the basis of the prologue to the Fourth Gospel, Justin established a foundation from which to communicate to the Greeks the affirmation that Christ is the truth. But although this offered the possibility of converting Greek thought to Christianity and made all Christians debtors to the apologists, it was nevertheless full of danger for the Christian gospel. This becomes clear when we consider the question of truth.

In declaring that Christ is the truth just because He is the *logos*, in and through whom the world was made and existence finds its foundations and meaning, Justin developed an idea of truth similar if not identical to that of Platonism. God, as ultimate truth, is understood to be "he who is always the same in himself and in relation to all things,"[16] and who is known "only through the mind."[17] Truth is thus taken in the Platonic sense of something fixed which establishes its links with the world in and through the mind. This mind (νοῦς) was given, according to Justin, simply "in order to contemplate (καθορᾶν) that same being who is the cause of all intelligent beings (νοητῶν)."[18]

The significant point about this way of approach to truth is that the possibility of knowing God, the truth, for Justin is due to the συγγένεια (relationship of an ontological character) between God and the soul or νοῦς.[19] In a typically Platonic manner, Justin attributes error, or ψεῦδος, entirely to the presence of things of the senses, and to the body especially. The νοῦς is present equally for all men, and the bond (συγγένεια) between God the truth and man is permanent. It suffices that man should liberate himself from the influences of the body in order to "behold" truth.[20] From what we have just said, it is clear that underlying Justin's way of understanding truth is not only the dualism between things

[16]Justin, *Dial.* 3, 5: "Τὸ κατὰ τὰ αὐτὰ καὶ ὡσαύτως ἀεὶ ἔχον" c.f. Plato, *Republic* 6.4846: "τοῦ ἀεὶ κατὰ τὰ αὐτὰ ὡσαύτως ἔχοντος." The reading τὸ ὂν instead of Θεόν, which is preferred by some, does not affect in any essential way what we are seeking to show here.

[17]*Ibid.* 3, 7 "τὸ θεῖον . . . μόνον νῷ καταληπτόν." Compare this with the Greek Fathers' idea of the "incomprehensibility" (ἀκατάληπτον) of divine nature.

[18]*Ibid.* 4, 1.

[19]*Ibid.* 4, 2.

[20]*Ibid.* 4, 3.

of the senses and of the intellect but—more importantly—
the ontologically necessary link between God and the world.[21]
The permanent συγγένεια between God and man through
the medium of νοῦς leads us to take the idea of *logos*, employed by Justin in a christological sense, as the bond between
God and the world, between truth and the mind. Christ, as
the *logos* of God, becomes this very link between truth and
the mind, and the truth of philosophy is nothing less than
part of this *logos*.[22]

The danger of monist ontology is evident in all this, but
in this case the danger was not apparent at the level of constituting a problem for the Church. The reason is probably
that Justin neither elaborated theologically upon the basis of
this monism nor claimed any official place for philosophy in
the life of the Church. This was done by Clement of Alexandria, who introduced philosophy officially into the Church,[23]
and by Origen, who tried to elaborate a theological system
starting from Greek philosophy. The application of the *logos*
concept in this context led to the crisis of Arianism, which
compelled the Church to revise the concept radically.

Clement's way of understanding truth develops along the
direction mentioned in connection with Justin.[24] The influence

[21]This must be emphasized as against attempts to dissociate Justin from
Platonism. See e.g. J.N. Hydahl, *Philosophie und Christentum: Eine Interpre-
tation der Einleitung zum Dialog Justins* (1966). As H. Chadwick says in
Early Christian Thought and the Classical Tradition (1966), p. 12: "For a
Platonist to accept Christianity, as Justin himself has done, is no revolutionary
step involving a radical rejection of his earlier world view."

[22]Hence Justin's idea of the λόγος σπερματικὸς (*Apol. I*, 44, 10). He
considers that philosophers depart from the truth only when they disagree with
one another (*ibid.*). The distinction between the λόγος σπερματικὸς
and the σπέρματα τοῦ λόγου made by R. Holte ("*Logos Speermatikos,*
Christianity and Ancient Philosophy according to St. Justin's Apologies," in
Studia Theologica 12 [1958] p. 170ff.) and which led J. Daniélou
(*Message evangelique et culture béllénistique* [1961] p. 45) to a kind
of deplationization of Justin, must be seen within the framework of the
συγγένεια between mind and God which Justin seems to hold to. Whether
the Logos implants the seed of truth or whether these seeds are part of the
human *logos*, the fact remains that for Justin it is this fundamental συγγένεια
which makes the work of the incarnate Logos possible.

[23]Cf. G. Kretschmar, "Le développement de la doctrine du Saint-Esprit du
Nouveau Testament à Nicée," in *Verbum Caro* 22 (1968) p. 20.

[24]The idea that truth exists "partially" (μερικῶς) outside Christ (cf. p.

of Greek thought on Clement's conception of truth can be seen in his way of envisaging the idea of God—truth as the "nature" of being. This viewpoint was to have a decisive importance for later theology in the East, as we shall see,[25] and equally in the West. In the fragments of Clement which the works of St Maximus the Confessor have preserved for us, "nature" is equivalent to "the truth of things."[26] This concept of truth as "nature" leads Clement to understand the nature of God as "spirit" (based on Jn. 4:24).[27] Consequently, "spirit" is defined as "nature" which leads to the idea developed by Origen that "spirit" is God's corporal "substance."[28]

Origen, by contrast with Clement, did not wish to be a philosopher but an *ecclesiasticus,* a man of tradition. He therefore tried to construct a system based on the creed, denying nothing which the Church professed, but attempting to explain tradition in a philosophical manner. Whether he managed to do this while preserving the biblical perspective on truth can be decided only after examining two fundamental aspects of his teaching: the doctrine of creation, and the interpretation of Scripture.

Despite his doctrine of creation *ex nihilo,* Origen connected the idea of God so closely with that of creation that he came to speak of eternal creation, arguing that God would not be eternally omnipotent with no object on which to exercise his power.[29] God thus becomes eternally a creator, and the link between the *logos* of God and the *logoi* of creation thus comes to be organic and unbreakable, as in the Greek idea of truth.[30] The interpretation of the Scriptures in Origen

58 n. 4) continues to play a fundamental role, also in Clement. See J. Daniélou, *op. cit.* pp. 50ff and 67ff.

[25] See below, section II § 3.

[26] Maximus the Confessor, *Op. th. et pol.,* PG 91: 254: "φύσις ἐστὶν ἡ τῶν πραγμάτων ἀλήθεια."

[27] See *Fragm.* in the edition of O. Staehlin, *Clemens Alexandrinus* (1909), p. 220.

[28] Origen, *De Princ.* I, 1, 4. This is the result of Stoic influence (G. Kretchmar, *op. cit.* p. 23) but clearly displays the difficulties inherent in approaching God by means of His "nature." See below, section II, §§ 3-4.

[29] Origen, *De Princ.* I, 4, 3.

[30] See J. Daniélou, *Origéne* (1948), p. 258, on the Stoic influence on Origen in this area.

likewise implies an idea of truth which is essentially Greek. Although Origen does not deny the reality or historicity of the biblical events, what definitely counts when interpreting the Bible is the *meaning* of these events. Even the cross of Christ is the symbol of something higher, and only the *simpliciores* can be content with the pure fact of the crucifixion.[31] Truth resides in the meaning of things, and once this meaning has been grasped, the things bearing it lose their importance.[32] In quite an interesting way, this leads Origen to place the accent on eschatology, although this eschatalogy is oriented not towards a consummation of history, but towards the eternal significance of events.

This view of things has very clear implications concerning the understanding of Christ's claim to be the truth. Christ is "truth itself" (αὐτοαλήθεια),[33] but not because of his humanity. "No one among us is so simple minded as to think that the essence of truth was not in existence before the moment of its manifestation in Christ."[34] This does not mean that Christ's humanity is to be rejected, but that in its relation to truth, it is "true" only in so far as it *participates* in the truth.[35]

The crucial point enabling us to judge Origen's position on this delicate topic is precisely the importance for truth of the *historical* Christ. Interpreting John 1:17 (". . . the truth came (ἐγένετο) by Jesus Christ.") and attempting to reconcile this with John 14:6 ("I am the truth"), Origen writes: "Nothing is produced by its own intermediary. But this (i.e. the word ἐγένετο) must be taken as meaning that truth itself, the essential (οὐσιώδης) truth . . . the prototype of

[31]*In Jo.* I, 9: To preach "Christ and Christ crucified" is the "somatic gospel" aimed at the simple people, while for the "spiritual" the Gospel is that of the Logos and its being in God since the beginning. Cf. G. Florovsky, "Origen, Eusebius and the Iconoclastic Controversy," in *Church History* 19 (1950), pp. 77-96, esp. p. 88.

[32]Thus the Old Testament prophets in effect knew the truth essentially as much as the apostles themselves. See *In Jo.* I, 24, cf. G. Florovsky, *op. cit.* p. 89.

[33]*In Jo.* VI, 6.

[34]*Contra Celsum* VIII, 12.

[35]See H. Crouzel, *Origéne et la connaissance mystique* (1961), p. 34, on the idea of participation and its place in Origen's conception of truth.

the truth which is found in spiritual souls, this truth of which a kind of image has been imprinted in those who think according to the truth, *has not been produced by the intermediary of Jesus Christ, nor by any other intermediary, but has been actualized* (ἐγένετο) *by God.*"[36] Origen thus appears to understand the "came" of John 1:17 not as a historical event, such as the incarnation, but in cosmological terms;[37] the truth has been *directly imprinted by God*—evidently in the eternal creation of the world. For this reason, truth exists as the very nature of being (οὐσιωδῶς).[38] "Every man of wisdom, *in the measure of his participation in wisdom,* participates in the Christ who is wisdom."[39] Our remark here, delicate but fundamental, is that "wisdom" does not depend on the Christ-event, but, in a sense, Christ participates in wisdom. We cannot invert the assertion "Christ is the truth" and say "the truth is Christ," since the historical Christ appears to be the truth precisely because of his participation in truth, being the *logos* of creation—not because he is Jesus of Nazareth.

Thus, the problem which Origen and the whole current of *logos* theology leave unanswered is: how can we understand the *historical* Christ to be the truth? If the historical Christ is the truth by virtue of his being simultaneously the *logos* of God and of creation, it seems to indicate that the incarnation does not *realize* the truth in a fundamental way, but merely *reveals* a pre-existing truth. This idea of *revelation* seems to lie at the very heart of the problem, since revelation always unifies existence, through an idea or a meaning that is singular and comprehensive, forming a connection between created and uncreated rationality. One of the criticisms which modern theology can make of Origen is that if he undermined the historical Christ, it is because he was preoccupied above all

---

[36] *In Jo.* VI, Praef. 8.

[37] See E. Von Ivanka, *Hellenisches und christlisches in frühbyzantinischen Geistesleben* (1948), ch. I, on the essentially cosmological nature of Origen's thesis.

[38] Note how the idea of "nature" reappears when truth is approached from a cosmological viewpoint. Cf. above, and notes 15, 26, 28.

[39] *In Jo.* I, 34.

with revelation.[40] It is an essential point, and the criticism is
fully justified, because there appears to be an intrinsic contradiction between revelation and history,[41] in that the former
tends to lead to a unification of existence so that its meaning
can be apprehended, while the latter presents existence in the
form of fragmentations and antinomies. If an interest in truth
as revelation eclipses an interest in truth as history, it inevitably results in the human mind becoming the ground of truth,
the crucial bond between truth and creation. This brings us
back to the problem presented in our introductory comments,
regarding the synthesis between the idea of truth as being
and of truth as history. From what we have just seen,
we can state that the way in which the apologists and Origen
approached the problem did not succeed in creating this synthesis. Let us now pass on to other currents of Greek patristic
thought to see how the synthesis was performed.

2. The Eucharistic Approach

While an interest in knowledge and revelation and the
search for the meaning of existence led the *logos* theologians
of the first three centuries to understand truth in terms of
cosmology, the bishops' absorption in the life and struggles
of their communities led them into an entirely different approach to the idea of truth. Already in the writings of St
Ignatius of Antioch,[42] it is made clear that the idea of truth
is not primarily a matter of epistemology—in the strict sense
of the word—but is connected with what we might call *life.*
In our western minds the use of the word "life" implies
the idea of something "practical" as opposed to "contempla-
tive" or "theoretical," and thus the use of this word brings
us automatically back to the Old Testament idea of truth

[40]E. de Faye, *Origéne, sa vie, son oeuvre, sa pensée* III (1928), p. 230. Cf.
H. Koch, *Pronoia und Paideusis: Studien über Origenes und sein Verhältnis
zum Platonismus* (1932), p. 63.

[41]An important attempt in modern theology to overcome this contradiction
is found in W. Pannenberg; see especially his *Revelation as History* (London,
1969).

[42]Ignatius, *Magn.* 1, 2; *Eph.* 3:2, 7:2, 20:2; *Sm.* 4:1, etc.

as *praxis*. This takes us away from the ontological problem of truth and deprives the gospel of all real contact with Greek thought. But why should life be put in opposition to being? In actual fact, are not life and being identical?

The problem reappears along with the Greek conception of existence which has found a place in our western minds, particularly in its Aristotelian form. For Aristotle, life is *a quality added to being,* and not being itself. The truth of being is not found in life, but precedes it; a lifeless stone can claim for itself the verb "to be" just as much as an animal can. That an animal should *have* life, and the stone not have it, is something else. With being we use the verb *to be* while with life we use the verb *to have*: life is *possessed* by being, just as a movement or *telos* is possessed by things in general (en-tel-*echeia*).[43] It is precisely because life is something possessed, and cannot precede being, that truth as the meaning of being relates ultimately to being as such, and not to life. Now if a Greek mind was unable to say *in the same breath* "being and life," the Christian had to say both at once. This identification of being with life affected the idea of truth in a decisive way. This can be seen in the current of Greek patristic thought which developed in the second century. We have already pointed out that Ignatius of Antioch prefers to speak of truth in connection with life. In fact, this is only the continuation of the Fourth Gospel's definition of knowledge as "eternal life" or "true life." (Jn. 3, 15, 36; 14:6; 17:3).[44] But while the Johannine definition of knowledge lends itself to an understanding of truth as *praxis* in the Old Testament sense (an understanding which specialists tend to accept too readily, neglecting the differences between Old and New Testament thought), Ignatius' way of combining knowledge with life points more clearly towards an ontological approach to truth. It is this which should be seen in Ignatius' concern with immortality and incorruptibility. For Ignatius, life signifies not only *praxis* but *being for ever*: i.e. that which does

[43]Aristotle, *De Anima*, 402a-b, 431b, 434b.
[44]Cf. among others, C. Maurer, *Ignatius von Antiochien und das Johannes-evangelium* (1949), on Ignatius' knowledge of the Fourth Gospel.

not die.[45] Here we have the first profound identification of
being with life.

The theme re-appears in a more elaborate form in the
theology of St Irenaeus. The Greek concern with being
becomes more evident, yet the response to it remains entirely
biblical. Irenaeus likewise makes use of the idea of incorruptibility.[46] He sees Christ as being the truth not of the *mind*—
his fight against Gnosticism, the most rationalistic movement
of the period, leads him away from this—but of the *incorruptibility of being*. This was an extremely profound assimila-
tion of the Greek concept of truth as the "nature" of things
with the Johannine and Ignatian concept of truth as life.
Christ is the truth not because he is an epistemological principle which explains the universe, but because he is life and
the universe of beings finds its meaning in its incorruptible
existence in Christ,[47] who takes up into Himself (ἀνακε-
φαλαίωσις) the whole of creation and history. Being is
inconceivable outside of life, and because of this the ontological nature of truth resides in the idea of life.

This identification of being with life is so decisive for the
history of Christian theology that, in our opinion, it is solely
upon this basis that the great achievements of Trinitarian
theology of the fourth century can be judged to their full
value. It is therefore important to consider the reasons for
this phenomenon. What was it among the Greek Fathers that
made it possible to identify being with life?

This question cannot be answered by attempting to asso-
ciate the ideas of Ignatius and Irenaeus with some intellectual
movement, for the simple reason that such a movement did
not exist. What seems to have formed the foundation of these
two Fathers' thought is not an intellectual tradition, but their
common experience of the Church as a community, and especially as a *eucharistic* community. The role played by the
eucharist in the theology of Ignatius is so decisive that it
would be surprising if it had not had an influence on this

[45]Ignatius, *Eph.* 17:1, 20:2. Truth is identical with the "teaching of incorruptibility" (διδαχὴ ἀφθαρσίας) *Magn.* 6:2.
[46]E.g. Irenaeus, *Adv. Haer.* III, 19:1, IV, 38:4.
[47]*Ibid.*, IV, 36:7.

identification of existence with life. In fact, we meet the idea of immortality in his writings in connection with the eucharist.[48] In Irenaeus we find the same centrality of the eucharist, and there is no doubt that this is what influenced his conception of incorruptibilty,[49] with its ontological connotations, since this emerges from the relationship which he establishes between creation and the eucharist.[50]

How could a theology of the eucharist lead to an identification of existence with life? The answer is found firstly in the biblical roots of the relationship between the eucharist and life. The Fourth Gospel provides an adequate base to establish this relationship. Secondly, both Ignatius and Irenaeus have to fight on behalf of the reality within the eucharist—the former in combating docetism[51] and the latter in combating gnosticism.[52] If the eucharist is not *truly* Christ in the historical and material sense of the word "truth," then truth is not life and existence at the same time, since for both men the eucharist imparts life. Thus truth had to become historical without ceasing to be ontological.

Finally there was the understanding of the eucharist as community.[53] The life of the eucharist is the life of God Himself, but this is not life in the sense of an Aristotelian movement which flows out mechanically from the interior of existence. It is the life of *communion* with God, such as exists within the Trinity and is actualized within the members of the eucharistic community. Knowledge and communion are identical.[54]

All this leads naturally to the theological developments of

[48]Ignatius, *Eph.* 20:2.

[49]Note the remarkable parallel between the understanding of the eucharist as "medicine of immortality, an antidote against death" in Ignatius (ibid.), and its description in Irenaeus as *antidotum vitae* (*Adv. Haer. III*, 19:1).

[50]Irenaeus, *Adv. Haer.* IV, 18: 4-5, V, 2:2, IV, 17:5, IV, 18: 1, 4. Cf. A.W. Ziegler, "Das Brot von unseren Feldern: Ein Beitrag zur Eucharistielehre des hl. Irenäus," in *Pro mundi vita* (Festschrift zum eucharistischen Weltkongress 1960), pp. 21-43.

[51]Ignatius, *Sm.* 7:1.

[52]Irenaeus, *Adv. Haer.* IV, 20:5.

[53]For a detailed discussion of sources concerning this aspect of the problem, see J.D. Zizioulas, *The Unity of the Church in the Eucharist and the Bishop during the first three Centuries* (1965, in Greek) esp. pp. 87-148.

[54]Irenaeus, *Adv. Haer.* IV, 20:5.

the fourth century. But it must be strongly underlined that
without this foundation of the Church's eucharistic experience, such as exhibited in Ignatius and Irenaeus, the trinitarian theology of the fourth century would remain a problem.
We must therefore pause briefly on this point before passing
to the fourth century.

The identification of existence with life through the idea
of immortality and incorruptibility will lead naturally into
trinitarian theology. If incorruptibility is possible only in and
through communion with the life of God Himself, creation
or being can exist and live only insofar as the source of being
—God—is Himself life and communion. The eucharistic
experience implies that life is imparted and actualized only in
an event of communion,[55] and thus creation and existence in
general can be founded only upon this living God of communion. Thus the divine act that brings about creation implies
simultaneously, the Father, the Son and the Spirit.[56]

Irenaeus seems to stop here. He is concerned mainly with
created being and sees existence as ultimately dependent upon
the Trinity. But what about uncreated being? Could it not be
said, perhaps, that in the last resort, i.e. in our reference to
God as being, being *precedes* life and life springs from being?
Is it not possible, in other words, to postulate a divine nature
(φύσις—οὐσία) as the ultimate ontological truth, and to
make life and communion depend upon it under the form of
the Trinity? The answer to this question is given by the Greek
Fathers in their historic attempt to press the identification of
being and life with communion to the ultimate point of
existence, God Himself. This came about in the fourth century.

[55]This has to be emphasized in connection with Ignatius and Irenaeus. Both
these Fathers have been presented, especially by Biblical scholars, as having
introduced more or less pagan notions into the eucharist. One such case, for
example, would be Ignatius' famous expression "medicine of immortality."
A careful study of Ignatius' thought as a whole, however, reveals that the
eucharist for him is not φάρμακον ἀθανασίας by virtue of possessing in
its "nature" a potential for life or a possibility of life, in the sense suggested
by the Greek idea of φύσις. The eucharist as defined by Ignatius is above
all a communion expressed by the assembly of the community around the
bishop. The "immortality" of the eucharist is to be sought in this communion-
event and not in the "nature" of the eucharist as such.

[56]Irenaeus *Adv. Haer.* V, 28:4; cf. IV, *Praef.* 4.

3. *The Trinitarian Approach*

The Arian crisis highlighted the need for radical revision of Origen's teachings and the cosmological approach to truth. This could be achieved only through a revision of the doctrine of the *logos,* and Arianism provided the appropriate opportunity. Could the doctrine of the *logos* be of use in talking about ultimate being, the truth of the Greeks? For an instant, the Church found itself shaken with uncertainty, but the answer came from the great Alexandrian theologian St Athanasius. His answer, which was the theological basis for the definition of Nicaea, was in the affirmative, but subject to one essential condition: the doctrine of the *logos* can be maintained *only if the logos becomes identical with the Son as part of the Trinity.*

Athanasius' standpoint, which proved crucially important in the Church's struggle against Arianism, was a direct consequence of the ontology of communion formed within the current of eucharistic theology that connected Ignatius, through Irenaeus, up to Athanasius. That Athanasius belongs theologically to this movement, rather than to the catechetical tradition of Alexandria, follows clearly from a general study of his theology. It will be sufficient for our present purposes to consider his way of using ontological ideas in his struggle against Arianism. It is interesting to note the points where his thought is indebted to the ontological ideas of Ignatius and Irenaeus of which we have attempted a presentation in this study.

In his fight against Arianism, Athanasius developed an ontology whose characteristics are as follows:

First, he made a clear distinction between substance, which he regarded as ultimate, and will,[57] attributing to being the same ultimate character which it had always enjoyed in Greek thought. This distinction was needed in order to make it plain that the being of the Son in his relation to God was not of the same kind as the being of the world. The Son's

---

[57]*Contra Arianos* I:33, II:2, etc. Cf. G. Florovsky, "The Concept of Creation in St. Athanasius," in *Studia Patristica* IV (ed. F. L. Cross, 1962), pp. 36-57.

being belongs to the substance of God, while that of the
world belongs to the will of God. It was a distinction needed
in order to argue against the Arians, but its importance went
far beyond the particular occasion. Its wider significance
rests in the fact that, through this distinction between substance and will, Athanasius was in a position to break out
of the closed ontology of the Greeks which linked God to the
world by an ontological *syggeneia*. He thus avoided the trap
into which Justin and Origen had fallen, not by abandoning
ontological thought but, on the contrary, by raising it up to
the ultimate character which its nature requires.[58] *To be* is not
the same as *to will* or, hence, as *to act*. This assertion,
apparently Greek and not Hebrew, presented itself as the
means for protecting the biblical roots of the Gospel from
the dangers of Greek ontology. God's being, in an ultimate
sense, remained free in relation to the world, in such a way
that the Greek mind could identify it as "being" without having to link it with the world out of an ontological necessity.

But this was not all. By connecting the Son's being with
the very substance of God, Athanasius also transformed the
idea of substance. And it is here that his departure from the
cosmological thinking of Justin and Origen appears to be
actually an adoption of the eucharistic thinking of Ignatius
and Irenaeus. To say that the Son belongs to God's substance
implies that substance *possesses almost by definition a relational character*. "Has God ever existed without His own
(Son)?"[59] This question has an extreme ontological importance. The word "ever" in the sentence is used of course not
temporally but logically, or rather ontologically. It refers not
to a time in God, but to the nature of His being, to His being
qua being. If God's being is by nature relational, and if it can be
signified by the word "substance," can we not then conclude
almost inevitably that, given the ultimate character of God's
being for all ontology, substance, inasmuch as it signifies the
ultimate character of being, can be conceived only as communion?[60]

[58]*Ibid*. II:2.
[59]*Ibid*. I:20.
[60]The following passages, among others, support our interpretation of

Whether this involves a revolutionary change concerning the meaning of substance in Greek thought, or whether it actually has a basis in aspects of the latter which have escaped our attention, are questions which it is not the author's present intention to follow up.[61] However, a fairly clear conclusion emerges from a study of Athanasius, that a distinction between "primary" and "secondary" substance, which certain specialists have employed to interpret the Greek Fathers' trinitarian theology[62] is in fact erroneous. As we shall notice again in a brief treatment of the Cappadocians, such a distinction does not make sense and creates serious problems when considering the relationship within the Trinity between substance and person.

This is Athanasius' principal contribution to the development of Christian ontology. Aided by the idea of communion

Athanasius in a striking way. Without the relationship between the Father and the Son "the perfectness and fullness of the Father's substance is depleted (or eliminated = ἀφαιρεῖται)"; *Contra Arianos* I:20. This leads Athanasius to make the extraordinary statement "If the Son was not there before He was born; there would be no truth in God," which implies that *it is the Father-Son relationship that makes God be the truth eternally in Himself.*

Any identification between Platonic and Athanasian ontology (see, for example, E.P. Meijering, *Orthodoxy and Platonism in Athanasius: Synthesis or Antithesis* [1968]) collapses at this point. There are many similarities between Athanasian and Middle Platonic or Neoplatonic ontology. (Meijering's work is extremely successful in bringing these out.) But nowhere in Platonic or, for that matter, ancient Greek thought in general can we find the view that the perfectness and fullness of a substance is depleted (or eliminated), if a certain relationship is absent from it. Athanasius himself (*De Syn.* 51) is conscious of this difference between his ontology and that of the Greeks as he rejects any notion of divine substance *per se*, i.e. without its being qualified with the term *Father*, calling it the way of thinking "of the Greeks" (Ἑλλήνων ἑρμηνεῖαι). But "Father" is by definition a relational term (no father is conceivable without a son), and it is precisely this that makes the use of "substance" by Athanasius un-Greek. It is clear that we have here the emergence of a *new ontology* (cf. below).

[61]In his profound analysis of Aristotle's idea of substance, Prof. D.M. Mackinnon ("Aristotle's Conception of Substance," in R. Marbrough, ed., *New Essays on Plato and Aristotle*, [1965], pp. 97-11a) has revealed to us the subtleties of this idea in Aristotle, and it would be extremely wise for historians of doctrine to take these seriously into their consideration. See also his "Substance in Christology: A Crossbench View," in S.W. Sykes and J.P. Clayton, eds., *Christ, Faith and History* (Cambridge Studies in Christology, 1972), pp. 279-300.

[62]See G.L. Prestige, *God in Patristic Thought* (1936), p. 245 f., and J.N.D. Kelly, *Early Christian Creeds* (1950), p. 243f.

which had acquired an ontological significance in and through
the eucharistic approach to being, Athanasius develops the
idea that *communion belongs not to the level of will and
action but to that of substance.* Thus it establishes itself as
an ontological category. This was significant progress towards
an ontology founded on biblical premises, a decisive step
towards a Christianization of Hellenism. But without deni-
grating Athanasius' greatness or his importance as a theologian, we must recognize that in this ontology he left a number
of basic problems unanswered. One concerns the ontological
status, as it were, which we are to attach to that being which
does not come out of substance but out of will and action:
namely, creation. If the world's being is a product not of
God's substance but of His will, what is then its ontological
base?

If we say that this base is the will of God, do we not once
more risk attributing an ontological content to the will of
God, thus making almost useless the distinction that was
developed to confront the Arian position? This is such a
difficult and fundamental question as to lend support to the
ontological monism of the classical Greeks as a more sensible
alternative to a Christian ontology based on God's ontological otherness. It is the question of knowing whether
otherness can make sense in ontology, whether ontology can
do anything more than rest on the idea of totality. To a large
extent this is still an open question[63]—even though the first
attempt towards answering it was made long ago by St
Maximus the Confessor, when he employed (and radically
transformed) the idea of *ekstasis* from pseudo-Dionysius the
Areopagite.

The second problem raised by Athanasius' ontological basis
concerns the being of God Himself. Athanasius' ontology
rests, as we have just seen, on the assertion that between God
and the world there exists an otherness founded on the fact
that the world's being is based on the will, not the substance,
of God. In this sense, the use of the idea of substance in
theology played an indispensible part in the development of

[63]Here Christian theology can benefit considerably from E. Levinas' remarkable work *Totalité et Infini* (1971).

an ontology along biblical lines. But what about the otherness
within the very substance of God which is implied by Athansius' assertion that the Son has "always" belonged to God's
being? Athanasius demonstrated that ontological otherness
is an inevitable result of the distinction between will and
nature, but he does not show to what extent "interior" communion within one substance implies otherness at an ontological level.

Such a fundamental question cannot be answered without
clarifying further the idea of relational substance which was
developed in the eucharistic approach to ontology, and ex-
ploited by Athtanasius. This was to be the great contribution
of the Cappadocian Fathers. Let us now turn briefly to their
views.

One of the difficulties in developing an ontology of communion which possessed clarity was the fact that, as an ontological category, substance did not differ essentially from
hypostasis. Athanasius lets us clearly see that for him—and
for his contemporaries—*ousia* and *hypostasis* mean exactly
the same thing.[64] And so, if it is desired to speak of an "interior" otherness within one substance (i.e. an otherness not
based on will), how can this be expressed? Anyone who
studies the history of this period knows the confusion and
misunderstanding that terminology was able to generate then.
A term such as "person" smacked of Sabellianism and was
insufficiently ontological for some, while for others *hypostasis*
implied tritheistic views. But the significant thing is that the
solution developed by the Cappadocians led, in fact, to a
further stage in the revision of Greek ontology and the formation of a Christian ontology.

Up until the period when the Cappadocians undertook to
develop a solution to the trinitarian problems, an identifying
of *ousia* with *hypostasis* implied that a thing's concrete individuality (*hypostasis*) means simply that it *is* (i.e. its *ousia*).
Now, however, changes occurred. The term *hypostasis* was
dissociated from that of *ousia* and became identified with
that of *prosopon*. But this latter term is *relational*, and was
so when adopted in trinitarian theology. This meant that from

---

[64]See Athanasius, *Ep. ad episc.* etc., PG 26: 1036.

now on a relational term entered into ontology and, conversely, that an ontological category such as *hypostasis*
entered the relational categories of existence. *To be* and *to
be in relation* becomes identical. For someone or something
to *be*, two things are simultaneously needed: being itself
(*hypostasis*) and *being in relation* (i.e. being a person). It
is only in relationship that identity appears as having an
ontological significance, and if any relationship did not imply
such an ontologically meaningful identity, then it would be
no relationship.[65] Here is certainly an ontology derived from
the being of God.

What was the importance of this stage in ontology, reached
by the Cappadocians? Above all, it was that the being of God
became placed on a new and more biblical foundation. By
usurping, as it were, the ontological character of *ousia*, the
word *person/hypostasis* became capable of signifying God's
being *in an ultimate sense*. The subsequent developments of
trinitarian theology, especially in the West with Augustine
and the scholastics, have led us to see the term *ousia*, not
hypostasis, as the expression of the ultimate character and
the causal principle (ἀρχή) in God's being. The result
has been that in textbooks on dogmatics, the Trinity gets
placed after the chapter on the One God (the unique *ousia*)
with all the difficulties which we still meet when trying to
accommodate the Trinity to our doctrine of God. By contrast,
the Cappadocians' position—characteristic of all the Greek
Fathers—lay, as Karl Rahner observes,[66] in that the final
assertion of ontology in God has to be attached not to the
unique *ousia* of God but *to the Father*, that is, to a *hypostasis*
or person.

This identification of God's ultimate being with a person

---

[65]The Cappadocians arrived at this through their thesis that no nature exists
"in the nude" but always has its "mode of existence" (τρόπος ὑπάρξεως)
See e.g. Basil, *Ep.* 38:2, PG 45: 337.

It is interesting to take up G.L. Prestige's criticism (*op. cit.* p. 233) of
St Basil's idea that in God there is a coincidence between nature and person.
This, he says, makes it hard to defend the unity of the Godhead, because it
implies a shift of the meaning of substance from the sense of primal substance
into that of secondary substance. But this shows precisely why the application
of this distinction becomes questionable in the case of the Greek Fathers.

[66]See K. Rahner, *The Trinity* (1970), *passim* and esp. p. 58f.

rather than with *ousia* not only makes possible a biblical doctrine of God (= the Father, in the Bible), but also resolves problems such as those inherent in the *homoousion* concerning, for example, the relation of the Son to the Father. In making the Father the "ground" of God's being—or the ultimate reason for existence—theology accepted a kind of subordination of the Son to the Father without being obliged to downgrade the *Logos* into something created. But this was possible only because the Son's otherness was founded on the *same substance*. So, whenever the question of the ontological relationship between God and the world is raised, the idea of *hypostasis,* from now on ontological in an ultimate sense, must be completed with that of substance if we do not wish to fall back into ontological monism. The identification of God with the Father risks losing its biblical content unless our doctrine of God includes not just the three persons, but also the unique *ousia.*[67]

4. The "Apophatic" Approach

In the development of apophatic theology, the Platonic/ Origenist understanding of truth was recovered only to be denied at its very heart, in its epistemological and ontological claims. While for Origen the highest way of indicating and expressing truth is by means of the prefix αὐτο- ("itself": e.g. αὐτοαλήθεια, αὐτο δικαιοσύνη, etc.), for the apophatic theologians the preferred expression is the prefix ὑπερ- ("beyond," "above": e.g. ὑπεραλήθεια, ὑπερουσία etc.). This implies a radical reorientation in regard to knowledge and a removal of truth from its Greek base. For Greek thought was satisfied with indicating truth through the term *auto-* and furthermore it would never have proceeded beyond

---

[67]The *homoousion* presupposes that *ousia* represents the ultimate ontological category. There seems to be no doubt that this is the view of Athansius. If, however, we take into account the relational character of *ousia* in Athanasius, we can conclude that the Cappadocians do not depart from Athanasius' thought but simply draw the consequences that Athanasius' theology had for the doctrine of God's being. Athanasius' relational notion of substance becomes through the creative work of the Cappadocians an ontology of personhood.

the *nous* which, for the Greeks was permanently attached to truth as to its ultimate ontological ground.[68]

The message of apophatic theology was precisely that the closed Greek ontology had to be broken and transcended, since we are unable to use the concepts of the human mind or of creation, for signifying God—the truth. The absolute otherness of God's being which is found at the heart of biblical theology is affirmed in such a manner that the biblical approach to God contrasts acutely with that of the Greeks.[69] Apophaticism rejects the Greek view of truth, emphasizing that what we know about being—about creation, that is—must not be ontologically identified with God. God has "a simple, unknowable existence, inaccessible to all things and completely unexplainable, *for He is beyond affirmation and negation.*"[70] And therefore truth lies beyond the choice between affirmation and negation.[71] Neoplatonic imagery of a "hierarchy" used

[68]It is true that philosophers of the Platonic, Neoplatonic and Gnostic schools spoke of a "departure" (ἐκδημία) of beings, some of them using the prefix ὑπὲρ in their vocabulary. But the significant thing is that for these philosophers, the "departure" was *not a movement beyond the nous, but always a movement away from other things to enable the nous to arrive at its pure state.* (It is in this sense that we must understand also the well-known phrase ἐπέκεινα τῆς οὐσίας).

In the Greek philosophical tradition, at this point, also including Origen and his followers, the *nous* always remains capable of knowing God (cf. above). Apophatic theology parted radically from this position as is shown by the fact that truth, for it, resides not in the *nous* but beyond it. (See Ps. Dionysius, *De myst. theol.* 1:3, PG 3:1001A. Cf. I. Hausherr, "Ignorance infinie," *Orientalia Christiana Periodica* (1936), p. 357; also for the texts R. Roques, "Contemplation, extase et ténébre selon le Ps. Denys," in *Dict. Spir.* (1952), col. 1898.

[69]The lively opposition between this apophaticism and the Greek approach to God appears clearly in an examination of the idea of God in Plato. In Plato, we arrive at the idea of God by firstly considering the "soul," especially as it becomes "generation," providing "a continual flow of being," and then by considering 'the order inherent in the movement of the stars"—that is, "the intelligence that establishes the whole in order" (*Laws* 966d).

[70]Maximus, *Myst., Praef.*

[71]The deeper meaning of this idea rests in detaching truth from a fallen sitation where choice imposes itself between the "true" and the "false" (cf. below, section III, 1-2). This is essential for maintaining the identification of truth with God Himself, since God exists beyond the possibility of choosing between the "true" and the "false." In a profound passage (*Amb.*, PG 91:1296C) Maximus makes precisely this remark about truth: The Logos is ὑπὲρ ἀλήθειαν because there exists nothing which may be examined beside

in the writings of Dionysius the Areopagite has misled those specialists who have spoken of a Neoplatonic influence on his writings. The importance of this imagery is not in the imagery itself, but in the meaning which it clothes in these writings. The essential point concerning this imagery is that, by contrast with the emanations of the Neoplatonists, the Dionysian "hierarchy" does *not* imply the emergence of lower existence out of a higher one.[72]

This can be better understood only through a careful consideration of two characteristic features of apophatic theology which appear especially in Dionysius and Maximus the Confessor, namely the ideas of *ekstasis* and of the distinction between *essence* and *energy* in God.

The idea of *ekstasis* signifies that God is love, and as such He creates an immanent relationship of love *outside Himself*. The emphasis placed on the words "outside Himself" is particularly important, since it signifies that love as ekstasis gives rise not to an emanation in the neoplatonic sense, but to an *otherness* of being which is seen as responding and returning to its original cause.[73] In Maximus this idea receives a more complete and definite treatment, because his approach is not ultimately related to cosmology, as in Dionysius, but to the trinitarian being of God.[74] Likewise, the distinction between essence and energy in God serves to indicate the relationship between God and the world as ontological otherness bridged by love, but *not* by "nature" or by "essence."[75]

Him and compared with Him, whereas the "truth" of which we have experience is opposed to "falsehood."

[72]See R. Roques, *L'univers dionysien: Structure hiérarchique du monde selon le Ps. Denys* (1954), p. 77 n. 6 and p. 135 n. 3.

[73]Dionysius the Areopagite, *De div. nom.* 4:14, also Maximus, *Amb.* 23: "God moves inasmuch as He implants an immanent relationship of eros and love in those capable of receiving it; He moves in attracting naturally the desire of those who are moved towards Him."

[74]Cf. P. Sherwood, *St. Maximus the Confessor: The Ascetic Life—The Four Centuries on Charity* (Ancient Christian Writers 21, 1955), p. 32.

[75]The roots of this distinction are to be found in Gregory of Nazianzus (*Or.* 38:7). Its development leads to the theology of St Gregory Palamas. Cf. V. Lossky, *The Mystical Theology of the Eastern Church* (1957). The intention behind this distinction was to safeguard the otherness between Creator and creation: see P. Sherwood, *op. cit.* p. 32 and J. Meyendorff, *The Byzantine Legacy in the Orthodox Church,* [1982] pp. 191 ff.

This distinction, moreover, joined to the idea of ekstasis, represents the first attempt in the history of Christian thought to reconcile on a philosophical basis the biblical idea of God's otherness with the Greeks' concern for the unity of existence. This is a philosophically worked out development of what was implicit in the eucharistic and trinitarian approaches which we have studied above. The importance of all this will become better apparent when we consider the relationship between truth and human existence.

Thus, the apophatic theology of this period by no means implies a theological agnosticism, if carefully studied in its essential aims.[76] The principal object of this theology is to remove the question of truth and knowledge from the domain of Greek theories of ontology in order to situate it within that of *love* and communion. That apophatic theology founds itself on love is something so evident as to be the necessary key to its understanding and assessment. The perspectives offered by an approach to being through love, as arrived at by the mystical and ascetic theologians of the period, led by another route to the same conclusion that the eucharistic and trinitarian approaches of the previous period reached: it is only through an identification with *communion*[77] that truth can be reconciled with ontology. That this implies neither agnosticism nor a flight outside matter and history emerges from the thought of Maximus the Confessor. The great achievement of this thinker was to attain the most developed and complete reconciliation between the Greek, Jewish and Christian concepts of truth. It is in this father's theology that the question we asked in our introduction seems to find its most all-encompassing answer.

[76]To equate "apophatic" with "negative" can lead to error. See Dionysius' repeated expressions οὐ κατ' ἔλλειψιν (*De div nom.* 3:2, PG 3:869A) μὴ κατὰ στέρησιν (*Ep.* 1, PG 3:1065A) etc., through which he seeks to indicate the *positive* content of theology, which is theology καθ' ὑπεροχὴν (*De div. nom.* 312). It is a theology that transcends the opposition "positive versus negative" or "knowledge versus ignorance," etc.

[77] Note the importance of the prefix συν- in Ps. Dionysius' use of *ekstasis* (*De div. nom.* 3:1-2, PG 3:681, 684). It signifies communion within which each partner's distinctness is maintained. Cf. R. Roques, "Contemplation," (n. 68 above), col. 1899 ff.

5. *The Christological Approach*

We have seen that in the theology of the first three centuries, the approach to the idea of truth through the *logos* failed in two ways in its attempt to link the biblical concept of truth with that of Greek thought: it did not reconcile the Greek concept of being with the ontological otherness of God's being, and it did not fully identify the ontological content of truth with Christology in its historical aspect. The idea of *logos* helped to explain the unity of God and creation, but not the difference that there is between the two. Thus patristic theology was led to abandon this idea, and the problem remained unanswered: how can the truth of created and historical existence be an *ontological* truth while fully maintaining the ontological otherness of God's being in relation to creation and history? How, in other words, can ultimate truth be linked up ontologically with creation and history in such a way that creation may keep its own, distinct being, while God remains the ultimate truth of being?

The solution to this fundamental problem, as we have seen, was not completely absent from Greek patristic thought before St Maximus, but lacked development and, above all, explanation in philosophical terms. We have tried to show that the beginnings of a solution to the question were found in the eucharistic theology of Ignatius and Irenaeus, with whom we find for the first time the identification of being with life; and that this solution was then made deeper by the fourth century trinitarian theologians, through the identification they made between life, communion and the being of God Himself. But if truth is in the last resort identifiable with being only in and through communion, what prevents us from returning to the Greek ontology of the *logos,* and uniting God with the world precisely by virtue of the identification of being with communion? In fact, it was because of the idea of *participation* that Origen made wide use of the idea of the *logos* to link God with the world. This led to the question: in what way does "participation" differ from "communion"?

The answer to this crucial question was given in the fourth

century by the way in which the two terms "participation" (μετοχή) and "communion" (κοινωνία) were employed. At first sight these terms seem to be interchangeable in the Greek Fathers; however a clear distinction was deliberately and significantly made in their use: participation is used only for creatures in their relation with God, and never for God in his relation to creation.[78] This became especially apparent in the fourth century in connection with the christological controversies and their implications for the eucharist.[79] If we consider what this distinction entails for the idea of truth, our conclusion has to be: the truth of creation is a *dependent* truth, while the truth of God's being is *communion* in itself.

As well as the ontological priority of the divine truth, this conclusion implies that reality or the truth of created existence cannot affirm itself by itself. *God and the world cannot be ontologically placed side by side as self-defined entities.* Creaturely truth is dependent upon something else, in which it participates; this is truth as *communion by participation* (as compared with God, who is truth as *communion without participation*[80]). Thus we cannot say that creation is truth according to its own "nature." Once more, the idea of truth leads us ultimately not to the "nature" of things, as with the Greeks, but to life and communion of beings.

These remarks, which can be derived from a study of the fourth century Greek Fathers, seemingly offer an explanation for the way in which ultimate ontological truth links to the truth of creation without destroying the otherness of God's being. The question remaining unanswered here is that of the relationship between truth and history. How does ultimate ontological truth link up with that of creation when the latter is approached not as a static thing but as a movement in time

---

[78]E.g. Athanasius, *Contra Arianos* I:9, 46-48, III:40; Basil *Contra Eun.* 2:22. Cf. A. Houssiau, *"Incarnation et communion chez les Péres grecs,"* in *Irénikon* 45 (1972), pp. 457-468.

[79]Cf. H. Chadwick, "Eucharist and Christology in the Nestorian Controversy," in *Journal of Theological Studies* N.S. 2 (1951) pp. 145-164. Also A. Houssiau, *op. cit.,* p. 463 ff.

[80]Cf. St Cyril of Alexandria's distinction between "communion κατὰ φύσιν (Christ's communion with God), and "communion κατὰ μετοχήν" (our participation in the incarnation). For the texts see Houssiau, *op. cit.* p. 477.

and as decay? It seems that St Maximus the Confessor was the first in the history of Christian thought to work out an answer to this question.

The way by which the Greek Fathers distinguished themselves in their approach to history is that they considered the latter in close connection with ontology. In contrast with the approach to this problem found in the West since St. Augustine,[81] the problem of the relationship between truth and history is tackled not from the viewpoint of time in relation to eternity, but from that of being and life in relation to death and decay. And the crucial point of this approach lies in the idea of *movement of being*: Can there be truth in the movement of being, when in history this movement is associated with death and decay?

Maximus had inherited from Origenism a description of creation as a triad—becoming-rest-motion (γένεσις-στάσις-κίνησις)—in which the ultimate characteristic of movement (placed after rest) is understood to offer an indication of the sinful nature of creation which, according to Origen's mythology of the Fall, was patterned after eternal rest or stillness.[82] This view of things is consciously wrecked by Maximus, who places rest after motion (γένεσις-κίνησις-στάσις).[83] This change has a twofold result. On the one hand it makes history into something provisional, and therefore impossible to take within the existence of God; while on the other, it makes history meaningful because it possesses a πέρας, that is to say an end in the positive sense of this word ("fulfilment").[84]

This takes the concept of history back to its Old Testament basis, with the difference however that history is now viewed ontologically. The truth of history is identical with that of creation itself, both being oriented towards the future. Per-

---

[81]With the idea of history removed since St Augustine from ontology to psychology, the path was prepared for the modern conflict between history and nature, the former being exclusively a characteristic of the human being.

[82]Cf. P. Sherwood, *op. cit.* p. 47 ff.

[83]*Ibid.*

[84]Maximus based all this on the idea that *will* involves *motion*. Helped by Aristotle, he defines motion as "a natural force tending towards its own end"; he qualifies this, however, with the ideas of will and love, which take motion away from its Aristotelian foundation. See esp. *Amb.* 1 and 23. Cf. above, the distinctiveness of the idea of *ekstasis* (section II § 4).

fection is not an original state to which creation is bidden
to return, but a πέρας which summons from ahead.[85] The
truth of time is not as it were an ontologically inexplicable
intermediary between beginning and end, the domain of a
psychological *anamnesis* of the past and an equally psychological expectation of the end. The truth of history lies in the
future, and this is to be understood in an ontological sense:
history is true, despite change and decay, not just because it
is a movement *towards* an end, but mainly because it is a
movement *from* the end, since it is the end that gives
it meaning. If the consummation of historical existence
is not an existence without decay and death (such is the
significance of placing the στάσις *after* the movement),
then it is inevitable that being should come to cease to be, and
we should have to conclude that history leads to non-entity
and non-truth. The truth of history is identified thus with
the truth of being simply because history is the movement of
being towards and from its end which gives it meaning.

But if the meaning of history is understood in this way,
how do we find the proper and decisive place owing to
Christology in our conception of truth? The problem becomes
complex when a connection with ontology is sought: how can
the "end" of history be identical, as truth, with history's own
process (the incarnation) and also with the permanence of
being?

The importance and unique character of Maximus' theology
rest in his success in developing a christological synthesis
within which history and creation become organically interrelated. Helped by his courageous salvaging of the *logos*
concept from its long period of disuse due to the dangers
accompanying it, Maximus arrived at this christological
synthesis: Christ is the *logos* of creation and one must
find in him all the *logoi* of created beings.[86] The apolo-

---

[85]See esp. *Quest. ad. Thae.* 60. Here Maximus essentially recovers Irenaeus'
theme about Adam's childhood, on which basis he develops a theology of
history. Compare this with the Augustinian concept of man having been created
perfect.

[86]Cf. I. H. Dalmais, "La théorie des logoi des creatures chez S. Maxime le
Confesseur," in *Revue des Sciences Philosophiques et Théologiques* (1952),
pp. 244-249.

gists and Origen had also said this, but Maximus parted from them by making the *logos* concept pass from cosmology into the incarnation by means of the dynamical ideas of will and love.[87] In this way, neither the *logoi* of things nor the *logos* of God are conceivable apart from the dynamical movement of love. The substratum of existence is not being but love. The truth possessed by the *logos* of existence depends only upon love, and not upon some objective structure of a rational kind which might be conceivable in itself. This is extremely important for an understanding of the *logos* concept, for it leads to an identification of the *logoi* of things not with nature or being itself, but with the *loving will of God*. For example, if one approaches the *logos* concept from the viewpoint of "nature" one is forced to say that God knows created beings according to their own nature. Maximus puts his finger on the crucial point here and objects forcefully: "God does *not* know things according to their own nature, but He recognizes them as the realizations of His own will (ἰδία θελήματα) since He makes them through His will (θέλων)"[88] His knowledge is nothing other than His love. If He ceases to love what exists, nothing will be. Being depends on love.

This is a radical departure from the Greek idea of truth, because the *logoi* of things are no longer a necessity for God. But what is important is that this departure was performed christologically, and it is this which leads to a synthesis of truth as being and history simultaneously. Since God knows created beings as the realizations of His will, it is not being itself but the ultimate will of God's love which unifies beings and points to the meaning of being. And precisely here is the role of the incarnation. *The incarnate Christ is so identical to the utlimate will of God's love, that the meaning of created being and the purpose of history are simply the incarnate Christ.* All things were made with Christ in mind, or rather at heart, and for this reason *irrespective of the fall of man, the incarnation would have occurred.*[89] Christ, the *incarnate*

[87]See e.g. *Amb.* 23.
[88]*Amb.* θελήματα and προορισμοί are synonymous in the thought of Maximus. See e.g. *Quaest. ad Thal.* 60.
[89]A discussion of the texts will be found in G. Florovsky, "Cur Deus

Christ, is the truth, for He represents the ultimate, unceasing will of the ecstatic love of God, who intends to lead created being into communion with His own life, to know Him and itself within this communion-event.

All this removes truth from its Platonic unchangingness and, equally, from the necessity implicit in the Aristotelian "entelechy." History is neither banished in a platonic manner, nor transformed into a movement inherent in being or "nature" itself.[90] The truth of history lies simultaneously in the substratum of created existence (since all beings are the willed realizations of God's love); in the fulfilment or the future of history (since God's love, in His will and its expressions—namely, created existence—is identifiable with the final communion of creation with the life of God); and in the incarnate Christ (since on God's part the personification of this loving will is the incarnate Christ). Whereby Christ becomes the "principle" and "end" of all things, the One who not only moves history from within its own unfolding, but who also moves existence even from within the multiplicity of created things, towards the true being which is true life and true communion.

So truth is located simultaneously at the heart of history, at the ground of creation, and at the end of history: all this in one synthesis which allows us to say "Christ is the truth" for Jews and Greeks at the same time. It is perhaps the first time in the whole history of philosophy that such a thing could be expressed, because as far as we know, there is no other case where philosophical language has succeeded in uniting the beginning and the end of existence without creating in this way a vicious circle. Maximus succeeded in nothing less than the miracle of reconciling a circle with a straight line. The way whereby he worked out a relationship between ontology and love, and developed an ontology of love out of the idea of *ekstasis*, may have immense value even in the theology and philosophy of our own days.

Homo? The motive of the Incarnation in St. Maximus the Confessor," in *Eucharisterion* (Melanges H. Alivisatos, 1958), p. 76 ff.

[90]The idea of history as *Heilsgeschichte*, developed by O. Cullmann, leads in fact back to Aristotle, as is shown by J. McIntyre, *The Christian Doctrine of History*, (1957) pp. 42 ff.

6. *The Approach through the "Eikon"*

If Christ makes history into truth and truth into part of the unfolding of history, and if this is simply because Christ is the "end" of history, the truth of history seems to remain paradoxical: determined by its end while the end is a part of its unfolding. How can this be expressed in theological terms? It will suffice to quote here a passage of Maximus. "The things of the Old Testament are shadow (σκιά); those of the New Testament are image (εἰκών); and those of the future state are truth (ἀλήθεια).[91]

At first sight, this is a curious assertion which makes the incarnation a less true reality than the second coming. Accustomed to an idea of reality determined by rationalism and historicism, we tend to consider as "truths" and "facts" the things which experience verifies or which correspond to certain norms and concepts "grasped" by us as true. But in the present case, the use of the term εἰκών does not signify this kind of factual truth, nor any lack of reality. For all the Greek Fathers except those of the Origenist school, εἰκών always means something *real* and as true as ἀλήθεια. The long fight over the place of icons in the Church during the eighth and ninth centuries was centered precisely on the question of ascertaining whether it is in any way possible to present truth in the form of an icon, and the demarcation line between the two parties lay precisely in the acceptance or rejection of the truth of the incarnation in its relationship to history and creation.[92] Those who fought against the icons took their arguments from the school of Origen, whose conception of history has been already discussed here; while those who defended the icons insisted precisely upon the fact that the incarnation makes it not merely possible, but quite unavoidable, to understand truth in the manner of an icon.[93] But if the εἰκών, or truth of history, is no less true than

[91]Maximus, *Sch. in eccl. hier.* 3, 3:2.
[92]See J. Meyendorff, *Christ in Eastern Christian Thought* (1969), pp. 132-148.
[93]For the sources, see J. Meyendorff, *ibid.*

that of the eschaton, in what sense is the word "truth" applied
to the "future state"?

The idea of εἰκών in the Greek Fathers is often understood
along Platonic lines. The passage of Maximus quoted above
shows clearly that this is wrong. In the Platonic way of
thinking, the image must not have its reality in the future;
it is always the past which is decisive, making truth a matter
of ἀνάμνησις, a connecting of the soul to the pre-existing
world of ideas. The authentic Greek patristic tradition never
accepted the Platonic notion—adopted by Origen and St
Augustine among others—in which perfection belongs to the
original state of things. The Greek patristic tradition also
showed no tendency to understand the εἰκών in a retrospective psychological sense, and at the Council in Trullo explicitly rejected symbolism in iconography. In this crucial
passage, Maximus shows once more that truth in Greek patristic thought is very different from that of Platonism. We must
search elsewhere for the roots of the iconological language
of the Fathers.

Of course this is a very complex problem, and cannot
properly be dealt with here. Suffice it to say by way of suggestion, that the iconological language of the Greek Fathers
makes increased sense if seen in the light of primitive apocalyptic theology, such as first developed within the primitive
Syro-palestinian tradition and penetrated throughout the
eucharistic liturgies of the East. This tradition presents truth
not as a product of the mind, but as a "visit" and a "dwelling"
(cf. Jn. 1:14) of an eschatological reality entering history to
open it up in a communion-event. This creates a *vision* of
truth not as Platonic or mystical contemplation understands
it but as picturing a new set of relationships, a new "world"
adopted by the community as its final destiny.

So, through its apocalyptic roots, iconological language
liberates truth from our "conception," "definition" "compre-
hension," of it and protects it from being manipulated and
objectified. It also makes it relational, in the sense that the
truth of one being is able to be "conceived" only in and
through the mirror of another. To use a remarkable explanation of the idea of εἰκών given by Athanasius, when he

refers it to God, the Son is the εἰκὼν of the Father precisely because it is in Him that the Father sees Himself as "truth."[94] Iconological language emerges after truth becomes identified with communion. *Eikon* is the final truth of being communicated in and through an event of communion (liturgical or sacramental), anticipating the "end" of history from within its unfolding.

* * *

In summarizing this attempt at a synthesis of Greek patristic thought concerning truth, we can say that the Greek Fathers' main success in this area rests in the identification of truth with communion. Here we must clearly emphasize the word *identification*, because this synthesis must not be confused with other associations of truth with communion which have arisen during the history of Christian theology. If communion is conceived as something *additional* to being, then we no longer have the same picture. The crucial point lies in the fact that being is *constituted* as communion; only then can truth and communion be mutually identified.

This identification forms theology's hardest problem, as is to be observed in the application of truth to human existence. Our state of fallen existence is characterized precisely by the fact that in our approach to truth, being is constituted *before* communion. Salvation through the truth thus depends in the last resort upon the identification of truth with communion. The next part of our study will be dedicated to this problem. The Greek patristic synthesis which we have attempted to present in this section will serve as a background to the two following sections.

III. *Truth and Salvation: The Existential Implications of Truth as Communion*

1. *Truth and Fallen Existence: the Rupture between Being and Communion*

For the Greek Fathers the fall of man—and for that matter,

---

[94]Athanasius, *Contra Arianos* I:20-21.

sin—is not to be understood as bringing about something new (there is no *creative* power in evil), but as *revealing and actualizing the limitations and potential dangers inherent in creaturehood, if creation is left to itself*. For since the fall results from the claim of created man to be the ultimate point of reference in existence (to be God), it is, in the final analysis, the state of existence whereby the created world tends to posit its being ultimately with reference to itself and not to an uncreated being, God. Idolatry, i.e. turning created existence into an ultimate point of reference, is the form that the fall takes,[94a] but what lies behind it is the fact that man refuses to refer created being to communion with God. In other words, viewed from the point of view of ontology, the fall consists in *the refusal to make being dependent on communion,* in a rupture between truth and communion.

This rupture between being and communion results automatically in the *truth of being* acquiring priority over the *truth of communion*. This is *natural* for created existence. It is inevitably the case when you have a created being as the ultimate point of reference, because "created" means "given": man may wish to make communion ultimate but the fact of existence is a "datum" with which he is presented, and thus he can never escape from the fact that being precedes relationship. The "substance" or *ousia* of things becomes the ultimate content of truth, if truth is to relate to being. The only alternative to this would be to make communion *constitutive* of being, but in this case a denial of the fall—or a redemption from it—would be implied.

Given the fact that communion is no longer constitutive of being in a fallen state of existence, and that the *being* of things must be recognized before a relationship can take place, every single being acquires an ontological status, so to say, on its own merit. Thus the world consists of *objects,* of things whose ontological status one has to recognize before one can relate to them. The truth of these "objects" becomes, therefore, a provocation for the knower; the known and the knower exist as two opposite partners; the *res* and the *intel-*

[94a]Cf. L. Macquarrie, *Principles of Christian Theology,* 1966, p. 238 f.

lectus must somehow reach an *adaequatio*;[95] the subject and the object constitute a pair whose presence determines epistemology.

Inherent in all this is the decisive role of the notion of *individuality* in ontology. This, too, must be ultimately explained by reference to the rupture between being and communion. Since the *being* of things is ultimate and prior to communion, and everything that exists posits its own being as something "given" to man, the world ultimately consists of a fragmented existence in which beings are particular *before* they can relate to each other: you first *are* and then relate. This ultimacy of the individual in ontology is connected, as we shall see, with the problem of creation *par excellence*, which is death, but it also results in the challenge that truth represents for the *freedom* of man. For he is asked to *submit* to, i.e. compulsorily to acknowledge, the truth of being of whatever is other than himself, whether fellowman or thing. The authority of truth becomes in this way authoritarian and repulsive, but because, as we have noted, it is so firmly grounded upon the nature of created existence, upon the truth of being, any attempt to ignore or reject it amounts to absurdity. Ever since Kierkegaard,[96] modern existentialist thought has not ceased to underline the impasse which created existence reaches whenever truth and freedom have to come to terms with each other.[97] Again, everything seems to go back to the rupture between being and communion, which implies the priority of the former over the latter.

Another consequence of this situation is displayed in the relationship between truth and love. In associating truth with

[95]Cartesian philosophy provides a good example of this. When Kant defines the *ad aequatio* as "agreement with the laws of the intellect" (*Critique of Pure Reason*, B, 350) he introduces the transcendental dimension of truth. However, this does not rescue the concept of truth from what is described here as the fallen condition of existence, since according to Kant it is the integrated unity of human experience which determines in the last resort what truth is (*ibid.* B, 197).

[96]According to Kierkegaard (see e.g. *Existence* I, II) truth is the act of an individual, and its basis is existence; but "doing the truth' is an existential paradox which makes faith and christianity as a whole incompatible with reason.

[97]See below, notes 103 and 105.

the nature or substance of things and with the kind of understanding which is inherent in this individualism of existence,
man restricts himself to reaching a relationship between communion and love only after obtaining a knowledge of the
"object" of his love. The "other," whether in the form of a
"person" or a "thing," is present as an object of knowledge
before any relationship of communion can take place. Knowledge precedes love, and truth precedes communion. One can
love only what one knows, since love comes out of knowledge,
(except that this happens in our fallen condition, and ought
not to be turned into an element of our metaphysical anthropology or, even less, of our approach to trinitarian theology,
as in the case of Thomas Aquinas[98]). This dichotomy between
love and knowledge implies a separation not just between
person and nature, but also between thought and action in
the very heart of human existence. And since the possibility
of knowledge appears to precede the act of communion
(love) and to be independent of it, it becomes possible for
man to dissociate his thought from his action and thus to
falsify truth. Man thus becomes a *hypocrite,* and it is indeed
only man, i.e. a person, that is capable of hypocrisy.

The consequences of this appear clearly when one considers
the problem of the relationship between truth and action or
praxis. "Doing the truth," which is a biblical theme, becomes
impossible for man precisely because faith and praxis in his
fallen existence are able to coincide only for "a moment,"
and this "moment of existence" simply reveals what "existence" implies but does not attain. Kierkegaard's discovery of
the authentic moment of existence struck the greatest blow
against the West's subject-object structuring of truth, but led
only to an identification of truth with doubt. In this situation
an alternative has been offered to man, if he wishes to identify
truth with *praxis,* to arrive at a Marxist identification of truth
with human activity in the form of the development of man
in his society.[99]

We could continue to list the consequences of the indi-

[98]See Thomas Aquinas, *Summa Theol.* Ia IIae 4.   This derives from Augustine (*De Trin.* 10).

[99]According to Marx (see e.g. his *Second Thesis on Feuerbach*) truth arises
from praxis in its evolution with society.

vidualization of being in our fallen existence in relation to truth, but the most tragic of them must be seen in the fact of *death*. There is no plainer falsification of truth on the ontological level than a "dying being"; this is a contradiction in the absurdest terms. The problem of death is connected with truth in existence precisely through the truth's identification with nature itself, accompanied by the individualization and fragmentation of this nature. When we are told that Adam died because he fell by making himself into God, we are being correctly told that making onself God—i.e. the ultimate reference-point of existence—is something on the level of ontology, not psychology. Death intervenes not as the result of punishment for an act of disobedience but as a result of this individualization of nature to which the whole cosmos is subjected. In other words, there is an intrinsic connection between death and the individualization into which we are born through the present form of procreation, and it is this which shows precisely what it means to have a life which is not the *"true* life" (ζωὴ ἀληθινή).

To be saved from the fall, therefore, means essentially that truth should be fully applied to existence, thereby making life something *true*, i.e. undying. For this reason the Fourth Gospel identifies eternal life, i.e. life without death, with truth and knowledge. But it can be accomplished only if the individualization of nature becomes transformed into communion—that is, if communion becomes identical with being. Truth, once again, must be communion if it is to be life.

2. *Truth and the Person*

The most immediate area for passing beyond the state of fallen existence just described is the reality of the person. The significance of the person rests in the fact that he represents two things simultaneously which are at first sight in contradiction: particularity and communion. Being a person is fundamentally different from being an individual or a "personality," for a person cannot be imagined in himself but only within his relationships. Taking our categories from our fallen state of existence, we usually identify a person with the "self" (individual) and with all it possesses in its qualities and experiences (the personality). But modern philosophers recall with good reason that this is not what being a person means. What is the relationship between personal existence and truth, in its particularity and in its communion?

The essential thing about a person lies precisely in his being a revelation of truth, not as "substance" or "nature" but as a "mode of existence."[100] This profound perception of the Cappadocian Fathers[101] shows that true knowledge is not a knowledge of the essence or the nature of things, but of how they are connected within the communion-event. We saw above that the theme of *ekstasis* was a key idea in the Greek patristic concept of truth, but in its application to the idea of "person" it needs to be completed by another theme, that of *hypostasis*. While *ekstasis* signifies that a person is a revelation of truth by the fact of being in communion, *hypostasis* signifies that in and through his communion a person affirms his own identity and his particularity; he "supports his own nature" (ὑπο-στάσις) in a particular and unique way. The person is the horizon within which the truth of existence is revealed, not as simple nature subject to individualization and recombination but as a unique image of the whole and the "catholicity" of a being. In this way, if one sees a being as a person, one sees in him the whole of human nature. Thus to destroy a human person is to commit an act of murder against all humanity: in the final analysis, a denial of the truth of man's being. The mystery of being a person lies in the fact that here otherness and communion are not in contradiction but coincide. Truth as communion does not lead to the dissolving of the diversity of beings into one vast ocean of being, but to the affirmation of otherness in and through love. The difference between this truth and that of "nature in itself" lies in the following: while the latter is subject to fragmentation, individualization, conceptualization, compre-

[100]On this point, see Ch. Yannaras, *The Ontological Content of the Theological Concept of the Person* (1970, in Greek). The distinction which he makes between *ousia* and *par-ousia* is particularly illuminating for the subject.

[101]Cf. *supra*, section II, § 3 and ch. I of this book.

hension, etc., the person is not. So in the context of person-hood, *otherness* is incompatible with *division*.[102]

This identification of otherness with unity is incompatible with fallen existence, into which we are born as individuals with a clear tendency to seize, dominate and possess being. This individualized and individualizing Adam in us is our original sin, and because of it the "other," i.e. beings existing outside ourselves, in the end becomes our enemy and "our original sin" (Satre).[103] A human being left to himself cannot be a person. And the *ekstasis* of beings towards humanity or towards creation alone leads to "being-into-death."[104] For this reason, all attempts to define truth as "being-into-life" require automatically the idea of being *beyond* created exist-ence.

3. *Truth and the Savior*

When Christ says He is the truth and at the same time the life of the world, He introduces into truth a content carrying ontological implications. If the truth saves the world it is because it is life. The christological mystery, as declared by the Chalcedonian definition, signifies that salvation as truth and life is possible only in and through a person who is ontologically *true*, i.e. something which creation cannot offer, as we have seen. The only way for a true person to exist is for being and communion to coincide. The triune God offers in Himself the only possibility for such an identification of being with communion; He is the revelation of true person-hood.

Christology is founded precisely upon the assertion that only the Trinity can offer to created being the genuine base

---

[102]The distinction between "otherness" (διαφορά) and "division" (διαίρεσις) is developed by St Maximus on the basis of Chalcedonian Chris-tology. Concerning these terms and their synonyms in Maximus, see L. Thun-berg, *Microcosm and Mediator: The Theological Anthropology of Maximus the Confessor* (1965), p. 54 ff. Cf. also Yannaras, *op. cit.*, p. 73 ff.

[103]J.-P. Sartre, *L'Être et le Néant* (1949), p. 251.

[104]This observation of M. Heidegger is of great importance for an ontology of the world *taken as it is*, i.e. without reference to a beyond.

for personhood and hence salvation. This means that Christ
has to be God in order to be savior, but it also means something more: *He must be not an individual* but a true person.
It is impossible,within our experience of individualized existence to find any analogy whatsoever with an entity who is
fully and *ontologically personal.* Our experience of personhood through communion and love gives an idea of this kind
of existence, but without offering full ontological content.
True life, without death, is impossible for us as long as our
being is ontologically determined by creaturehood. Thus,
with the aid of love as an analogy, we shall be able to reach
an understanding of the Christology of the cross (a person
who loved us so much as to die for us); but without an
ability to follow it into the resurrection (a person who conquered death) Christology brings with it nothing ontological.
Christ is the truth precisely because in Himself He shows not
just being, but the persistence, the *survival of being;* through
the resurrection, Christology shows that created existence can
be so true that not even human freedom can suppress it;[105] as
was actually attempted on the cross. Truth and being are
existentially identified only in Christ's resurrection, where
freedom is no longer fallen, i.e. no longer a threat to being.

Christology, therefore, removes the problem of truth from
the realm of the individual and of "nature" to the level of
the person.[106] One must see in Christ a person in whom the

[105]Dostoevsky unveils the ontological implications of freedom in presenting
the attempt to terminate existence by self-annihilation as an expression of
human freedom of self-affirmation. As it is put by Kirilov in *The Possessed,*
man can prove that he is God—i.e. the ultimate reference-point of existence—
only if he can put an end to his existence by killing himself. The fact that
existence continues despite a man's capacity to kill himself is the ontological
proof that man is subject to individualization and not the final ground of
being, despite the threat he represents for being in having the possibility of
destroying beings by death. We should note the importance of all this for the
ontological implications of the cross and resurrection of Christ.

[106]A defence of the use of the term substance in Christology will be found
in D. M. Mackinnon, "Substance in Christology," pp. 279-300. The purpose
of this defence is to show the immediate and direct character of God's presence
in Christology and to answer the fundamental question: How can a particular
act be that of one who is related to the Father, identical to the Father, if it is
not within the nature of His relationship? One cannot but positively appreciate these aims, in the context of western thinking which tends to separate
being or *ousia* from relationship and personhood. What we are trying to show

division of "natures" is changed into an otherness through communion.[107] This shift of Christology away from our individualized existence seems to many to lead to a picture of a Christ who is not "human"; nevertheless, what we have just said shows that, unless in Christology this "de-individualization" of Christ takes place, its existential implications will no longer have any ontological importance.[108]

The fact that an individualization of Christ creates insurmountable problems in Christology, in view of the existential implications of the assertion that Christ is the truth, can be seen clearly in relation to ecclesiology. For if Christ's being is established after the manner of an individual, i.e. as an entity conceivable in itself, the inevitable question arises: How can man, and creation in general, be connected with this individual existentially, i.e. not just psychologically or morally, but ontologically?[109] This whole problem is linked with the relationship between Christology and pneumatology, and we must look at it before we are able to see how the Church can take up her position in presenting Christ as truth and communion.

here on the basis of Greek patristic thought (cf. *supra*, section II, § 3) is that being and relationship must be mutually identified and that it is only within the "mode of existence" that "nature" or "substance" is truth.

[107]The patristic idea of *hypostatic union,* such as developed principally by Cyril of Alexandria, makes the *person* (*hypostasis*), and not the natures, the ultimate ground of Christ's being. Here there is a subtle but significant distinction to be made between this view and that suggested by the idea of *communicatio idiomatum,* which seems to assign, or at least to assume, an ontological status in each nature taken in itself.

[108]All christologies wishing to take the *human* person as the basis of Christ's identity may offer a soteriology of the *ethical* or *psychological* type, but remain irrelevant for ontology. The problem of death as a threat to personal being cannot be resolved if the *hypostasis* of the Savior is subject to the individualism and the ontological necessity of the biological hypostasis (see Chapter I).

[109]The problem also involves logical and experiential difficulties which Christology cannot resolve for man today as long as it pictures Christ as an individual. How can an individual who lived in Palestine so many years ago have a relationship with me *here and now?* To introduce the Holy Spirit as a *deus ex machina* to resolve this problem creates extra ones which it does not resolve, and in any case does not seem persuasive at the existential or the ontological level. The only obvious alternative in the context of this individualistic type of Christology is to understand our relationship with Christ as an *imitatio Christi,* or in terms of substitutional theories of soteriology. Any

110 BEING AS COMMUNION

IV. *Truth and the Church: Ecclesiological Consequences of the Greek Patristic Synthesis*

1. *The Body of Christ formed in the Spirit*

The christological starting point of our understanding of truth, or rather the identification of our concept of truth with Christ, raises the question as to what kind of Christology we have in mind when making this identification. It is possible to envisage at least two kinds of Christology here. Firstly, we may understand Christ as an individual, seen objectively and historically, presenting Himself thereby for us as the truth. With this way of understanding Christ, the distance between Him and us is bridged by the aid of certain means, which serve as vehicles for truth to communicate itself to us: for example, His spoken words incorporated within the Scriptures and perhaps tradition—transmitted, interpreted, or even expounded through magisterium—all being realized *with the assistance or under the guidance of the Holy Spirit.*

Secondly, it is possible to envisage a type of Christology in which Christ, although a particular person, cannot be conceived in Himself as an individual. When we make the assertion that He is the truth, we are meaning His *whole personal existence, in this second type* of Christology; that is, we mean *His relationship* with His body, the Church, ourselves. In other words, when we now say "Christ" we mean a person and not an individual; we mean a relational reality existing "for me" or "for us."[110] Here the Holy Spirit is not one who *aids* us in bridging the distance between Christ and ourselves, but he is the person of the Trinity who actually realizes in history

attempt to understand the relationship as ontological necessarily leads to the abandonment of an individualistic conception of Christ (cf. the biblical idea of "corporate personality").

[110]Cf. the Christology of D. Bonhoeffer (*Gesammelte Schriften* III 1960, pp. 166, 242) where this is used as a key expression. This view of Bonhoeffer's is very important in that it steers clear of Reformation theories of soteriology and theology based more on Christ's activity than his person. The pneumatological dimension, however, is lacking throughout all Bonehoeffer's work, and this makes the idea of "pro-me" into a scheme without ontological content.

that which we call Christ, this absolutely relational entity, our Savior. In this case, our Christology is *essentially* conditioned by Pneumatology, not just secondarily as in the first case; in fact it is *constituted* pneumatologically. Between the Christ-truth and ourselves there is *no gap to fill* by the means of grace. The Holy Spirit, in making real the Christ-event in history, makes real *at the same time* Christ's personal existence as a body or community. Christ does not exist *first* as truth and *then* as communion; He is both at once. All separation between Christology and ecclesiology vanishes in the Spirit.

Such a pneumatologically constituted Christology is undoubtedly biblical. In the Bible Christ becomes a historical person only *in the Spirit* (Matt. 1:18-20; Luke 1:35) which means that Christology's very foundations are laid pneumatologically. The Holy Spirit does not intervene *a posteriori* within the framework of Christology, as a help in overcoming the distance between an objectively existing Christ and ourselves; he is the one who gives birth to Christ and to the whole activity of salvation, by anointing Him and making Him Χριστός (Luke 4:13). If it is truely possible to confess Christ as the truth, this is only because of the Holy Spirit (I Cor. 12:3). And as a careful study of I Cor. 12 shows, for St Paul the body of Christ is literally composed of the charismata of the Spirit (charisma = membership of the body).[111] So we can say without risk of exaggeration that Christ *exists only pneumatologically,* whether in His distinct personal particularity or in His capacity as the body of the Church and the recapitulation of all things. Such is the great mystery of Christology, that the Christ-event is not an event defined in itself—it cannot be defined in itself for a single instant even theoretically—but is *an integral part of the economy of the Holy Trinity.* To speak of Christ means speaking at the same time of the Father and the Holy Spirit.[112] For the Incarnation, as we have just seen, is formed by the work of

[111]Cf. Chapter VI below.

[112]The unity of the divine activity *ad extra* is emphasized very strongly by the Fathers. See e.g. Athanasius, *Ad. Serap.* I:20; Basil, *De Spir.* 19:49; Cyril of Alexandria, *In Jo.* 10 etc. This is also true of the Western Fathers. Cf. Y. Congar, "Pneumatologie ou 'Christomonism' dans la tradition Latine?" in *Ecclesia a Spiritu Sancto edocta* (Melanges G. Philips, 1970), pp. 41-63.

the Spirit, and is nothing else than the expression and realization of the will of the Father.

Thus the mystery of the Church has its birth in the entire
economy of the Trinity and in a pneumatologically constituted
Christology. The Spirit as "power" or "giver of life" opens
up our existence to become relational, so that he may at the
same time be "communion" (κοινωνία, cf. II Cor.
13:13). For this reason the mystery of the Church is essentially none other than that of the "One" who is simultaneously "many"—not "One" who exists first of all as "One"
and *then* as "many," but "One" and "many" at the same
time.[113]

In the context of a Christology constructed in this pneumatological manner, truth and communion once more become
identical. This happens on the historical and anthropolgical
levels alike. While the Christ-truth, as existence in the Spirit,
cannot be imagined individualistically, truth itself is inevitably
and constantly realized in the Spirit, i.e. in a pentecostal event.
In the description of Pentecost in Acts 2, the significance of
the event seems related as much to history as to anthropology:
through the outpouring of the Spirit, the "last days" enter
into history, while the unity of humanity is affirmed as a
diversity of charisms. Its deep significance seems to lie in the
fact that this takes place in Christ, viewed both historically and also anthropologically, as a here-and-now reality.
The objectivization and individualization of historical
existence which implies distance, decay and death is transformed into existence in communion, and hence eternal life
for mankind and all creation. In a like manner, the individualization of human existence which results in division and
separation is now transformed into existence in communion
where the otherness of persons ("on each of them separately,"
Acts 2:3) is identical with communion within a body.[114]
Christ's existence, as described above, is thus made historical
and personal through the same movement of the Spirit of
God which made Christ Himself into a historical being. The

[113]This is discussed at greater length in J.D. Zizioulas, *"Die Pneumatologische Dimension der Kirche,"* in *Communio* (1973).
[114]Cf. above, section III, 1.

truth seen as Christ and the truth seen as the Holy Spirit are identical, and therefore the Spirit himself is called "the Spirit of truth" (Jn. 14:17, 15:26, 16:13). Only the mode of the operation of truth differs, a Christ-mode and a Spirit-mode, such that the one divine love may accommodate itself (the economy) to our needs and limitations.

Now, the description of the pentecostal event in Acts 2 proceeds to show the same thing more concretely. Christ's existence is applied to our historical existence not *in abstracto* or individualistically, but in and through a *community*. This community is formed from out of ordinary existence, through a radical conversion from individualism to personhood in baptism. As death and resurrection in Christ, baptism signifies the decisive passing of our existence from the "truth" of individualized being into the truth of personal being. The resurrectional aspect of baptism is therefore nothing other than *incorporation into the community*. The existential truth arising from baptism is simply the truth of personhood, the truth of communion. A new birth (ἀναγέννησις) is required for this, simply because birth by normal procreation, as stated in the previous chapter, is for created beings a cause of individualization and is thus a birth of beings destined to death. Eternal life needs the new birth of baptism as a "birth in the Spirit," just as Christ's own birth was "in the Spirit," so that each baptized person can himself become "Christ,"[115] his existence being one of communion and hence of true life.[116]

[115]Cf. Cyril of Jerusalem, *Catech.* 21:1; Terullian, *De Bapt.* 7-8; *Const. Apost.* III, 16.

[116]This "de-individualization" of Christ, His identification with a pneumatic "body," makes sense only if the echatological realities are introduced into history. The Spirit is associated with the "last days" (Acts 2:17) and a pneumatic Christology draws its "truth" only from the fact of the *resurrected* Christ, i.e. from the historical "verification" of this eschatological truth. If one accepts the resurrected Christ, then it is no longer possible to have an individualistic Christology. Any reference to the person of Christ will inevitably imply what we have called here a de-individualization, i.e. it will present Christ as a *person* (not an individual), as a being whose identity is established in and through communion. The New Testament was written by those who had accepted Jesus' resurrection as a historical fact, and therefore Christ's identity is always presented in the New Testament in pneumatological terms (for some Gospel writers, such as Matthew and Luke, even from the moment of

The application of Christ's existence to ours then amounts
to nothing other than a realization of the community of the
Church. This community is born as the Body of Christ and
lives out of the same communion which we find in Christ's
historical existence. His 'true life" is identical with the eternal
life of the Triune God; the community itself thus becomes
"the pillar of truth" in an existential sense. All this, having
its ἀλήθεια in the *eschata,* is given to it sacramentally as
an "eikon,"[117] so that it may realize in itself the truth of
Christ in the form of faith, hope and love, as a foretaste of
eternal life, making it aspire towards the transfiguration of
the world within this communion which the Church herself
experiences.

But this experience of truth in the Church's existence is
realized to its maximum, in the course of her historical life,
in the eucharist. The eucharistic community is the Body of
Christ *par excellence* simply because it incarnates and realizes our communion within the very life and communion of
the Trinity, in a way that preserves the eschatological character of truth while making it an integral part of history.
So if we wish to see how Christ the truth is united to the
Church we can only begin by considering the holy eucharist.

2. *The Eucharist as the Locus of Truth*

How does the eucharist reveal Christ as the truth? What
does the statement that Christ is the truth mean for the life
and structure of the Church, in the light of its eucharistic
experience? Here we will make the following observations:

(a) The eucharist reveals the Christ-truth as a "visitation"
and as the "tabernacle" (Jn. 1:14) of God in history and

Jesus' biological conception). Given this, it was now impossible for the
Church to speak of Christ other than in terms of communion, i.e. identifying
Him with the "communion of the saints." The pneumatological and eschatological approaches to Christ equally imply His community. The raised Christ
is unimaginable as an individual; He is the "first-born of many brothers,"
establishing His historical identity in and through the communion-event which
is the Church.

[117]Cf. *supra,* section II, § 6.

creation, so that God can be beheld in the glory of His truth and partaken of within His communion of life. The Church has therefore no other reality or experience of truth as communion so perfect as the eucharist. In the eucharistic assembly God's Word reaches man and creation not from outside, as in the Old Testament, but as "flesh"—from inside our own existence, as part of creation. For this reason, the Word of God does not dwell in the human mind as rational knowledge or in the human soul as a mystical inner experience, but as communion within a community. And it is most important to note that in this way of understanding Christ as truth, Christ Himself becomes revealed as truth not *in* a community, but *as* a community. So truth is not just something "expressed" or "heard," a propositional or a logical truth; but something which *is,* i.e. an ontological truth: the community itself becoming the truth.

Because the Christ-truth is not only revealed but also realized, in our existence, as communion within a community, truth is not imposed upon us but springs up from our midst. It is not authority in the sense of *auctoritas* but is grace and love, embracing us in its being which is bound to us existentially. Yet this truth is not the product of a sociological or group experience; it comes clearly from another world, and as such is not produced by ourselves.

(b) This kind of truth does not come to us simply as the result of a *historical transmission.* The problem here becomes very delicate, and needs careful consideration.

It is certain that Christianity is founded on historical fact, and the Church Fathers were those Christians of their era who thought most along historical lines, if we compare them with the heretics whom they fought against. (Heresy, for the Fathers, is "innovation"). Nevertheless history understood in the light of eucharistic experience is not the same as history as normally understood; it is conditioned by the *anamnetic* and *epicletic* character of the eucharist which, out of distance and decay, transfigures time into communion and life. Thus history ceases to be a succession of events moving from past to present linearly, but acquires the dimension of the future, which is also a *vertical* dimension transforming history into charismatic—pentecostal events. Within history thus pictured, truth does not come to us solely by way of *delegation* (Christ —the apostles—the bishops, in a linear development). It comes as a pentecostal event which takes linear history up into a charismatic present-moment. The ordination of a bishop takes place exclusively during the eucharist (and in the Eastern liturgy, the feast of Pentecost is celebrated at each episcopal ordination) for this reason.

This illuminates our understanding of the Church's "infallibility" and its expression through certain ministries. Already Irenaeus speaks of bishops as possessing a certain *charisma veritatis;* the primitive Church developed the idea of apostolic succession though the bishops just as it did conciliarity, also through the bishops. Why was the bishop from the earliest days associated with *veritas?* In the approach presented here, this association cannot be understood as a delegation of the truth to official ministers. The fact that every bishop receives the *charisma veritatis* only within the eucharistic community, and as a Pentecost-event, shows that the apostolic succession has to pass to the community through communion. *The bishop in his function is the apostles' successor inasmuch as he is the image of Christ within the community:* the primitive church was unable to see the two aspects (Christ-apostles) separately.[118] Similarly, the councils were expressions of the truth simply because the bishops were the heads of their communities, which is why diocesan bishops alone can take part in councils. The communities' *unity in identity* is the foundation of conciliar infallibility.

(c) Similar observations could be made about the *formulation* of truth in the Church. If truth as communion is not to be separated from the ontology of life, then dogmas are principally *soteriological* declarations; their object is to free the original εἰκὼν of Christ, the truth,[119] from the distortions of certain heresies, so as to help the Church community to

---

[118]This is particularly clear in Hippolytus, *Trad. Apost.* 3 (prayer of ordination of a bishop).

[119]Cf. W. Elert, *Der Ausgang der alt-kirchlichen Christologie* (1957), where the important point is made concerning the role of the *Christusbild* as contrasted with that of the *Christusbegriff* in the development of classical Christology.

maintain the correct vision of the Christ-truth and to live in and by this presence of truth in history. The final intention of all this is to lead to communion with the life of God, to make truth into communion and life. This is why the ancient councils ended their definitions with anathemas, as if the main aim of the council were not so much definition as anthema. Excommunication had from then on a pastoral basis, that of protecting the community from distortions of the εἰκὼν of truth, so as not to endanger the truth's soteriological content. If communion was no longer possible after a council's definition and anathema, it was because the eucharist requires a common vision (εἰκὼν) of Christ. The councils' aim was eucharistic communion, and in producing or adopting creeds the intention was not to provide material for theological reflection, but to orientate correctly the eucharistic communities. Thus it may be said that the credal definitions carry no relationship with truth in themselves, but only in their being doxological acclamations of the worshiping community.

However, the "definitions" do have a certain reality of their own. What relationship with truth do these forms bear, in the light of the eucharistic vision of truth? We have here another delicate problem to consider. Throughout this account, we have insisted that truth is not "comprehensible" and thus cannot be objectified and defined. How are dogmas to be seen if not as "formulations" or "definitions" of the truth, making this truth a captive to the bonds of historical and cultural forms?

If we start our reflection from the understanding of dogmas in their soteriological and doxological character mentioned above, then these dogmas represent a form of *acceptance, sanctification,* and also *transcendence* of history and culture. It is a form similar to that of the eucharist itself, borrowing its basic elements from creation and the ordinary life of the people, and transcending them in communion. What happens in a dogmatic formulation, as it passes through the charismatic process of a council, is that certain historical and cultural elements become elements of communion, and thus acquire a sacred character and a permanence in the life of the Church. Here, history and culture are accepted but at

the same time eschatologized, so that truth shall not be sub-
jugated through being incarnated in history and culture. To
illustrate this, we can again return to certain terms and concepts which the Church borrowed from Greek culture for
dogmatic purposes. Take, for example, the term καθολικὸς
or πρόσωπον or ὑπόστασις. Historically and culturally,
they are Greek words. Would Aristotle have understood their
meaning, had he been given the Nicene Creed to read? He
would have if the words were history and culture solely. If
not, as one has the right to suspect, then something crucial
must have happened to these historical and cultural elements
through the fact of their being associated with the thought-
structure and life of the Church. It is in this sense that we
would understand faithfulness to dogmas. Not because they
rationalize and set forth certain truths or the truth, but because they have become expressions and signs of communion
within the Church community. Communion, being relational,
is inescapably of an incarnational nature, which is why it actualizes truth *hic et nunc* by accepting history and culture.
At the same time, there is a prophetic and critical element
in truth as communion. This comes about through the acceptance, not the rejection, of historical forms. Christ, the truth, is
judge of the world, by the very fact of having taken it upon
Himself.

This means that any breaking of the bond between dogma
and community amounts to a breaking of the bond between
truth and communion. Dogmas, like ministries, cannot survive as truth outside the communion-event created by the
Spirit. It is not possible for a concept or formula to incorporate
the truth within itself, unless the spirit gives life to it in
communion. Academic theology may concern itself with doctrine, but it is the communion of the Church which makes
theology into truth.[120] This type of approach to the dogmas
maintains the vigilance which the Greek patristic synthesis
held against conceptualizing truth, yet without leading to any
rejection of the truth's historicity.

[120]This explains the fact that the primitive Church expressed its faith officially through councils *of bishops*, i.e. of the presidents of eucharistic communities, and not through theologians.

(d) The eucharist shows that truth is not just something concerning humanity alone, but has profound *cosmic* dimensions. The Christ of the eucharist is revealed as the life and recapitulation of all creation. One of the basic difficulties inherent in the Greek conception of truth is that it implies that truth can be grasped and formulated by human reason. But, as the eucharistic reveals, this human "reason" must be understood as the element which unifies creation, and refers it to God through the hands of man, so that God may be "all in all." This eucharistic or priestly function of man reconnects created nature to infinite existence, and thus liberates it from slavery to necessity by letting it develop its potentialities to the maximum. If as we have insisted in this account, communion is the only way for truth to exist as life, the nature which possesses neither personhood nor communion "groans and is in travail" in awaiting the salvation of man, who can set it within the communion-event offered in Christ. Man's responsibility is to make a eucharistic reality out of nature, i.e. to make nature, too, capable of communion. If man does this, then truth takes up its meaning for the whole cosmos, Christ becomes a cosmic Christ, and the world as a whole dwells in truth, which is none other than communion with its Creator. Truth thereby becomes the life of all that *is*.

The implications of this go beyond theological truth, in the narrow sense of "theological," and extend to the truth of the natural sciences. Science and theology for a long time seemed to be in search of different sorts of truth, as if there were not one truth in existence as a whole. This resulted from making truth subject to the dichotomy between the transcendent and the immanent, and in the final analysis from the fact that the "theological" truth and the "scientific" truth were both disconnected from the idea of communion, and were considered in terms of a subject-object framework which was simply the methodology of analytical research. The revolution that Einstein effected in science, however, has meant a radical re-orientation of the scientific search for truth.[121] The final consequences are still to be realized,

[121]Cf. T. F. Torrance, *Space, Time and the Incarnation* (1969).

but one thing seems clear, which is that the Greek conception of being has been critically affected by the idea of relationship: for the natural sciences in the post-Einstein period, existence has become relational.[122] This essentially leads scientific truth back to the final position of the Greek Fathers[123] on the philosophical level, and makes it possible to speak of a unique truth in the world, approachable scientifically or theologically. If theology creatively uses the Greek patristic synthesis concerning truth and communion and applies it courageously to the sphere of the Church, the split between the Church and science can be overcome. The scientist who is a Church member will be able to recognize that he is carrying out a *para-eucharistic work,* and this may lead to the freeing of nature from its subjection beneath the hands of modern technological man. The eucharistic conception of truth can thus liberate man from his lust to dominate nature, making him aware that the Christ-truth exists for the life of the whole cosmos, and that the deification which Christ brings, the communion with the divine life (II Peter 1:4), extends to "all creation" and not just to humanity.[124]

(e) Finally, a eucharistic concept of truth shows how truth becomes *freedom* (Jn. 8:32). As we remarked in connection with the relation between truth and the fallen condition of existence, freedom normally means in this context a choice between different possibilities or between negation and affirmation, good and evil. The possibility of choice is based on the individualizations and divisions within being, which are born

[122]Einstein showed that certain aspects of reality are intrinsically *relational,* rather than absolute, as a Greek might have expected. These comprise certain attributes of a thing—position, velocity, etc.—which now are definable only in relation to other things. However, two reservations need to be made: (a) the basic ontology of the thing is unaffected by all this, since it still retains an "identity" in absolute terms; and (b) the subject-object distinction also remains unchanged. A further step towards the kind of rapprochement between science and theology envisaged here may perhaps be found in quantum mechanics. In this branch of physics, it is shown that the observer is *involved* in his measurement in an essential way. Subject and object are now related, thus bridging the hitherto unbrigeable gap between the two. However it must be added that the philosophical interpretation of quantum mechanics is still a matter of some dispute (P. J. Bussey).

[123]Cf. T.F. Torrance, *op. cit.*

[124]Cf. Athanasius, *Ad. Serap.* I, 23.

out of man's insistence on referring all of being ultimately to himself. The overcoming of these divisions is the precise meaning of what we call the "catholicity" of existence within Christ and His Body, the catholic Church. It is this sort of catholicity of existence which the eucharistic community exhibits in its own structure.[125] And the freedom given by the Christ-truth to creation is precisely this freedom from division and individualization, creating the possibility of otherness within communion.

But if this is truth's foundation as freedom within the Church, then clearly a new concept of freedom is being born, determined not by choice but by the movement of a constant affirmation, a continual "Amen." The people of God gathered together in the eucharist realize their freedom under the form of affirmation alone: it is not the "yes" and the "no" together which God offers in Christ, but only the "yes," which equates to the eucharistic "Amen" (II Cor. 1:19, 20).[126] So it is clear that the eucharist contains an idea of truth which is not of this world, and which seems unrealistic and inappli-

---

[125]A more detailed discussion of this point will be found in Chapter IV below.

[126]In the light of Greek patristic thought as we have attempted to present it in this study, freedom is situated higher than what we call "moral freedom." The possibility of choice which defines moral freedom arises from the individualization of being, inherent in the fall (see above, Section III, 1) and is in fact a limitation of freedom because it rests on possibilities that are *given* and, consequently, constraining. In placing God's being above the level of will (Athanasius) or above affirmation and negation (Maximus)—see above, Section II, 3-4—the Greek Fathers were wishing to situate freedom itself above the limitations inherent in choice and in the "given." God is truly free because He is confronted with nothing "given" before Him, so that He exists above all affirmation and negation. But this must not remain a negative statement. God is truly free in a positive sense, because "eternally" (i.e. without being confronted with anything "given," as any being would be who had a beginning). He *affirms* His existence by a communion-event. He is the Father because He eternally has a Son through whom He affirms Himself as Father, and so on. So the being of God appears truly free as regards "given" things, and through an otherness which is not individualization. A freedom of this kind is offered to man in Christ as the eschatological "glory" of the "children of God." The Spirit allows a "foretaste" to be had of this as he leads the community of the Church in history, and in this sense the eucharistic communion, which is the Church's eschatological event *par excellence*, is an affirmation, an "Amen," and reveals a state of existence free from the possibility of denial, and even free as regards that denial of being and life which is death. A freedom resting on affirmation through communion is

cable to life. But as we have emphasized above in connection
with Christology, you do not do justice to truth's ontological
content by implying that our fallen state of existence is all
there is. The individualization of existence by the fall makes
us seek out security in objects or various "things," but the truth
of communion does not offer this kind of security: rather, it
frees us from slavery to objective "things" by placing all
things and ourselves within a communion-event. It is there
that the Spirit is simultaneously freedom (II Cor. 3:17) and
communion (I Cor. 13:13).

Man is free only within communion. If the Church wishes
to be the place of freedom, she must continually place all
the "objects" she possesses, whatever they may be (Scripture,
sacraments, ministries, etc.) within the communion-event to
make them "true" and to make her members free in regard
to them as objects, as well as in them and through them as
channels of communion. Christians must learn not to lean
on objective "truths" as securities for truth, but to live in an
epicletic way, i.e. leaning on the communion-event in which
the structure of the Church involves them. Truth liberates
by placing beings in communion.

a freedom in regard to individualization and death, and is trus an affirmation
of *being*. This is not moral but ontological freedom, deriving from the identification of being and truth with communion.

3.

Christ, the Spirit and the Church

I. Introduction

One of the fundamental criticisms that Orthodox theologians expressed in connection with the ecclesiology of Vatican II concerned the place which the council gave to Pneumatology in its ecclesiology. In general, it was felt that in comparison with Christology, Pneumatology did not play an important role in the council's teaching on the Church. More particularly, it was observed that the Holy Spirit was brought into ecclesiology *after* the edifice of the Church was constructed with Christological material alone. This, of course, had important consequences for the teaching of the council on such matters as the sacraments, ministry and ecclesial institutions in general.

This criticism may be on the whole a valid one, but when we come to the point of asking what its *positive* aspect is, namely what the Orthodox would in fact like to see the council do with Pneumatology in its ecclesiology, then we are confronted with problems. In one of his articles Fr Congar quotes two Orthodox observers to the council, whose names he politely refrains from mentioning, as having said to him that "if we must propose a schema *De Ecclesia*, two chapters would suffice: one on the Holy Spirit and another on Christian man."[1] This quotation is in itself a clear indication that Orthodox theology needs to do a great deal of reflection on the relationship between Christology and Pneumatology, and that

[1]Y. Congar, "Actualité d'une pneumatologie," in *Proche-Orient Chrétien* 23 (1973), 121-132 (121).

the actual state of Orthodox theology in this respect is by no means satisfactory.

A quick look at the history of modern Orthodox theology concerning this subject leads us back to the critique of Western thought by Khomiakov in the previous century and the famous idea of *sobornost* which resulted from it.[2] Khomiakov was not explicit on the problem we are discussing here, but his views can make sense only if a strong dose of Pneumatology is injected into ecclesiology. In fact this dose—which, by the way, had already been generously given to ecclesiology by Khomiakov's Roman Catholic contemporary Johannes Möhler through his work *Die Einheit*[3]—was so strong as to make of the Church a "charismatic society" rather than the "body of Christ." This led later Orthodox theologians, notably the late Fr Georges Florovsky, to reiterate with particular emphasis that the doctrine of the Church is "a chapter of Christology."[4] By so doing Florovsky indirectly raised the problem of the synthesis between Christology and Pneumatology, without however offering any solution to it. In fact there are reasons to believe that far from suggesting a synthesis, he leaned towards a Christological approach in his ecclesiology.

The Orthodox theologian who was destined to exercise the greatest influence on this subject in our time was Vladimir Lossky. His views are well known, but two points need to be mentioned in particular. The first is that there is a distinct

[2]A. S. Khomiakoff, *L'Eglise Latine et le Protestantisme au point de vue de l'Eglise d'Orient*, 1872; W. I. Birkbeck (ed.), *Russia and the English Church during the Last Fifty Years*, I, 1895; G. Florovsky, "Sobornost: The Catholicity of the Church" in *The Church of God. An Anglo-Russian Symposium*, 1934; A. Gratieux, *A. S. Khomiakov et le Movement slavophile*, I-II, 1939; E. Lanne, "Le mystère de l'Eglise dans la perspective de la théologie orthodoxe," in *Irénikon* 35 (1962) 171-212; esp. E. Suttner, *Offenbarung, Gnade und Kirche bei A. S. Chomiakov*, 1967; and recently, P. O'Leary, *The Triune Church. A Study in the Ecclesiology of A. S. Komiakov*, 1982.

[3]J. A. Möhler, *Die Einheit in der Kirche, oder das Prinzip des Katholizismus*, 1825. Cf. Y. Congar, "La pensé de Möhler et l'ecclésiologie orthodoxe" in *Irénikon* 12 (1935), 321-329.

[4]G. Florovsky, "Le corps du Christ vivant," in *Le sainte Eglise universele. Confrontation oecumenique*, 1948, p. 12. See also the study of J. Romanides, "Orthodox Ecclesiology according to Alexis Khomiakov" in *The Greek Orthodox Theological Review* 2 (1956), 57-73.

"economy of the Holy Spirit" alongside with that of the Son.[5] The other is that the content of Pneumatology, as contrasted with that of Christology, should be defined in ecclesiological terms as concerning the "personalization" of the mystery of Christ, its appropriation by the faithful, what could be called the "subjective" aspect of the Church (the other one, the "objective," being proper to Christology).[6] Thus, with the help of the scheme "nature versus person," Lossky would develop the view that both Christology and Pneumatology are necessary components of ecclesiology, and would see in the sacramental structure of the Church the "objective" Christological aspect which has to be constantly accompanied by the "personal" or "subjective" aspect. The latter is related to the freedom and integrity of each person, his inner "spiritual life," deification etc. This seems to offer material for a synthesis between Christology and Pneumatology in ecclesiology. And yet its actual schematization makes Lossky's position extremely problematic, as we shall see later. For the same reasons his first point, too, concerning a distinct "economy of the Spirit," becomes questionable and in fact renders the synthesis so difficult that it must be abandoned.

Lossky did not draw conclusions from the implications of his views for the actual structure and institutions of the Church. The problem *how* to relate the institutional with the charismatic, the Christological with the Pneumatological aspects of ecclesiology, still awaits its treatment by Orthodox theology.

Two other Orthodox theologians of our time who have insisted on the importance of Pneumatology in ecclesiology have recognized the difficulties inherent in any dissociation of Pneumatology from Christology. Nikos Nissiotis and Fr Boris Bobrinskoy have stressed that the work of the Holy Spirit and that of Christ belong together and should never be seen in separation. This is an important corrective of the views expressed by Khomiakov and to a large extent also Lossky, although the priority given to Pneumatology is still

[5]See V. Lossky, *The Mystical Theology of the Eastern Church,* 1957, esp. pp. 135ff.; 156ff and 174ff.

[6]See *Ibid;* also his *In the Image and Likeness of God,* 1974, esp. ch. 9.

preserved in both Nissiotis and Bobrinskoy.[7] The question, however, remains still open as to *how* Pneumatology and Christology can be brought together into a full and organic synthesis. It is probably one of the most important questions facing Orthodox theology in our time.

As this brief historical survey, suggests Orthodox theology has no ready-made answers to offer to the problems at hand. It is often assumed that Orthodoxy can be helpful in the ecumenical discussions by contributing its Pneumatology to them. This may be true to some extent, especially if the Orthodox contribution is taken as a corrective to Western excesses in ecclesiology. But when it comes to the point of doing justice to the basic components of the Orthodox tradition itself or—and this is more important—to the point of facing our actual ecumenical problems with positive propositions, it becomes clear that Orthodox theology needs to work closely together with Western theology if it is to be really helpful to itself and to others. This brief study will reflect problems and concerns relating to Orthodoxy itself, which is by no means immune from the post-Vatican II *problematique*. A proper synthesis between Christology and Pneumatology in ecclesiology concerns Orthodoxy as much as the West.

II.   *The Problem of the Synthesis between*
      Christology and Pneumatology

What would a proper synthesis between Christology and Pneumatology have to include? This question must be asked before any attempt is made to tackle the problem of ecclesial institutions. We shall discuss it only in those aspects which concern ecclesiology.

Few people if any would question the statement that

─────────────
[7]See N. Nissiotis, "The Importance of the Doctrine of the Trinity for Church Life and Theology" in A. J. Philippou (ed.), *The Orthodox Ethos*, 1964, esp. p. 62f.; *Id.*, "Pneumatologie orthodoxe" in F. J. Leenhard *et al.*, *Le Saint-Esprit*, 1963; B. Bobrinskoy, "Le Saint-Esprit dans la liturgie," in *Studia Liturgia* 1 (1962), 47-60; *Id.* "Présence réelle et communion eucharistique," in *Revue des Sciences philosophiques et théologiques* 53 (1969), 402-420.

Christology and Pneumatology belong together and cannot be separated. To speak of "Christomonism" in any part of the Christian tradition is to misunderstand or be unfair to this part of tradition. (Fr. Congar has shown this with regard to the Roman Catholic Western tradition.)[8] The problem is not whether one accepts the importance of Pneumatology in Christology and vice versa; it arises in connection with the following two questions: (i) The question of *priority*: should Christology be made dependent on Pneumatology or should the order be the other way around? (ii) The question of *content*: when we speak of Christology and Pneumatology, what *particular* aspects of Christian doctrine—and Christian existence—do we have in mind?

First, the question of priority. That this is a *real* question and not the product of a theological construction is to be seen in the fact that not only the entire history of theology in what concerns the East-West relationship, but even the most primitive theology and liturgical practice we know of are conditioned by this problem.[9] In the New Testament writings themselves we come across both the view that the Spirit is given *by* Christ, particularly the risen and ascended Christ ("*there was no Spirit yet,* for Christ had not yet been glorified")[10]; and the view that there is, so to say, *no Christ* until the Spirit is at work, not only as *a forerunner* announcing his coming, but also as the one who *constitutes his very identity as Christ,* either at his baptism (Mark) or at his very

[8]Y. Congar, "Pneumatologie ou 'Christomonisme' dans la tradition latine" in *Ecclesia a Spiritu Sancto edocta*, Mélanges G. Philips, 1970, pp. 41-63. In his important three-volume work *Je crois en l'Esprit Saint*, 1980 (recently in English translation: *I believe in the Holy Spirit*, 1983) Father Congar shows clearly and convincingly the central place that Pneumatology has occupied in Western theology throughout the centuries. It is a work of particular significance and deserves special attention at the present time when the theological dialogue between the Roman Catholic and the Orthodox Churches is taking place. Another important recent study showing the place of Pneumatology in Western thought is that of Father Louis Bouyer, *Le Consolateur*, 1980. The importance of the problem of Pneumatology is made explicit also in an article by the Roman Catholic theologian, W. Kasper, "Esprit-Christ-Eglise" in *L'expérience de l'Esprit*, Mélanges E. Schillebeeckx, 1976, pp. 47-69.

[9]For a more detailed discussion see my "Implications ecclésiologiques de deux types de Pneumatologie," in *Communio Sanctorum*, Mélanges J.-J. von Allmen, 1982, pp. 141-154.

[10]John 7:39.

biological conception (Matthew and Luke). Both of these views could co-exist happily in one and the same Biblical writing, as is evident from a study of Luke (Gospel and Acts), John's Gospel, etc. On the liturgical level these two approaches became quite distinct very early with the development of two traditions concerning the relationship between baptism and confirmation (or chrismation).[11] It is well known that in Syria and Palestine confirmation *preceded* baptism liturgically at least until the fourth century, while in other parts, the practice of the Church which finally prevailed everywhere was observed, namely the performance of confirmation *after* baptism. Given the fact that confirmation was normally regarded as the rite of the "giving of the Spirit," one could argue that in cases where confirmation preceded baptism we had a priority of Pneumatology over Christology, while in the other case we had the reverse. And yet there is also evidence suggesting that baptism itself was inconceivable in the early Church without the giving of the Spirit,[12] which leads to the conclusion that the two rites were united in one synthesis both liturgically and theologically, regardless of the priority of any of the two aspects over the other.

It seems, therefore, that the question of priority between Christology and Pneumatology does not *necessarily* constitute a problem, and the Church could see no problem in this diversity of approach either liturgically or theologically for a long time. Thus there is no reason why things should be different today, as some Orthodox seem to suggest. The problem arose only when these two aspects were *in fact* separated from each other both liturgically and theologically. It was at this point in history that East and West started to follow their separate ways leading finally to total estrangement and division. Not only baptism and confirmation were

[11]Cf. T. W. Manson, "Entry into Membership of the Early Church" in *Journal of Theological Studies* 48 (1947), 25-33.

[12]See G. Lampe, *The Seal of the Spirit,* 1951. Lampe's controversy with G. Dix on this matter (the latter insisted that the Spirit is given in confirmation only), proves to be pointless given this variety in liturgical use. In any case, baptism and confirmation formed a liturgical unity in the early Church and for that reason the Holy Spirit was involved in the entire process of christian initiation.

separated liturgically in the West, but Christology tended little by little to dominate Pneumatology, the *Filioque* being only part of the new development. The East while keeping the liturgical unity between baptism and chrismation, thus maintaining the original synthesis on the liturgical level, did not finally manage to overcome the temptation of a *reactionary* attitude towards the West in its theology. The atmosphere of mutual polemic and suspicion contributed a great deal to this situation and obscured the entire issue. What we must and can see clearly now, however, is that so long as the unity between Christology and Pneumatology remains unbreakable, the question of priority can remain a "theologoumenon." For various reasons which have to do with the idiosyncrasy of the West (concern with history, ethics etc.), a certain priority will always be given by it to Christology over Pneumatology. Indeed, there are reasons to suppose that this could be spiritually expedient, especially in our time. Equally, for the East Pneumatology will always occupy an important place given the fact that a liturgical meta-historical approach to Christian existence seems to mark the Eastern ethos. Different concerns lead to different emphases and priorities. As long as the essential *content* of both Christology and Pneumatology is present, the synthesis is there in its fulness. But in what does this "content" consist? From what exactly does ecclesiology suffer if the content of Christology or Pneumatology is deficient?

It is difficult to make distinctions when a unity is involved. Our task at this point is somewhat delicate and involves the risk of separating where we should be only distinguishing. We must bear in mind that according to patristic tradition, both Eastern and Western, the activity of God *ad extra* is one and indivisible: Wherever the Son is there is also the Father and the Spirit, and wherever the Spirit is there is also the Father and the Son. And yet the contribution of each of these divine persons to the economy bears its own distinctive characteristics[13] which are directly relevant for ecclesiology in which

---

[13]The unity of divine operations *ad extra* is, according to the Fathers, indivisible but *not undifferentiated*. See J. McIntyre, "The Holy Spirit in Greek Patristic Thought" in *The Scottish Journal of Theology* 7 (1954), esp. pp. 357ff.

they have to be reflected. Let us mention some of these concerning the Son and the Spirit in particular.

The most obvious thing to mention is that only the Son is
incarnate. Both the Father and the Spirit are involved in
history, but only the Son *becomes* history. In fact, as we shall
see later, if we introduce time and history into either the
Father or the Spirit we automatically deny them their par-
ticulars in the economy. To be involved in history is not the
same as to *become* history. The economy, therefore, in so far
as it assumed history and has a history, is *only one* and that
is the *Christ event.* Even "events" such as Pentecost which
seem to have an exclusively pneumatological character at
first sight should be attached to the Christ event[14] in order to
qualify as part of the *history* of salvation; otherwise they
cease to be pneumatological in the proper sense.

Now if *becoming* history is the particularity of the Son in
the economy, what is the contribution of the Spirit? Well,
precisely the opposite: it is to liberate the Son and the economy
from the bondage of history. If the Son dies on the cross,
thus succumbing to the bondage of historical existence, it is
the Spirit that raises him from the dead.[15] The Spirit is the
beyond history,[16] and when he acts in history he does so in
order to bring into history the last days, the *eschaton.*[17] Hence
the first fundamental particularity of Pneumatology is its
eschatological character. The Spirit makes of Christ an eschatological being, the "last Adam."

Another important contribution of the Holy Spirit to the
Christ event is that, because of the involvement of the Holy
Spirit in the economy, Christ is not just an individual, not
"one" but "many." This "corporate personality" of Christ is
impossible to conceive without Pneumatology. It is not insignificant that the Spirit has always, since the time of Paul,

----

[14]In the Fourth Gospel, for example, Pentecost is seen as the return of
Jesus through the outpouring of the Holy Spirit. See R. E. Brown, *The Gospel
according to John,* 1970, p. 1139. Similarly in the Fathers, e.g. in Cyril of
Alexanderia, *In Jo.* X, 2 and XI, 2 (PG. 74, 433-436; 453-456).

[15]Romans 8:11.

[16]Cf. H. U. von Balthasar, "Der Unbekannte penseits des Wortes" in
Interpretation der Welt, Festschrift R. Guardini, 1966, pp. 638-645.

[17]Acts 2:17.

been associated with the notion of *communion* (κοινωνία).[18]
Pneumatology contributes to Christology this dimension of
communion. And it is because of this function of Pneumatology that it is possible to speak of Christ as having a "body,"
i.e. to speak of ecclesiology, of the Church as the Body of
Christ.

Now there have been also other functions attached to the
particular work of the Spirit in Christian theology, e.g. in-
spiration and sanctification. The Orthodox tradition has attached particular significance to the latter, namely the idea
of sanctification, perhaps because of the strong Origenist influence that has always existed in the East. This is evident
in Monasticism as a form of what is normally called "spirituality." But monasticism—and the notions of "sanctification"
and "spirituality" that lie behind it—has never become a
decisive aspect of *ecclesiology* in the East. Ecclesiology in the
Orthodox tradition has always been determined by the liturgy,
the eucharist; and for this reason it is the first two aspects
of Pneumatology, namely *eschatology* and *communion* that
have determined Orthodox ecclesiology. Both eschatology
and communion constitute fundamental elements of the Orthodox understanding of the eucharist. The fact that these
two things are, as we have just seen, also fundamental aspects
of Pneumatology shows that if we want to understand Orthodox ecclesiology properly, and its relation to Pneumatology, it is mainly to these two aspects of Pneumatology that we
must turn, namely to eschatology and communion.[19]

Now, all this needs to be qualified with another funda-
metal point. It is not enough to speak of eschatology and
communion as necessary aspects of Pneumatology and ecclesiology; it is necessary to make these aspects of Pneumatology

[18] 2 Corinthians, 13:13.

[19] In saying this I do not wish to undermine the importance of personal
sanctification, especially as this is understood by Monasticism. Orthodox
Monasticism is, in any case, tied up with eschatology so closely that it becomes in this way deeply related with ecclesiology. What I wish to underline,
however, is that no "spirituality" is healthy and truly christian unless it is
constantly dependent on the event of ecclesial communion. The eschatological
community *par excellence* is to be found in the eucharist, which is thus the
heart of all ecclesiology.

constitutive of ecclesiology. What I mean by "constitutive" is that these aspects of Pneumatology must qualify the very ontology of the Church. The Spirit is not something that "animates" a Church which already somehow exists. The Spirit makes the Church *be.* Pneumatology does not refer to the well-being but to the very being of the Church. It is not about a dynamism which is added to the essence of the Church. It is the very essence of the Church. The Church is *constituted* in and through eschatology and communion. Pneumatology is an ontological category in ecclesiology.

III.   *Implications of the Synthesis for Ecclesiology*

All this sounds somewhat theoretical. If we try to apply this to the concrete existence of the Church, some of the peculiarities of Orthodox ecclesiology will become easier to explain.

1. *The importance of the local Church in ecclesiology.* This has been brought out with particular force in our time mainly since the work of N. Afanasiev and his "eucharistic ecclesiology." But it has not yet been justified in terms of Pneumatology. Let me make a first attempt here by referring to what I have just said about the constitutive character of Pneumatology in both christology and ecclesiology.

The Church is the Body of Christ, which means that she is instituted through the one Christological event: she is one because Christ is one and she owes her being to this one Christ. If Pneumatology is not ontologically constitutive of Christology, this can mean that there is first one Church and *then* many Churches. K. Rahner, for example, has argued that the "essence" of the Church lies in the universal Church; it is the "existence" of the Church that makes it local.[20] However, if Pneumatology is made constitutive of both Christology and ecclesiology, it is not possible to speak in these terms. The Spirit is in this case the one who actually brings about, constitutes ontologically, the Body of Christ. The Pentecostal event is an ecclesiologically constitutive event. The one Christ

[20]K. Rahner—J. Ratzinger, *Episkopat und Primat,* 1962, p. 26.

event takes the form of *events* (plural), which *are as primary ontologically* as the one Christ event itself. The local Churches are as primary in ecclesiology as the universal Church. No priority of the universal over the local Church is conceivable in such an ecclesiology.

Ever since Afanasiev this idea has become current in Orthodox theology. But there is a danger in it which Afanasiev did not see and which many Orthodox theologians fail to see too. Because of the lack of a proper synthesis between Christology and Pneumatology in Orthodox ecclesiology, it is often too easily assumed that eucharistic ecclesiology leads to the priority of the local Church over the universal,[21] to a kind of "congregationalism." But as I have tried to argue in another study of mine,[22] Afanasiev was wrong in drawing such conclusions, because the nature of the eucharist points not in the direction of the priority of the local Church but in that of the *simultaneity* of both local and universal. There is only *one* eucharist, which is always offered in the name of the "one, holy, catholic and apostolic Church." The dilemma "local or universal" is transcended in the eucharist, and so is any dichotomy between Christology and Pneumatology.

To make this even more concrete, let us turn to the question of how *in fact* this simultaneity works in ecclesiology. This leads us directly to the question of the ecclesial institutions: *what ecclesial structures and institutions exist which help the Church to maintain the right balance between local and universal?* And how must these structures and institutions be interpreted so as to do justice to the proper synthesis between Christology and Pneumatology which we have been advocating here?

2. *The significance of conciliarity.* That Orthodoxy does not have a Pope is in fact true. But that it has councils *instead* is wrong. The council is not present in Orthodox theology as a substitute for the Roman Catholic Pope, and this for the simple reason that the council cannot play the role of the Pope or replace his ministry. The true nature of conciliarity in Orthodox theology can be understood only in the light of

[21]Cf. below ch. 5, n. 111.
[22]See ch. 4 below.

what I have called here the *constitutive* role of Pneumatology
in ecclesiology, and of the fact that Pneumatology implies
the notion of communion.

The theological *raison d'être* of conciliarity—or of the
institution of the synod—is to be found in the idea that communion (which, as we have seen, is a characteristic of Pneumatology) is an *ontological* category in ecclesiology. At this
point the relevance of trinitarian theology for ecclesiology
becomes clear. There seems to be an exact correspondence
between the trinitarian theology, as it was developed particularly by the Cappadocian Fathers—especially St Basil—
and Orthodox ecclesiology. Let me say a few words on this
point, because I think that this is essential and not so widely
appreciated.

One of the striking peculiarities of St. Basil's teaching on
God, compared with that of St Athanasius and certainly with
that of the Western Fathers, is that he seems to be rather un-
happy with the notion of substance as an ontological category
and tends to replace it—significantly enough for our subject
here—with that of κοινωνία. Instead of speaking of the unity
of God in terms of His one nature, he prefers to speak of it
in terms of the *communion of persons*: communion is for
Basil an ontological category. The *nature* of God is communion.[23] This does not mean that the persons have an ontological priority over the one substance of God, but that the
one substance of God coincides with the communion of the
three persons.

In ecclesiology all this can be applied to the relationship
between local and universal Church. There is one Church, as

[23]See, for example, Basil, *De Sp. s.* 18, (PG 32, 194C): "The unity (of
God) is in the *koinonia tes theotetos.*" Cf. *ibid.*, 153A and 156A. A careful
study of Basil shows that for him the meaning of *homoousios* is better
expressed in terms such as οἰκεία καὶ συμφυὴς καὶ ἀχώριστος κοινωνία,
i.e. by the employment of the term *koinonia* (*De Sp. S.* 68; *Ep.* 52, 3; *C. Eun.*
II, 12 etc.). Cf. on this A. Jevtich, "Between the 'Niceans' and the 'Eastern-
ers'. The Catholic Confession of Saint Basil" in *St Vladimir's Theological
Quarterly* 24 (1980), 244. For further discussion cf. my "The Teaching of
the Second Ecumenical Council on the Holy Spirit in Historical and Ecumenical Perspective" in *Credo in Spiritum Sanctum* (Atti del congresso teo-
logico internationale di pneumatologia, Roma 22-26, marzo 1982), ed. by
José Saraiva Martins, Vatican City, 1983, vol. I, pp. 29-54.

there is one God. But the expression of this one Church is the communion of the many local Churches. Communion and oneness coincide in ecclesiology.

Now, when we look at the institutional aspect of ecclesiology, it follows that the institution that is supposed to express the unity of the Church must be an institution which expresses *communion.* Since there is no institution which derives its existence or its authority from anything that precedes the event of communion, but from the event of communion itself (this is what it means to make communion ontologically *constitutive*), the institution of universal unity cannot be self-sufficient or self-explicable or prior to the event of communion; it is dependent on it. Equally, however, there is no communion which can be prior to the oneness of the Church: the institution which expresses this communion must be accompanied by an indication that there is a ministry safeguarding the oneness which the communion aims at expressing.

We can now become more concrete and try to interpret our view of synodality in the light of these theological principles.

The canonical institution of the synod is often misunderstood in Orthodox theology. Sometimes the synod is called "the highest authority in the Church," as if Orthodoxy were the "democratic" opposite of the "monarchical" Rome. Many Orthodox think of the council in terms of late Medieval Western *Konziliarismus.* The true significance of the synod in Orthodox tradition, however, seems to me to be given in the canon 34 of the so-called *Apostolic Canons;* and its meaning is based on two fundamental principles put forth by this canon. The first principle is that in every province there must be *one* head—an institution of unity. There is no possibility of rotation or of collective ministry to replace this one head. The local bishops-Churches can do nothing without the presence of the "one." On the other hand the same canon provides a second fundamental principle, namely that the "one" cannot do anything without the "many."[24] There is no

---

[24]The text of the canon is as follows: "The bishops of every nation (region = ἔθνος) ought to know who is the first one (πρῶτον) among them, and to esteem him as their head, and not to do any great thing without his consent; but every one to manage only the affairs that belong to his own

ministry or institution of unity which is not expressed in the form of communion. There is no "one" which is not at the same time "many"—is this not the same as the pneumatologically conditioned Christology, which we mentioned earlier? Pneumatology, by being constitutive of both Christology and ecclesiology, makes it impossible to think of Christ as an individual, i.e. of Christ without his Body, the "many," or to think of the Church as one without simultaneously thinking of her as "many."

To conclude this point, Orthodox theology is wrongly understood if we simply think of the Church as a confederation of local Churches. The Orthodox view of the Church, in my understanding at least, requires an institution which expresses the *oneness* of the Church and not simply its multiplicity. But the multiplicity is not to be subjected to the oneness; it is constitutive of the oneness. The two, oneness and multiplicity, must coincide in an institution which possesses a twofold ministry: the ministry of the πρῶτος (the first one) and the ministry of the "many" (the heads of the local Churches).

3. *The Bishop and the community.* We can now turn to a consideration of the institutions on the level of the local Church itself, always bearing in mind the same theological principles. Here again communion is ontologically constitutive. But as has been already observed in connection with the universal Church, the proper relationship between the "one" and the "many" must be maintained. In the case of the local Church the "one" is represented through the ministry of the bishop, while the "many" are represented through the other ministries and the laity. There is a fundamental principle in Orthodox ecclesiology going back to the early centuries and reflecting the proper synthesis between Christology and Pneumatology which I have been advocating here. This principle is that the "one"—the bishop—cannot exist without the

diocese and the territory subject to it. But let him (i.e. the first one) not do anything without the consent of all the other (bishops); for it is by this means that there will be unanimity, and God will be glorified through Christ in the Holy Spirit." The original text in F. X. Funk, *Didascalia et Constitutiones apostolorum,* 1905, pp. 572-574.

"many"—the community—and the "many" cannot exist without the "one."

First, the principle that the "one" is inconceivable without the "many." In practical canonical terms this is expressed in various ways: (a) there is no ordination to the episcopate outside the community.[25] Since ordination is an act which is ontologically constitutive of episcopacy, to condition the ordination of the bishop by the presence of the community is to make the community *constitutive* of the Church. There is no Church without the community, as there is no Christ without the Body, or the "one" without the "many." (b) There is no episcopacy without a community attached to it.[26] Here a detail must be stressed because it points to a peculiarity of Orthodoxy compared with Roman Catholic theology: the mention of the name of the community takes place in the prayer of ordination of a bishop. Since in the Orthodox Church there is no *missio canonica* or a distinction between *potestas ordinis* and *potestas iurisdictionis,* the fact that the community is mentioned in the prayer of ordination means that *the community forms part of the ontology of episcopacy:* there is no bishop, not even for a moment or theoretically, who is not conditioned by some community. The "many" condition ontologically the "one."

But again this is not the whole story. The opposite is also true, namely that the "many" cannot exist without the "one." This in concrete terms is expressed in the following ways: (a) There is no baptism, which is the constitutive act of the community, i.e. the ontological basis of the laity, without the bishop. The "many" cannot be "many" without the "one." (b) There is no ordination of any kind without the presence of the bishop; the bishop is a condition for the existence of the community and its charismatic life.

4. *The "iconic" character of the ecclesial institutions.* This mutual interdependence between the "one" and the "many," this twofold structure of the Church is placed under one further condition for its existence: both the ordination of the bishop, which requires the community, and the ordination of

---

[25]See chs. 5 and 6 below.
[26]*Ibid.*

the laity (baptism) or of any other minister, which requires
the presence of the bishop, both of these have to be attached
to the *eucharist*. This seems to me to imply that it is not
enough to place the ecclesial institutions in the context of the
proper synthesis between the "one" and the "many." This is
only one of the components of Pneumatology. The other one,
which has been mentioned earlier, is *eschatology*, and to my
mind this aspect is expressed through the fact that both
baptism and ordination have to take place in the context of
the eucharist. The eucharist, in the Orthodox understanding at
least, is an eschatological event. In it, not only the "one"
and the "many" co-exist and condition each other, but something more is indicated: the ecclesial institutions are *reflections of the Kingdom*. First, they are *reflections*: the nature
of the ecclesial institutions is "iconic," i.e. their ontology
does not lie in the institution itself, but only in relation to
something else, to God or Christ. Secondly they are reflections
of the Kingdom: all ecclesial institutions must have some
justification by reference to something ultimate and not simply
to historical expedience. There are, to be sure, ministries
which are meant to serve temporal historical needs. But these
cannot claim ecclesial status in a fundamentl structural sense.
History is never a sufficient justification for the existence of
a certain ecclesial institution, be it with reference to tradition,
apostolic succession, scriptural foundation or actual historical
needs. The Holy Spirit points *beyond* history—not, of course,
against it, though it can and must often point against history
as it actually is, through a prophetic function of the ministry.
The ecclesial institutions by being eschatologically conditioned
become *sacramental* in the sense of being placed in the dialectic
between history and eschatology, between the already and the
not yet. They lose therefore their self-sufficiency, their individualistic ontology, and exist *epicletically*, i.e. they depend
for their efficacy constantly on prayer, the prayer of the community. It is not in history that the ecclesial institutions find
their certainty (their validity) but in constant dependence on
the Holy Spirit. This is what makes them "sacramental," which
in the language of Orthodox theology may be called "iconic."

IV. *Conclusions*

Let me now conclude by summarizing the main points which I have tried to make and by placing what I have said in the light of the actual situation of Orthodoxy in our time. I have been discussing Christology, Pneumatology and ecclesial institutions in *Orthodox theology*—not in Orthodox practice. What I have said however, is not just theory; it derives from historical experience, even if this historical experience tends to be a somewhat remote memory from the past. My points have been the following:

1. Orthodox theology has not yet worked out the proper synthesis between Christology and Pneumatology. Without this synthesis it is impossible to understand the Orthodox tradition itself or to be of any real help in the ecumenical discussion of our time.

2. The important thing about this synthesis is that Pneumatology must be made *constitutive* of Christology and ecclesiology, i.e. condition the very being of Christ and the Church, and that this can happen only if two particular ingredients of Pneumatology are introduced into the ontology of Christ and the Church. These ingredients are: eschatology and communion.

3. If the Church is *constituted* through these two aspects of Pneumatology, all *pyramidal* notions disappear in ecclesiology: the "one" and the "many" co-exist as two aspects of the same being. On the universal level this means that the local Churches constitute one Church through a ministry or an institution which composes *simultaneously* a *primus* and a synod of which he is a *primus*. On the local level, this means that the head of the local Church, the bishop, is conditioned by the existence of his community and the rest of the ministries, particularly the *presbyterium*. There is no ministry which does not need the other ministries; no ministry possesses the fullness, the plentitude of grace and power without a relationship with the other ministries.

4. Equally, a pneumatological conditioning of the being of

the Church is important for the opening-up of ecclesial institutions to their eschatological perspective. Too much historicity is often attached to the ecclesial institutions. Orthodoxy often suffers from meta-historicism; the West usually suffers from a historization of its ecclesial institutions. The liturgical ethos of Orthodoxy will probably never make it possible for her to be fully involved in history, although it has not prevented such eruptions of liberation movements as those of the Greek war of independence in the last century. But the justification of any *permanent* ecclesial institution certainly needs an eschatological perspective; history is not enough.

5. Finally, if Pneumatology is made constitutive of ecclesiology, the notion of *institution* itself will be deeply affected. In a christological perspective alone we can speak of the Church as *in-stituted* (by Christ), but in a pneumatological perspective we have to speak of it as *con-stituted* (by the Spirit). Christ *in-stitutes* and the Spirit *con-stitutes*. The difference between these two prepositions: *in*—and *con*—can be enormous ecclesiologically. The "institution" is something presented to us as a fact, more or less a *fait-accomplit*. As such, it is a provocation to our freedom. The "con-stitution" is something that involves us in its very being, something we accept freely, because we take part in its very emergence. Authority in the first case is something imposed on us, whereas in the latter it is something that springs from amongst us. If Pneumatology is assigned a constitutive role in ecclesiology, the entire issue of *Amt und Geist,* or of "institutionalism," is affected. The notion of communion must be made to apply to the very ontology of the ecclesial institutions, not to their dynamism and efficacy alone.

And now, how about the present, actual situation: how much of this in fact exists, and how much of it can still exist or be made to exist? The fact that Orthodoxy has not experienced situations similar to those of the Western Churches, such as the problem of clericalism, anti-institutionalism, Pentecostalism, etc. may be taken as an indication that *for the most part* Pneumatology has saved the life of Orthodoxy up to now. There is no sign of anti-establishment tendencies in the Orthodox Church, although in Greece at the moment such signs can be observed here and there. But the actual situation in Orthodoxy both theologically and canonically no longer does full justice to the tradition of which my exposé has been a reflection. The synodical institutions no longer reflect the true balance between the "one" and the "many," sometimes because the "one" does not operate or even exist, and sometimes because the "one" or the "ones" ignore the "many." The same is true about local Church life: the community has almost disappeared and the number of titular bishops is increasing rapidly. The only level on which the proper balance between the "one" and the "many" is still maintained is the *liturgical*: is it the liturgy that still saves Orthodoxy? Perhaps this is the case. But for how long? As Orthodoxy shares Western culture more and more, it will eventually share the problems of the Western Churches too. The problem of ecclesial institutions will thus soon become, existentially speaking, an ecumenical problem.

But what can be done? Vatican II has given hope and promise to many people that something can be done. I am not an expert on the theology of the council, but I feel that one of the directions in which it has pointed can be particularly important, namely the introduction of the notion of communion into ecclesiology. This, combined with the rediscovery of the importance of the λαός of God and the local Church, can help even the Orthodox themselves to be faithful to their identity. But much more needs to be done, for Vatican II has not completed its work. What an Orthodox sharing the views of this exposé would like to be done— perhaps by a "Vatican III"—is to push the notion of communion to its ontological conclusions. We need an ontology of communion. We need to make communion condition the very being of the Church, not the well-being but the being of it. On the theological level this would mean assigning a constitutive role to Pneumatology, not one dependent on Christology. This Vatican II has not done, but its notion of communion can do. Perhaps this will transform the ecclesial institutions automatically. It will remove any pyramidal structure that may still remain in the Church. And it may even place the stumbling block of ecclesial unity, the ministry of the

Pope, in a more positive light. So much and perhaps much more depends on the proper synthesis between Christology and Pneumatology in ecclesiology.

4.

Eucharist and Catholicity

The lines that follow represent an attempt to see the concept of the catholicity of the Church in the light of the eucharistic community. It is not an accident that in adopting the term "catholic" from Aristotelian language[1] the early Christians did not conceptualize it, but instead of speaking of "catholicity," as we do today,[2] they spoke of a "catholic Church" or even—and this is more significant—of "catholic Churches" in the plural.[3] This means that we cannot speak of "catholicity" and ignore the concrete local Church.

[1]The Aristotelian use of the term καθόλου as contrasted with the κατὰ μέρος or καθ' ἕκαστον survived at the time of the primitive Church mainly under the form of the adjective καθολικὸς (see e.g. Polybius, VI, 5, 3; Dionysius Halicarn., *Comp.*, 12; Philo, *Vita Moesis*, II, 32, etc.).

[2]Such conceptualizations have occurred not only in western theology, but also within that of the Orthodox Church, as we see, for example, in the well-known idea of *sobornost,* which appeared in nineteenth-century Russian theology, mainly through the works of Khomiakov. This idea is a conceptualization made on the basis of a translation of καθολικὴ by *sobornaia* in the Slavonic Creed and under the influence of eighteenth-century philosophical trends. It would be very interesting to study the exact meaning of this Slavonic term at the time of its first appearance, because it is possible that at that time the word meant precisely the *concrete gathering together,* i.e. a σύνοδος not in the technical sense of the councils but in that of συνέρχεσθαι ἐπὶ τὸ αὐτὸ as we find it in Paul (I Cor. 11:20 f.) and Ignatius (*Eph.,* 5, 2-3), and as it was explicitly used even in the time of Chrysostom when σύνοδος could simply mean the eucharistic gathering (see Chrysostom, *De Proph. obsc.,* 2, 5, PG 56:182; cf. below, note 22). If that is the case, then it is interesting to note that not only ideas such as the identification of "catholic" with "universal" as it developed in the West, but even that of *sobornost* as it developed in the East did nothing but obscure the original *concrete* meaning of the καθολικὴ ἐκκλησία.

[3]During the first three centuries at least, the term "catholic Church" was

Already in the book of the *Didache* in the later first or
early second century the idea was clearly expressed that in the
celebration of the eucharist the Church experiences that which
is promised for the *Parousia,* namely the eschatological unity
of all in Christ: "Just as this loaf was scattered all over the
mountains and having been brought together was made one,
so let your Church be gathered from the ends of the earth
in your Kingdom."[4] This conviction was not irrelevant in the
application of the term "catholic Church" to the local community. It was a clear indication that, although the catholicity
applied almost exclusively to the local Church. Ignatius in his well-known
passage in *Smyrn.,* 8, where the term appears for the first time in our
sources, seems to contrast the local episcopal community with the "catholic
Church" in a way that has led many scholars (Zahn, Lightfoot, Bardy, etc.)
to identify the latter with the "universal Church." But there is not a single
indication in the text that would suggest this identification. It is clear from
Ignatian ecclesiology as a whole that not only does a "universal Church" not
exist in Ignatius' mind but, on the contrary, an identification of the whole
Christ and the whole Church with the local episcopal community constitutes
a key idea in his thought (cf. below at note 24). In the *Martyrium
Polycarpi* the expression ἡ κατὰ τὴν οἰκουμένην καθολικὴ ἐκκλησία
has led scholars to similar conclusions in a way which seems to overlook
the fact that, if one translated καθολικὴ by "universal" in this text one would
be confronted with an impossible tautology which would read something
like: "The universal Church which is in the universe"! That in this document there is no such contrast between "local" and "universal" is shown by
the fact that it speaks of Polycarp as being the bishop "of the catholic
Church which is in Smyrna" (16, 2) precisely because the local Church is
the "dwelling place" (παροικία) of the whole Church (*inscr.*). In the same
way Tertullian can use the term "catholic Churches" in the plural. (*Praescr.
haer.,* 26, 4, PL 2, 38; see comments by Labriolle-Refoulé in the edition
"Sources Chrétiennes" 46, 1957, p. 126, n. 4), while Cyprian can write "on
the unity of the catholic Church" having in mind probably the Church
of Carthage (see Th. Camelot, "Saint Cyprian et la primauté" in *Istina* 2
[1957], p. 423, and M. Bevenot, *St Cyprian: The Lapsed—The Unity of the
Catholic Church* [Ancient Christian Writers 25, 1957], pp. 74-5), and
the Roman confessors in the middle third century can speak of "one
bishop in the catholic Church" (Cyprian, *Ep.,* 49 [46], 2-4; Eusebius,
Hist. Eccl., VI, 43, 11). It was probably only in the fourth century and out
of the struggle of such theologians as Optatus of Milevis (*Adv. Parm.,* 2, 1)
and Augustine (*Ep.,* XCIII, 23; *De Unit.,* 6, 16, etc.) against the provincialism of the Donatists that the term "catholic" came to be identified with
"universal." Cf. P. Batiffol, *Le Catholicisme de Saint Augustin* (1929), p.
212. During the same century in the East catholicity receives a *synthetic* definition, in which "universality" is one of the elements that constitute catholicity.
(See Cyril of Jerusalem, *Catech.,* 18, 23, PG 33:1044.)
    [4]*Didache,* 9, 4. Cf. 10, 5. For the fact that these are eucharistic texts see
J. P. Audet, *La Didache: Instruction des Apôtres* (1948), p. 407.

of the Church is ultimately an eschatological reality, its nature is revealed and realistically apprehended *here and now* in the eucharist. The eucharist understood primarily not as a *thing* and an objectified means of grace but as an *act* and a *synaxis* of the local Church,[5] *a "catholic" act of a "catholic" Church,* can, therefore, be of importance in any attempt to understand the catholicity of the Church.

In the following lines we shall first briefly study the eucharistic community as it developed in the early Church with attention fixed on those aspects which were related to catholicity. We shall then try to draw from this study some general conclusions concerning our discussions about catholicity today.

I. *The "One" and the "Many" in the Eucharistic Consciousness of the Early Church*

In his first letter to the Corinthians (10:16-17) and in connection with the celebration of the Lord's Supper Paul writes: "The cup of blessing which we bless is it not a communion (κοινωνία) of the blood of Christ? The bread which we break is it not a communion of the body of Christ? Because there is one bread, we who are many are one body, for we all partake of the one loaf." This is not the only time that Paul speaks of the "many" as being "one" in Christ, and not just a neuter "one" but a masculine "one."[6]

The idea of the incorporation of the "many" into the "one," or of the "one" as a representative of the "many" goes back to a time earlier than Paul. It is an idea basically connected with the figures of the "Servant of God" and the "Son

[5]This aspect of the eucharist had been forgotten for a long time. It has been emphasized in the West by such scholars as O. Casel, G. Dix, etc. For the ecclesiological implications of the eucharist see also H. Fries, "Die Eucharistie und die Einheit der Kirche," in *Pro Mundi Vita: Festschrift zum eucharistischen Weltkongress* (1960), p. 176; J. M. R. Tillard, *L'Eucharistie, Pâque de l'Eglise* (*Unam Sanctam,* no. 44, 1964); J. J. von Allmen, *Essai sur le repas du Seigneur* (1966), pp. 37f.; and the works of N. A. Afanasiev, A. Schmemann and J. Meyendorff (the latter's *Orthodoxy and Catholicity,* 1966).

[6]Gal. 3:28. Cf. II Cor. 11:2; Eph. 2:15 etc.

of Man."[7] But what is significant for us here is that this idea was from the beginning connected with the eucharistic consciousness of the Church. Paul in writing those words to the Corinthians, was simply echoing a conviction apparently widely spread in the primitive Church.

Thus with regard to the tradition of the Servant of God the texts of the Last Supper, in spite of their differences on many points, agree on the connection of the Supper with the "many" or "you" "for" or "in the place of" (ἀντί, περί) whom the one offers himself.[8] This relation of the eucharist to the tradition of the Servant of God in whom the many are represented established itself in the liturgical life of the Church already in the first century. In the most ancient liturgical prayer of the Roman Church, which is found in *I Clement,* we come across the idea of the Servant of God many times in connection with the eucharist.[9] The same is true about the *Didache,* where this idea finds its place in an even more explicit manner.[10]

Similar observations can be made about the connection of the eucharist with the "Son of Man" tradition. If the sixth chapter of the Fourth Gospel refers to the eucharist, it is significant that the prevailing figure of the Son of Man is connected there with the eucharist. He is the one who gives "the food which remains to eternal life."[11] Unlike the manna which God gave to Israel through Moses, this bread is "the true bread" which, having come down from heaven, is nothing else but "the Son of Man" himself.[12] It is significant that Christ appears here as the Son of Man, and not in another capacity, as he identifies himself with "the true bread."

[7]This contributed to the appearance of the well-known theory of "corporate personality" in the Bible. On this theory cf. among others: S. Pedersen, *Israel: Its Life and Culture* (1926); H. Wheeler Robinson, *The Hebrew Conception of Corporate Personality* (1936), p. 49 ff.; A. R. Johnson, *The One and the Many in the Israelite Conception of God* (1942); and J. de Fraine, *Adam et son lignage: Etudes sur la "personalité corporative" dans la Bible* (1959).

[8]See Mark 14:24; Matt. 26:28; Luke 22:20 and I Cor. 11:24.

[9]*I Clem.,* 59:2-4.

[10]*Didache,* 10, 2; 9, 2. Cf. above, note 4.

[11]John 6:27.

[12]John 6:27, 51.

Hence the eating of this bread is called specifically the eating of "the flesh of the *Son of Man*"[13] who takes into himself every one who eats this bread,[14] thus fulfilling his role as the corporate Son of Man.

It is precisely this idea that prevails in chapters 13-17 of the same Gospel, where the eucharistic presuppositions of the Last Super are so deeply connected with the eschatological unity of all in Christ, finding their climax in the prayer that "they all may be one."[15] It is impossible to see all this outside a eucharistic context in which the idea of the unity of the "many" in the "one" prevails. Because of this the Fourth Gospel not only allows itself to be taken as a eucharistic liturgy,[16] but it is also characterized by such otherwise inexplicable expressions as the strange exchange of first person singular with first person plural in 3:11-13—"Truly, truly *I* say unto you, *we* speak of what *we* know and bear witness to what *we* have seen; but you do not receive *our* testimony. If *I* have told you earthly things and you do not believe, how can you believe if *I* tell you heavenly things? No one has ascended into heaven but he who descended from heaven, *the Son of Man*." It should be noted that it is again a Son of Man text that contains such a philological phenomenon which can only be understood in an ecclesiological sense.[17]

All this shows the early and deep connection of the idea of the unity of the "many" in the "one" with the eucharistic experience of the Church. It would fall outside the scope of this study to discuss here whether or not this connection offers an explanation of the ecclesiological image of "the Body of Christ."[18] But it is certainly true that neither the identification of the Church with the Body of Christ nor the ultimate unity

[13] John 6:53.

[14] John 6:56.

[15] John 17.

[16] Ph. H. Menoud, *L'évangile de Jean d'après les recherches récentes* (1947), p. 247.

[17] Cf. E. Schweizer, *Gemeinde und Gemeindeordnung im Neuen Testament* (1959), §11a.

[18] For such an explanation see A. D. J. Rawlinson, "Corpus Christi," in *Mysterium Christi* (ed. G. A. Bell and A. Deissmann, 1930), p. 225 ff.

of the "many" in the "one" can be understood apart from
the eucharistic word "this is my Body."[19]

The ecclesiological consequences of this can be clearly seen
in the sources of the first three centuries. The first of these
consequences is that the local eucharistic community receives
the name ἐκκλησία or even ἐκκλησία τοῦ Θεοῦ already
in the letters of St Paul. A careful study of I Cor. 11 reveals
that the term ἐκκλησία is used in a dynamic sense: "when
you come together into, i.e. when *you become,* ἐκκλησία,"
(v. 18.) This implies clearly what in the following verses becomes explicit, namely that the eucharistic terms "coming
together," "coming together ἐπὶ τὸ αὐτό," "Lord's Supper,"
etc., are identified with the ecclesiological terms "ἐκκλησία"
or "ἐκκλησία of God." The other consequence which, I
think, is of great importance for later developments of the
idea of catholicity is that this local community is called
ὅλη ἡ ἐκκλησία, i.e. *the whole Church,* already by Paul
again.[20] Now, whether this idea had anything to do with the
idea of the "catholic Church" to appear a few generations
later will not occupy us here, interesting as it is from a historical point of view.[21] What remains a fact, in any case, is
that, in the literature of the first three centuries at least, the
local Church, starting again with Paul, was called the
ἐκκλησία τοῦ Θεοῦ or the "whole Church" or even the
καθολικὴ ἐκκλησία and this not unrelated to the concrete
eucharistic community.[22] As the ecclesiology of Ignatius of

[19]Cf. C. T. Craig, *The One Church in the Light of the New Testament*
(1951), p. 21.

[20]Rom. 16:23.

[21]This is discussed in my book *The Unity of the Church in the Eucharist
and the Bishop during the First Three Centuries* (1965—in Greek).

[22]It is not accidental that the term "catholic" came to be applied to the
cathedral, i.e. the main church where the bishop would celebrate and the
entire episcopal community would be present (Council in Trullo, canon
59). The terms *ecclesia major, ecclesia senior* and *ecclesia catholica*
became synonymous expressions by which the cathedral was distinguished
from the parishes from the fourth century on (such evidence appears for
example in the *Etheriae Peregrinatio,* ed. by H. Pétré, in Sources chrétiennes 21, 1948; and in the lectionaries of the Church of Jerusalem,
ed. by M. Tarchnisvilli in 1959, etc.). It is probably from this use of the
word "catholic" that the term *katholikon* came to be applied to the main
church in a Byzantine monastery, since this was the place where all the

Antioch makes clear, even the context in which the term καθολικὴ ἐκκλησία appears is a eucharistic one, in which Ignatius'
main concern was the unity of the eucharistic community.[23]
Instead of trying, therefore, to find the meaning of the
"catholic Church" in this Ignatian text in a contrast between
"local" and "universal," we would be more faithful to the
sources if we saw it in the light of the entire Ignatian ecclesiology, according to which the eucharistic community is
"exactly the same as" (this is the meaning I would give to
ὥσπερ *which* connects the two in the Ignatian text) the
whole Church united in Christ.[24]

Catholicity, therefore, in this context, does not mean anything else but the *wholeness* and *fulness* and *totality* of the
body of Christ "exactly as" (ὥσπερ) it is portrayed in the
eucharistic community.

II. *The Composition and Structure of the Eucharistic
Community as Reflections of Catholicity*

With such a view of the eucharistic community in the background it would have been impossible for the composition
and the structure of this community to be different from
what it actually was in the first centuries. A different composition and structure would mean a different ecclesiology.
It is, therefore, important for us in order to understand this
ecclesiology, especially as it concerns the aspect of "catholicity," to bear in mind this composition and structure.

monks would gather for the celebration of the eucharist. The significance
of these usages for the connection between the eucharistic community and
the "catholic Church" in the early centuries hardly needs to be emphasized.

[23]*Smyrn.*, 8: ". . . Let that be deemed a valid eucharist which is under
the leadership of the bishop or one to whom he has entrusted it. Wherever
the bishop appears let there be the multitude of the people be, just as wherever
Jesus Christ is there (is) the catholic Church."

[24]Any contrast between the "local" and the "universal" in this text would
mean that the "universal" Church is united around Christ whereas the
"local" is united *not* around Christ *but* around the bishop. This kind of
theology is foreign to Ignatius who, on the contrary, sees no difference
between the unity in Christ and the unity in the bishop (e.g. *Eph.*, 5, 1;
Magn., 3, 1-2; cf. *Polyc. inscr.*), and this not by way of metaphor but in a
mystical sense of real identification.

As a combination of the existing fragmentary liturgical evidence of the first centuries allows us to know, the "whole Church"[25] "dwelling in a certain city"[26] would "come together"[27] mainly on a Sunday[28] to "break bread."[29] This *synaxis* would be *the only one* in that particular place in the sense that it would include the *"whole Church."*[30] This fact, which is not usually noted by historians, is of paramount ecclesiological significance, for it immediately draws the line of demarcation between the Christian and the non-Christian pattern of unity at the time of the early Church.

Coming together in brotherly love was certainly not a Christian innovation. In the Roman Empire it was so common to form "associations" that there was need for special laws concerning such associations signified under the name of *collegia*.[31] The brotherly love which prevailed among the members of the *collegia* was so strong and organized that each one of them would contribute monthly to a common fund and would address the other members by the title "brethren" (*fratres, sodales, socii*).[32] Apart from the pagans, the Jews who lived in the Roman Empire were also organized in special communities under their own ethnarch[33] and their brotherly love was so strong that in cases of special groups, like the Essenes, it was based on principles of common property. To

[25]Rom. 16:23.

[26]I Cor. 1:2; II Cor. 1:1; I Thess. 1:1; Acts 11:22 etc.

[27]I Cor. 11:20, 33, 34. Cf. Ignatius, *Eph.*, 5, 2-3.

[28]The observance of Sunday was almost identical with the eucharistic *synaxis*. Cf. W. Rordorf, *Sunday—The History of the Day of Rest and Worship in the Earliest Centuries of the Christian Church* (1968), pp. 177 ff., and 238 ff.

[29]Acts 2:46; 20:7.

[30]The existence of the "Churches in the household" does not present a problem in this respect, even if these Churches are understood as eucharistic assemblies, for there are strong reasons to believe that—significantly enough—there was no more than one such "Church in the household" in each city. These reasons are presented in my *The Unity of the Church . . .,* pp. 64 ff.

[31]Tacitus, *Ann.*, 14, 17; Plinius, *Ad Traj.*, 34, 97; Menucius Felix, *Oct.*, 8-9; Origen, *Con. Cels.*, 1, 1. Cf. J. P. Waltzing, *Etude historique sur les corporations professionels des Romains* I, pp. 113-29.

[32]Cf. F. X. Kraus, "Fraternitas," in *Realencyclopaedie der christlichen Alterthümer* I (1880), col. 540.

[33]Cf. E. Schürer, *Geschichte des jüdischen Volkes* (1914), pp. 14-17.

speak, therefore, of the unity of the early Christians in terms of brotherly love would be to miss the unique point of this unity and perhaps even to expose it to a comparison from which it would certainly not gain much, especially in the light of such evidence as that provided by texts like Gal. 5:5, I Cor. 11:21, etc.!

Certainly there was a basic difference in faith that distinguished Christians from their environment.[34] But there was also a certain distinctiveness in the manner of their gathering together, which should not pass unnoticed. This distinctiveness lay in the composition of these gatherings. Whereas the Jews based the unity of their gatherings on race (or, in the later years, on a broader religious community based on this race) and the pagans with their *collegia* on profession, the Christians declared that in Christ "there is neither Jew nor Greek,"[35] "male or female,"[36] adult or child,[37] rich or poor,[38] master or slave,[39] etc. To be sure the Christians themselves soon came to believe that they constituted a *third race*, but this was only to show that in fact it was a "non-racial race," a *people* who, while claiming to be the true Israel, declared at the same time that they did not care about the difference between a Greek and a Jew once these were members of the Christian Church.

This attitude which transcended not only social but *also natural* divisions (such as age, race, etc.) was portrayed in the eucharistic community *par excellence*. It is very significant that, unlike what the Churches do today in an age marked by a tragic loss of the primitive ecclesiology, there was never a celebration of the eucharist specially for children or for

[34]Confessions of faith were very early attached to the liturgy so that an interaction between the two was established. Cf. K. Federer, *Liturgie und Glaube—Eine theologiegeschichtliche Untersuchung* (1950), p. 59 ff.

[35]Gal. 3:28; Col. 3:11. Cf. I Cor. 12:13.

[36]Gal. 3:28.

[37]Matt. 19:13. Cf. 14:21. The question of the participation of children in the eucharistic assemblies of the early Church is, of course, connected with the problem of paedobaptism at that period, on which the work of J. Jeremias, *Die Kindertaufe in den ersten vier Jahrhunderten* (1958), continues to be illuminating.

[38]James 2:2-7; I Cor. 11:20f.

[39]I Cor. 12:13; Gal. 3:28; Eph. 6:8.

students, etc., nor a eucharist that could take place privately and individually.[40] Such a thing would destroy precisely the catholic character of the eucharist which was *leitourgia,* i.e. a "public work" for all Christians of the same city to which —significantly enough—for a long time and in places as crowded as Rome in the second century even the people from the country would come to participate.[41] The eucharistic community was in its composition a *catholic community* in the sense that it transcended not only social but also natural divisions,[42] just as it will happen in the Kingdom of God[43] of which this community was a revelation and a real sign.[44]

This "catholicity" of the eucharistic community was also reflected in its structure. As far as we can reconstruct this structure from the pieces of evidence that we possess, we can see that in the center of the *synaxis* of the "whole Church"[45] and behind the "one altar"[46] there was the throne of the "one bishop"[47] seated "in the place of God"[48] or

[40]The gradual individualization of the eucharist with the introduction of private eucharistic prayers into the structure of the liturgy and finally with the prevalence of the "private mass" in the West, represents a historical development which should be examined in close connection with the development of ecclesiology.

[41]Justin, *Apol.,* I, 67. Cf. 65. This situation must have lasted at least until the middle of the third century when the first indications of the formation of parishes appear. The entire problem with its ecclesiological implications is discussed in my *The Unity of the Church* . . ., pp. 151-88.

[42]Cf. above, note 37.

[43]Matt. 22:30; Mark 12:25; Luke 20:34 f.

[44]The presuppositions of faith and love for communion were, of course, creating limitations to this community. It is important to study how a closed liturgical community, which the early Church undoubtedly was, can be related to the "catholic Church." For this a special study would be necessary. Cf. the works of W. Elert, *Abendmahl und Kirchengemeinschaft in der alten Kirche hauptsächlich des Ostens* (1954), and S. L. Greenslade, *Schism in the Early Church* (no date).

[45]See above.

[46]The connection of the "one Church" with the "one eucharist," the "one bishop" and the "one altar," clearly established already in the teaching of Ignatius (*Philad.,* 4; *Magn.,* 7, 2; *Eph.,* 5, 2; *Tral.,* 7, 2, etc.), continues through Cyprian (*Ep.,* 43 [40], 5; *De unit.,* 17, 14, etc.) well into the fourth century with the idea of a μονογενὲς θυσιαστήριον (Eusebius, *Eccl. Hist.,* X, 4, 68) and a number of deeply meaningful liturgical practices like the *fermentum,* the *antimension,* etc.

[47]Ignatius, *Philad.,* 4. Cf. previous note.

[48]Ignatius, *Magn.,* 6, 1; 3, 1-2; *Tral.,* 3, 1.

understood as the living "image of Christ."[49] Around his throne were seated the presbyters,[50] while by him stood the deacons helping him in the celebration, and in front of him the "people of God,"[51] that *order*[52] of the Church which was constituted by virtue of the rite of initiation (baptism-chrismation) and considered the *sine qua non* condition for the eucharistic community to exist and express the Church's unity.

A fundamental function of this "one bishop" was to express in himself the "multitude" (πολυπληθεία)[53] of the faithful in that place. He was the one who would offer the eucharist to God in the name of the Church, thus bringing up to the throne of God the *whole Body of Christ.* He was the one in whom the "many" united would become "one," being brought back to him who had made them, thanks to their redemption from Satan by the one who took them upon himself. Thus the bishop would become the one through whose hands the whole community would have to pass in its being offered up to God in Christ, i.e. in the highest moment of the Church's unity.

The decisive pre-eminence of the bishop in the idea of a "catholic Church" was thus developing from within the heart of the eucharistic community. Not only the multiplicity of the people but also the plurality of orders ought to cease to be a division and be transcended into a diversity like the one given by the Holy Spirit who distributes the gifts without destroying the unity. This was the function of *ordination.* Ordination means *order.* and therefore creates *orders.* This was nothing strange to the primitive eucharistic gatherings,

---

[49]The idea that the bishop is "the image of Christ" lasted at least until the fourth century (cf. *Pseudo-Clem. Homil.,* 3, 62). For material see O. Perler, "L'Evêque, représentant du Christ . . ." in *L'Episcopat et l'Eglise universelle* (ed. Y. Congar, *et al., Unam Sanctam* 39, 1962), pp. 31-66.

[50]Rev. 4:4. Cf. Ignatius, *Smyrn.,* 8, 1; *Eph.,* 20, 2, and the arrangement of the eucharistic assembly presupposed in such sources as Hippolytus, *Ap. Trad.* (ed. Dix, pp. 6 and 40 ff.).

[51]See Justin, *Apol.,* 65, 67, and previous note.

[52]*I Clem.,* 40, 5; 41, 7. The idea that the "layman" is not a "non-ordained" person but one who through baptism and chrismation belongs to his own order in the Church is fundamental in the correct understanding of the eucharistic synaxis and its ecclesiological implications.

[53]Ignatius, *Eph.,* 1, 3; *Tral.,* 1, 1: the "multitude" of Tralles could be seen in the person of their bishop.

which were structured by such orders. But a distribution of
gifts and ministries, and the creation of *orders* could mean a
destruction of unity, as it can in the natural world. By restrict-
ing all such ordinations to the eucharistic community and
making it an exclusive right of the bishop, *not as an individual but as the head of this eucharistic community,* to
ordain, the early Church saved the catholic character of its
entire structure. The bishop with his exclusive right of ordination and with the indispensable restriction of ordaining only
in the eucharistic context took it upon himself to express the
catholicity of his Church. But it was the eucharistic community and the place he occupied in its structure that justified
this.

III. *The Eucharistic Community and the
"Catholic Church in the World"*

But there was a paradox in the way the eucharistic community lent itself to the formation of the "catholic Church"
in the first centuries. The paradox lay in the fact that although
the eucharistic community, being a *local* entity, led inevitably
to the idea of a *catholic local Church,* it led at the same time
to a transcendence of the antithesis between local and universal, thus making it possible to apply the term "catholic"
both to the local and the universal realms at the same time.
This was possible for reasons that are rooted both in the
very nature and in the structure of the eucharistic community.

The nature of the eucharistic community was determined by
its being "eucharistic," i.e. by the fact that it consisted in the
communion of the Body of Christ in its totality and in its
inclusiveness *of all.* What each eucharistic community, therefore, was meant to reveal, was not part of Christ but the whole
Christ and not a partial or local unity but the full eschatological unity of all in Christ. *It was a concretization and localization of the general,* a real presence of the καθόλου in the
καθ' ἕκαστον in the true Aristotelian sense.[54] As it is indi-

[54]The relationship of the καθόλου to the καθ' ἕκαστον in Aristotle is
expressed very well in the example he gives: "as 'man' belongs to the

cated in the passage of the *Didache* we mentioned earlier,[55] the local eucharistic assembly understood itself as the revelation of the eschatological unity of all in Christ. This meant that *no mutual exclusion* between the local and the universal was possible in a eucharistic context, but the one was automatically involved in the other.

This principle found expression in the structure of the eucharistic community through the fact that the head of this community was related to the other eucharistic communities in the world by his very ordination. The fact that in each episcopal ordination at least two or three bishops from the neighboring Churches ought to take part[56] tied the episcopal office and with it the local eucharistic community in which the ordination to it took place with the rest of the eucharistic communties in the world in a fundamental way.[57] This fact not only made it possible for each bishop to allow a visiting fellow-bishop to preside over his eucharistic community[58] but must have been also one of the basic factors in the appearance of episcopal conciliarity.

The exact place that the "synod" or "council" occupied in the context of the catholicity of the early Church represents one of the most obscure and difficult problems. Were these councils intended, when they first appeared, to form a structure of a "universal catholicity" above the local Churches? Cyprian, one of the persons most involved in such conciliar activity, certainly did not think so. For him the authority of a council was moral and each bishop remained always directly respon-

καθόλου and Callias to the καθ' ἕκαστον" (*Interpr.*, 7, 17). Thus the καθ' ἕκαστον is not understood as a part of the καθόλου but as its concrete expression. In this way of thinking the dilemma between "local" and "universal" appears to make no sense.

[55]See above, note 4

[56]Hippolytus, *Apost. Trad.*, 2; Council of Arles, c. 20; I Nicaea, c. 4 and 6 etc.

[57]This is a fundamental point which N. Afanasiev has failed in his eucharistic ecclesiology to see and appreciate, as one may gather from the views expressed, for example, in his article "Una Sancta," *Irénikon* 36 (1963), pp. 436-75, and elsewhere.

[58]This we know, for example, from Polycarp's visit to Rome on the occasion of the paschal controversy (Eusebius, *Eccl. Hist.*, V, 24, 14-17). Cf. Syriac *Didascalia*, 12 (ed. Connolly, p. 122).

156   BEING AS COMMUNION

sible to God for his own community.[59] But the very fact of the
gradual acceptance of the "council" as a norm in the life of
the Church proves that its roots must have been very deep.

On another occasion too I tried to show that the phenomenon of early councils cannot be understood apart from a
primitive conciliarity which preceded the councils and which
again was not unrelated to the eucharistic community.[60] It
was not an insignificant thing that most, if not all, of the
earliest councils were ultimately concerned with the problem
of eucharistic communion[61] nor that the final admission of
supra-local conciliar structures with authority over the local
bishop was provoked by the pressing need to solve the problem
of eucharistic admission among the local Churches.[62] All this
meant that behind these developments stood a concept of
"catholicity" deeply rooted in the idea of the eucharistic
community. The various local Churches had to wrestle—perhaps unconsciously—with the problem of the relationship between the "catholic Church" in the episcopal community and
the catholic Church in the world. The moment they would
admit a supra-local structure over the local eucharistic community, be it a synod or another office, the eucharistic community would cease to be in itself and *by virtue of its eucharistic nature* a "catholic Church." The moment, on the other
hand, that they would allow each eucharistic community to
close itself to the other communities either entirely (i.e. by
creating a schism) or patrially (i.e. by not allowing certain

[59]Cyprian, *Ep.*, 55 (52), 21. The significant passage is: "Manente concor-
dia vinculo et perseverante catholicae ecclesiae individuo sacramento, actum
suum disponit et dirigit unusquisque episcopus rationem propositi sui Domino
redditurus." This makes it difficult to attribute to Cyprian the beginning of
a "universalist ecclesiology" as N. Afanasiev has done (cf. his "La doctrine
de la primauté à la lumière de l'ecclèsiologie," *Istina* 2 (1957), pp. 401-20).

[60]In my article "The Development of Conciliar structure to the Time of
the First Ecumenical Council," in *Councils and the Ecumenical Movement*
(World Council Studies, no. 5, 1968), pp. 34-51.

[61]Already in the first synods recorded in our sources. See Eusebius, *Eccl.
Hist.*, V, 16, 10. Cf. V, 24, 9; 28, 9.

[62]This is for the first time reflected in canon 5 of I Nicaea. This canon
is concerned with excommunications which took place in various local
Churches. Its deeper meaning lies in the idea that conciliarity is born out
of the Church's belief that eucharistic communion in a certain community
is a matter that concerns all communities in the world.

individual faithful from one community to communicate in another or by accepting to communion faithful excluded from it by their own community[63] they would betray the *very eucharistic nature of their catholicity* and the catholic character of the eucharist. The council was, therefore, an inevitable answer to this dilemma, and its genesis must be seen in the light of this situation.

Placed in this background, the councils represent in their appearance the most official negation of the division between local and universal, a negation which must be taken in all its implications. The eucharistic mentality which led to this solution would not allow any structure which would deny the fact that each eucharistic community revealed in a certain place *the whole Christ* and the ultimate eschatological unity of all in him. But the same mentality would not allow any provincialism that would fail to see the same reality in the other eucharistic communities. The whole Christ, the catholic Church, was present and incarnate in each eucharistic community. Each eucharistic community was, therefore, in full unity with the rest by virtue *not of an external superimposed structure* but of the whole Christ represented in each of them. The bishops as heads of these communities coming together in synods only expressed what Ignatius, in spite of—or perhaps because of—his eucharistic ecclesiology wrote once: "the bishops who are in the extremes of the earth are in the mind of Christ."[64] Thanks to a eucharistic vision of the "catholic Church" the problem of the relationship between the "one catholic Church in the world" and the "catholic Churches" in the various local places was resolved apart from any consideration of the local Church as being incomplete[65]

[63]See again canon 5 of I Nicaea where the problem lies in the historical background.

[64]Ignatius, *Eph.*, 3, 2.

[65]The idea that the local Church is a representative of the entire Church and therefore a full Church was a fundamental one in the consciousness of the early Church. Cf. B. Botte, "La collégialité dans le Nouveau Testament et chez les Pères apostoliques" in *Le Concile et les Conciles* (ed. B. Botte, *et al.*, 1960), p. 14 f., and J. Hamer, *L'Eglise est une communion* (1962), p. 38: "it is not in adding together the local communities that the whole community which constitutes the Church is born, but each community, however small, represents the whole Church."

or any scheme of priority of the one over the other, and in the sense of a *unity in identity*.[66]

IV. *Some General Conclusions*

In the light of this brief study of the "catholic" character of the eucharistic community as it developed in the early Church, the following thoughts may be of some relevance to the present-day ecumenical discussion on the catholicity of the Church.

(1) The primary content of "catholicity" is not a moral but a Christological one. The Church is catholic, not because she is obedient to Christ, i.e. because she does certain things or behaves in a certain way. She is catholic first of all because she is the Body of Christ. Her catholicity depends not on herself but on Him. She is catholic because she is where Christ is. We cannot understand catholicity as an ecclesiological notation unless we understand it as a Christological reality.[67]

To derive this assertion from a study of the eucharistic community means ceasing to understand it in the context of the problem of whether catholicity is a *given* reality or a

[66]The fundamental and crucial problem of the relationship between the "local" and the "universal" catholic Church must be solved apart from any notion of a *unity in collectivity*, and in the direction of a *unity in identity*. Schematically speaking, in the first case the various local Churches form *parts* which are added to one another in order to make up a whole, whereas in the latter, the local Churches are *full circles* which cannot be added to one another but *coincide* with one another and finally with the Body of Christ and the original apostolic Church. It is for this reason that any "structure of the unity of the Church in the Churches" (cf. the suggestion of Professor J.-J. von Allmen, *op. cit.*, p. 52) renders itself extremely difficult, once it is a *structure*. (It is not an accident that the ancient Church never realized such a *structure* in her life in spite of her conciliar activity.) The problem deserves a fuller discussion. With regard to the sources of the first three centuries, cf. the discussion in my book *The Unity of the Church . . .*, pp. 63-148.

[67]Christology as the starting point in ecclesiology in general has been stressed by G. Florovsky, "Christ and his Church, Suggestions and Comments," in *1054-1954, L'Eglise et les Eglises* II (1954), p. 164, and should not be understood as a negation of the pneumatological or the triadological aspect of the Church. For a clarification of this approach see Y. N. Lelouvier, *Perspectives russes sur l'Eglise: Un théologien contemporain, Georges Florovsky* (1968).

demand. This problem, which is often presented in the form of a dilemma, is strange to the eucharistic vision of catholicity because in such a vision whatever is given is revealed in *an existential way,* i.e. in the form of a presence *here and now,* a presence so fully incarnate in history that the ontological and the ethical cease to claim priority over each other. For example, to illustrate this ʼfrom our brief study of the eucharistic community, it is not possible to ask the question whether this community was composed in such a "catholic" way because she was conscious of a certain demand for that, or whether her being composed in such a way led to the consciousness of such a demand or such a concept of "catholicity." History is, in this respect, very instructive because there is perhaps nothing hidden so obscurely in the roots of Church history as the eucharistic structure of the first communities. To ask whether a certain belief preceded this structure, or if this structure led to this or that belief, would be asking a historically impossible question.

When, therefore, we say here that catholicity is not a moral but a Christological reality, we are not choosing between a "given" fact and a "demand," for the entire scheme of "given" versus "obtained" is far from being the context of discussion in a eucharistic vision of catholicity. The Christological character of catholicity lies in the fact that the Church is catholic not as a community which aims at a certain ethical achievement (being open, serving the world, etc.) but as a community which experiences and reveals the unity of all creation *insofar as this unity constitutes a reality in the person of Christ.* To be sure, this experience and this revelation involve a certain *catholic ethos.* But there is *no autonomous catholicity,* no catholic ethos that can be understood in itself.[68] It is *Christ's* unity and it is *His* catholicity that the Church reveals in her being catholic. This means that her catholicity is neither an objective gift to be possessed nor an objective order to be fulfilled, but rather a *presence,* a presence which unites into a single existential reality both what is given and what is demanded, the presence of Him who sums up in Him-

[68]Sociological views of catholicity must be only *derived* views and not *vice versa.*

self the community and the entire creation by His being existentially involved in both of them. The Church is catholic only by virtue of her being where this presence is (Ignatius), i.e. by virtue of her being inseparably united with Christ and constituting His very presence in history.

(2) To reveal Christ's whole Body in history means to meet the demonic powers of division which operate in history. A Christological catholicity which is seen in the context of this encounter with the anti-catholic powers of the world cannot be a *static* but a *dynamic catholicity*. This can happen only if we recognize in the catholicity of the Church a *pneumatological dimension*.

In the celebration of the eucharist, the Church very early realized that in order for the eucharistic community to become or reveal in it itself the wholeness of the Body of Christ (a wholeness that would include not only humanity but the entire creation),[69] the descent of the Holy Spirit upon this creation would be necessary. The offering up of the gifts and the whole community to the throne of God, the realization of the unity of the Body of Christ, was therefore preceded by the *invocation of the Holy Spirit*. "Send down thy Holy Spirit upon *us* and upon the *gifts* placed before thee."[70] For the world to become even symbolically a real sign of the consummation of all in Christ would be an impossibility without the Holy Spirit. The eucharistic community shows by its very existence that the realization of the Church's catholicity in history is the work of the Holy Spirit.

It is important to bear in mind that the Body of Christ, both in the Christological (incarnational) and in the ecclesiological sense, became a historical reality *through the Holy*

[69]This view of the eucharist has been a fundamental one in the eastern liturgies ever since Irenaeus' teaching, on which see A. W. Ziegler, "Das Brot von unseren Felder. Ein Beitrag zur Eucharistielehre des hl. Irenäus," in *Pro mundi vita: Festschrift zum Eucharistischen Weltkongress 1960* (1960), pp. 21-43.

[70]The liturgy of St John Chrysostom (prayer of consecration). The same prayer in the liturgy of St Basil makes it even clearer that the Holy Spirit is invoked not just for the consecration of the gifts but also for the realization of the unity of the community: "And to unite us all, as many as are partakers in the one bread and cup, one with another, in the communion of the one Holy Spirit."

Spirit.[71] For creation to lend itself to the *Logos* of God in order to bring about the incarnation would have been impossible without the intervention of the Holy Spirit. This is a fundamental scriptural assertion,[72] and the same is true about the realization of the community of the Church on the day of Pentecost.[73] To see these events retrospectively through the eyes of the Church means to place them in their pneumatological context, for that which made them a reality *eph hapax* namely the Holy Spirit, is that which makes them an existential reality, here and now, again. In this sense the eucharistic *anamnesis* becomes not a mere mental operation but an existential realization, a *re*-presentation of the Body of Christ,[74] thus revealing to us that the Church's existence as the Body of Christ and, therefore, her catholicity constitute a reality which *depends constantly* upon the Holy Spirit.

This means not only that human attempts at "togetherness," "openness," etc., cannot constitute the catholicity of the Church, but that no plan for a progressive movement towards catholicity can be achieved on a purely historical and sociological level. The eucharistic community constitutes a sign of the fact that the *eschaton* can only *break through* history but never be identified with it. Its call to catholicity is a call not to a progressive conquest of the world but to a "kenotic" experience of the fight with the anticatholic demonic powers and a continuous dependence upon the Lord and His Spirit. A catholic Church in the world, cognizant as she may be of

---

[71]See N. Nissiotis, "La Pneumatologie ecclésiologique au service de l'Unité de l'Eglise," *Istina* 12 (1967), pp. 322-40, where a discussion of the role of the Holy Spirit in ecclesiology is found. Cf. O. Clément, "L'Ecclésiologie orthodoxe comme ecclésiologie de communion," *Contacts* 20 (1968), pp. 10-36 (English translation in *One in Christ* 6 [1970], pp. 101-22).

[72]Luke 1:35; Matt. 1:18-20.

[73]Acts 1-2. Ever since, baptism and confirmation were inseparably united in the early Church and understood as the very operation of the Spirit in Christ's baptism and anointing (Luke 4:18) so that each baptized and chrismated Christian would become himself Christ (Tertullian, *De Bapt.*, 7-8; Theophilus of Antioch, *Ad Autol.*, 1, 12, and especially Cyril of Jerusalem, *Cat.*, 21, 1, PG 33:1089).

[74]This idea forms part of the emerging consensus on the Eucharist in the Ecumenical Movement today. See "The Eucharist in Ecumenical Thought" (a Faith and Order document) in *Study Encounter*, vol. IV, no. 3 (1968).

Christ's victory over Satan, lives in humility and service and above all in constant prayer and worship.

(3) The way the catholicity of the Church is revealed in the eucharistic community shows that the ultimate essence of catholicity lies in the transcendence of all divisions in Christ. This should be understood absolutely and without any reservations. It covers all areas and all dimensions of existence whether human or cosmic, historical or echatological, spiritual or material, social or individual, etc. The dichotomies in which life has been placed and conceived, unfortunately to a great extent by Christian tradition itself,[75] represent a betrayal of the catholic outlook so essential to the Church of Christ. One thinks in this respect, for example, of the dichotomy between the "sacred" and the "secular," or between body and soul. The eucharistic community with its understanding of the eucharist as *a meal*,[76] with its basic elements being material and not merely spiritual, with its long litanies and supplications in which man's everyday material and physical needs find their place etc., constitutes a sign of a "catholic" view of existence in which no dualistic dichotomies can be accepted. Man and the world form a unity in harmony and so do the various dimensions in man's own existence. An ecclesiological catholicity in the light of the eucharistic community suggests and presupposes a *catholic anthropology* and a *catholic view of existence* in general.

In such a catholic outlook the entire problem of the relationship of the Church to the world receives a different perspective. The separation and juxtaposition of the two can have no essential meaning because there is no point where the limits of the Church can be objectively and finally drawn. There is a constant interrelation between the Church and the world, the world being God's creation and never ceasing to belong to Him and the Church being the community which through the descent of the Holy Spirit transcends in herself the world and offers it to God in the eucharist.[77]

[75]Cf. A. Schmemann, *Sacraments and Orthodoxy* (1965), p. 14.

[76]Cf. again the ecumenical consensus in "The Eucharist in Ecumenical Thought" (note 74 above).

[77]This transcendence which is possible only "in the Spirit" presupposes a

(4) But how can this view of catholicity be reconciled with the fact that the eucharistic community itself is divided into *orders,* i.e. into categories and classes of people? History shows that there is a real problem here, because the divisions which have occurred on this basis are so deep that the Church is still suffering from them.[78] How can the situation which results from ordination into ministries and orders, into clergy and laity, be transcended in the way all divisions are transcended in the eucharistic community?

The fact that all ordinations were at a very early time incorporated in the eucharistic liturgy is, I think, of great importance in this respect. The first important implication of this fact is that there is no ministry which can be conceived as existing *parallel* to that of Christ but only as *identical* with it. In her being the Body of Christ, the Church exists as a manifestation of Christ's own ministry and as a reflection of this very ministry in the world. It is not an accident that the early Church applied to Christ all forms of ministries that existed. He was the apostle,[79] the prophet,[80] the priest,[81] the bishop,[82] the deacon,[83] etc. A Christologically understood ministry transcends all categories of priority and separation that may be created by the act of ordination and "setting apart."

Another fundamental implication is that no ministry in the Church can be understood outside the context of the community. This should not be explained in terms of representativeness and delegation of authority, for these terms being

baptismal purification of man and his world and in this sense it is important to bear in mind the "paschal" character of the eucharist (cf. J. M. R. Tillard, *op. cit.,* p. 164) and the intimate relationship between baptism and eucharist (see J.-J. von Allmen, *op. cit.,* p. 37 f.).

[78]We have in mind the whole issue of clericalism and anti-clericalism which has been a real problem, especially in the West. The East, by having kept for centuries a eucharistic vision of ecclesiology, did not experience this problem. It was only recently that, due to a replacement of this vision by later ecclesiological ideas, the problem appeared threatening in some Orthodox areas.

[79]Heb. 3:1.
[80]Matt. 23:8; John 13:13.
[81]Heb. 5:6; 8:4; 10:21; 2:17.
[82]I Peter 2:25; 5:4; Heb. 13:13. Cf. Ignatius, *Magn.,* 3, 1-2; *Polyc. inscr.*
[83]Rom. 15:8; Luke 22:27. Phil 2:7.

basically juridical finally lead to a separation of the ordained person from the community: to act *on behalf* of the community means to stand *outside* it because it means to act *in its place*.[84] But what is precisely denied by this communal dimension we want to point out here, is that there is no ministry that can stand *outside* or *above* the community.

To affirm that the ministry belongs to the community means, in the last analysis, to place the entire matter of ordination outside the dilemma of choosing between *ontological* and *functional*. It has been for a long time an object of discussion whether ordination bestows something indelible upon the ordained person, something that constitutes his individual possession (permanently or temporarily) or simply empowers him with an authority to function for a certain purpose. In the light of the eucharistic community this dilemma makes no sense and is misleading, for the terms of reference there, as we have had occasion to stress earlier here, are basically existential. There is no *charisma* that can be *possessed individually* and yet there is no *charisma* which can be conceived or operated *but by individuals*. How can this statement be understood?

Here, I think, we must seek illumination from a fundamental distinction between the *individual* and the *personal*. The distinction has already been made more than once in philosophy[85] but it has seldom been applied to theological problems such as those presented by ecclesiology. And yet the paradox of the incorporation of the "many" into the "one" on which the eucharistic community, as we have seen, and perhaps the entire mystery of the Church are based can only be understood and explained in the categories of *personal existence*. The individual represents a category that presupposes separation and division. "Individuality makes its

[84]In this sense terminology like that of "vicar," etc. when applied to the episcopate or the ministry in general may suggest a similar representation "outside" or "in the place of" someone who is absent.

[85]The distinction was already made, though from a different standpoint, by Thomas Aquinas and it was developed in modern times by J. Maritain, *Du Régime temporel et de liberté* (1933). Cf. N. Berdyaev, *Solitude and Society* (1938), p. 168. See also ch. I of this book.

appearance by its differentiation from other individualities."[86] The person represents a category that presupposes unity with other persons.[87] The eucharistic community, and the Church in general, as a *communion* (*koinonia*) can only be understood in the categories of personal existence.

Ordination to the ministry in the context of the eucharistic communion implies that the "seal of the Holy Spirit" which is given cannot exist outside the receiver's existential relationship with the community. It is not a mere function to be exercised outside a deep bond with this community. It is a bond of love,[88] such as every gift of the Spirit is, and its *indelible character* can only be compared with that which is possessed or given by love. Outside this existential bond with the community it is destined to die, just as the Spirit who gives this *charisma* once, and constantly sustains it, does not live outside this community because He is the bond of love. It is in this sense that the Spirit is exclusively possessed by the Church[89] and that all ministry is a gift of this Spirit.

All this means a transcendence of the divisions created by the variety of ministries and the distinctiveness of orders in the Church. It is in this context that the bishop's exclusive right to ordination must be viewed. If he came to possess such a right it was because of his capacity as the head of the eucharistic community—*hence his inability to ordain outside this community*—and in relation to his role as the one who offers the entire community in the eucharist to God. His exclusive right to ordain, in fact his whole existence as bishop, makes no sense apart from his role as the one through whom all divisions, including those of orders, are transcended. His

[86]M. Buber, *I and Thou* (1958), p. 62.

[87]*Ibid.*

[88]The Orthodox service of ordination to the priesthood is in many parts identical with that of matrimony. This does not only suggest an understanding of the ministry as a bond between the ordained, Christ and the community, but it indicates at the same time the *direction* in which theology should move in its attempts to understand the character of ordination.

[89]E.g. Cyprian, *Ep.*, 69 (66), 11; 75, 4, etc. In this sense the idea that there is no salvation outside the Church appears to be more than a negative statement. A fundamental truth behind it is that there is no possibility for an individualistic understanding of salvation: *unus christianus, nullus christianus.*

primary function is always *to make the catholicity of the Church reveal itself in a certain place.* For this he must himself be existentially related to a community. There is no ministry in the catholic Church that can exist *in absoluto.*

(5) The implications of such a view of the ministry and especially of the episcopate for the understanding of *apostolic succession* are clear. To speak of apostolic succession as a chain of episcopal ordinations going back to the apostolic times, without implying the indispensable bond of these ordinations with the community in whose eucharistic *synaxis* they have taken place, would amount to a conception of the ministry *in absoluto.* But if it is not a mere accident that the early Church knew of no episcopal ordination either outside the eucharistic context or without specific mention of *the place* to which the bishop would be attached,[90] we must conclude that there is no apostolic succession which does not go through the concrete community.

To assert that apostolic succession goes through the concrete episcopal community means to free one's mind from the bondage of historicity and place the entire matter in a wider church-historical perspective. It would be impossible and irrelevant to discuss here the problems that are related to the appearance of the idea of apostolic succession in the early Church. It is certainly true that this idea was from the beginning related to attempts at reconstructing episcopal lists, which means that the concern at that time was to prove the survival of orthodox teaching by means of strictly historical reconstruction. But why *episcopal* lists? The bishops were

[90]Already in the sub-apostolic times the bishop appears to be attached to the inhabitants of a certain city (Ignatius, *Magn.*, 15; *Polyc. Inscr.*). Later on, the existing evidence from acts of councils indicates that the bishop's name was attached to the name of a city (*Patrum Nic. nomina*, ed. by Gelzer, p. 61). What is most significant is that in the service of episcopal ordination the name of the area to which the bishop is assigned has entered the prayer of ordination: the divine grace . . . ordains this or that person to be a bishop of this or that diocese. Even when the institution of the so-called "titular" bishops—who are essentially bishops without a flock—was introduced, provision was made that the name of the diocese, even from among those which no longer existed, would be attached to the name of the bishop in his ordination. This, of course, amounts to a contradiction between theory and practice in ecclesiology, but it nevertheless reveals that the Church has never admitted in her consciousness an episcopate *in absoluto.*

not the only expounders of orthodox teaching—for a long time
their primary function was not considered to be that of
teaching[91]—while one could use a list of presbyters—they were
actually considered at that time to be teachers of the people[92]
—to prove the survival of orthodoxy in a certain place at least
equally well. Why is it that no attempt has been made for
such presbyterial lists? To raise such a question does not
mean to ignore the fact that the bishops were, at least at
the time of the appearance of the idea of apostolic succession,
considered to be the teachers *par excellence* and in any case
were the ones that bore ultimate responsibility for the orthodox teaching, especially since the time of Gnostic pressure
upon the Church. But even if we put aside the possibility
that the idea of apostolic succession goes back to a time earlier
than the middle second century and not necessarily in connection with the preservation of orthodox teaching,[93] the fact
that the lists of successions were exclusively episcopal—just as
in a similar case of the same period, i.e. in the appearance
of the councils, the composition was exclusively episcopal—
shows that the idea behind them was grounded on a reality
broader than the concern for proving the survival of orthodoxy, or to put it in other terms, that the concern for the
survival of orthodoxy was not isolated from the broader reality
of the Church's life as a community headed by the bishop.
The bishops as successors of the apostles were not perpetuators of ideas like the heads of philosophical schools,[94] nor
teachers in the same sense that the presbyters were, but heads

[91]In Ignatius (e.g. *Philad.*, 1, 2) the bishop was not necessarily the
teacher. In Justin (*Apol.*, I, 67) the bishop seems to be giving the sermon
in the eucharistic *synaxis*, but it was mainly from the time of the *Martyrium
Polycarpi* (16, 2) and afterwards that the stress on the bishop's teaching
appear clearly. Cf. G. Dix, "Ministry in the Early Church," in *The Apostolic
Ministry* (ed. K. E. Kirk, 1957), p. 204 f.

[92]Sources like the *Shepherd of Hermas* (Vis. 3, 4), Tertullian (*De Praescr.*,
2), Origen (*In Ezekiel*, 2, 2, PG 13, 682 C), etc., indicate that the
presbyters had teaching as one of their functions. The same is evident from
the prayers of ordination to the presbyterate (Hippolytus, *Apost. Trad.*, 8,
ed. G. Dix, p. 13), and from the existence of famous presbyters known as
teachers (Clement of Alexandria, Origen, etc.).

[93]*I Clem.*, 44, 2-4.

[94]Hippolytus, *Philos.*, 9, 12, 21 (PG 15, 3386): The "catholic Church"
was not a "school" (*didaskaleion*).

of communities whose entire life and thought they were supposed by their office to express. Their apostolic succession,
therefore, should be viewed neither as a chain of individual
acts of ordination nor as a transmission of truths but as a
sign and an expression of the *continuity of the Church's historical life in its entirety,* as it was realized in each community.

Such an understanding of apostolic succession explains
why in its first appearance this concept was so concretely conceived that the reference was made not to "apostolic succession"[95] in general but to apostolic "successions" (plural),[96]
exactly as in the language of that time the catholicity of the
Church was understood in the form of "catholic Churches"
(plural). The fundamental implication of this fact is that
each episcopal community reflects in itself not only the
"whole Church" but also the *whole succession of the
apostles.* Indeed, it is quite significant that each bishop was
at that time thought to be successor not of a particular apostle,
but of *all the apostles.*[97] This made each episcopal Church
fully apostolic[98] and each bishop an occupant of the *cathedra
Petri.*[99] This means that apostolic succession can never be a
result of *adding up* the various episcopal successions. The
apostolic college in its succesion was not divided into parts
so that each bishop would be ascribed to one part and all
bishops together to the whole of this college. Episcopal collegiality, therefore, does not represent a *collective* unity, but
a *unity in identity,* an organic unity. It is the identity of each
community with the Body of Christ expressed in historical

[95]It is noteworthy that for some ancient authors (e.g. Tertullian, *De
Praescr.,* 20, 2-5) apostolic succession is one "of apostolic churches rather
than of apostolic bishops," as it is pointed out by R. P. C. Hanson, *Tradition
in the Early Church* (1962), p. 158.

[96]Hegesippus quoted by Eusebius, *Eccl. Hist.,* I, 22, 3-5: "in each succession and in each city. . . ."

[97]Cf. F. Dvornik, *The Idea of Apostolicity in Byzantium and the Legend
of St Andrew* (1958).

[98]It is noteworthy how Tertullian (*De Praescr.,* 36, 2) refers to the various
Churches in connection with their apostolicity; in all the places he mentions
(Achaiá, Macedonia, Asia, Italy, Rome) "the very thrones of the apostles are
still pre-eminent in their places in which their own authentic writings are
still read, etc."

[99]Cyprian, *Ep.,* 69 (66), 5, and 43 (40), 5. Cf. *De Unit.,* 4.

terms through the continuity of the apostolic presence in the
locus apostolicus of each episcopal community.

Apostolic succession represents a sign of the historical
dimension of the catholicity of the Church. It serves to combine the historical with the charismatic and transcend the
divisions caused by time. In an understanding of the apostolic
succession stemming from the eucharistic community, where
the past and the future are through the Holy Spirit perceived
in one and the same reality of the present,[100] history and time
are fully accepted and eternal life is not opposed to them but
enters into them and transcends them as they affect man's
destiny and salvation. Thus the Church is revealed to be in
time what she is eschatologically, namely a catholic Church
which stands in history as a transcendence of all divisions
into the unity of all in Christ through the Holy Spirit to the
glory of God the Father.

[100]Cf. the liturgy of St John Chrysostom at the prayer of the anaphora:
"Commemorating this command of our Savior and all that was endured for
our sake, the cross, the grave, the resurrection after three days, the ascension
into Heaven, the enthronement at the right hand of the Father, and the
second and glorious coming again, thine own of thine own we offer to thee
in all and for all."

5.

Apostolic Continuity and Succession

Many factors have contributed to the theological consciousness of the Orthodox Churches with regard to the Church's continuity with her apostolic origins. Among these there are two which lie at the very basis of our subject. On the one hand, Orthodoxy is known for its devotion to *tradition*. This makes history acquire decisiveness in the consciousness of the Orthodox Churches, which is thus oriented towards the past with respect and devotion. On the other hand, Orthodoxy is known for the centrality and importance which it attributes to *worship* in its life and theology, and this leads it to a "theophanic" and in a sense "meta-historical" view of the Church.[1] Deep in these two aspects of Orthodox consciousness lie the seeds of a duality which could be easily turned into a dichotomy.[2]

In the following lines an attempt will be made to see how this duality of the traditional or historical and the theophanic or metahistorical elements affect the consciousness of the Church's continuity with the apostles. This attempt will be made especially in view of the fact that the implications of

---

[1]Cf. the remarks of Fr Y. Congar in *Le Concile et les Conciles* (ed. B. Botte *et al.*, 1960), p. 287: The East "suit beaucoup plus l'idée, très presente chez les Pères et dans la liturgie, d'une 'phanie,' d'une manifestation des réalités célestes, invisibles, sur la terre. Il s'ensuit une conception principalement sacramentelle et iconologique de l'Eglise."

[2]Thus it is a common phenomenon in ecumenical circles to regard the Orthodox both as "traditionalists" and as detached from the problems of history and preoccupied with the "triumphalism" of their liturgy.

this duality are quite relevant to non-Orthodox Churches as well, and are therefore related to many of the problems that both the Eastern and the Western Churches are facing today.[3] This is so because this duality is deeply rooted in the *beginning* of the Church and requires constantly a creative synthesis by theology so that it may not become a dichotomy.

I. *The Two Approaches, "Historical" and "Eschatological," to Apostolic Continuity*

1. In the early Biblical and patristic sources that we possess, we can distinguish two basic approaches to the idea of the Church's continuity with the apostles. Each of these two approaches is based on a corresponding image of the apostolate and bears specific implications for the theology and the structure of the Church.

It is of course true that the concept of the apostolate in the New Testament is a complex one, and it is extremely difficult to disentangle the various elements of which it is composed.[4] Nevertheless, it is possible to distinguish clearly two images used for the description of the nature and role of the apostles. On the one hand, the apostles are conceived as persons entrusted with a *mission* to fulfill. As such they are *sent* and thus *dispersed* in the world. This implies that they are understood as *individuals*[5] possessing a message and authority in a way that reminds one of the Jewish institution of the *shaliach*.[6] Because the angle from which the apostolate is

[3]E.g. the difficulty of integrating the sacramental conception of apostolic succession with the idea of linear historical transmission of authority in Vatican II. See B.-D. Dupuy, "La succession apostolique dans la discussion oecuménique," *Istina* 12 (1967), 391-401, esp. p. 391.

[4]For a discussion of these difficulties see R. Schnackenburg, "L'apostolicité: état de la recherche," *Istina* 14 (1969), 5-32; Engl. trans. in *One in Christ* 6 (1970), 243-273.

[5]The sending out of the apostles in pairs (Mark 6:7) need not occupy us here. On this peculiar Jewish-Palestinian feature see J. Jeremias, "Paarweise Sendung im Neuen Testament," in *New Testament Essays* (in memory of T. W. Manson, ed. by A.J.B. Higgins, 1959), pp. 136-43.

[6]Cf. K. H. Rengstorf "ἀπόστολος" in Kittel's *Theologisches Wörterbuch zum Neuen Testament* (1933), pp. 406-48. For a critical approach: G. Klein, *Die Zwölf Apostel* (1961), pp. 22-38. Cf. below, n. 80.

viewed in this approach is that of mission, the term "apostle" is thus applicable to all missionaries who possess the authority and the charisma of preaching the Gospel.[7] There are, of course, conditions attached to the use of the term "apostle" and it is still unclear how these conditions affect the notion of "apostle" in the New Testament.[8] But the point that interests us here is that in an approach inspired by the idea of mission, the apostles represent a *link* between Christ and the Church and form part of a historical process with a decisive and perhaps *normative* role to play. Thus the idea of mission and that of historical process go together in the New Testament and lead to a scheme of continuity in a linear movement: God sends Christ—Christ sends the apostles—the apostles transmit the message of Christ by establishing Churches and ministers.[9] We may, therefore, call this approach "historical."

2. On the other hand, the apostles are conceived as persons with an *eschatological function.*[10] In this case the imagery

[7]Hence the application of the term "apostle" to a group broader than the Twelve. Paul's apostolate constitutes part of this problem. On these and related questions see R. Schnackenburg, *op. cit.,* pp. 246ff.

[8]It is not, for example, clear whether the apostolate is related to "the historical Jesus" (Acts 1:22) or just to the Risen Christ (Gal. 1:1; II Cor. 10-13, etc.) or even to neither of the two (Rom. 16:7; Acts 14:14, etc.). The bibliography on these problems is enormous. See R. Schnackenburg, *op. cit.*

[9]This scheme is offered basically in the New Testament: John 20:21; Luke 10:16, etc. Christ Himself is an "apostle" (Heb. 3:1). See also John 17:7f; Mat. 28:18-20; Rom. 10:13-17; I John 1:1-13; II Tim. 2:2; Tit. 1:5, etc. It is on the basis of this "historical" or "missionary" scheme that transmission of apostolic authority to other persons for the continuation of this mission is mentioned already in the New Testament (Acts 20:17-35; I Tim. 5:22; 4:4; II Tim. 2:2; Tit. 1:4; 2:1-15, etc.). Cf. Ph. Menoud, *L'Eglise et son ministère selon le N. T.* (1949); J. Colson, "La succession apostolique au niveau du Ier siècle," *Verbum Caro* (1961), 138-72.

[10]The importance of eschatology for the understanding of the original concept of the apostolate became apparent with the discovery of the eschatological character of Christ's teaching through the works of J. Weiss and A. Schweitzer. Cf. E. M. Kredel, "Der Apostelbegriff in der neuren Exegese," *Zeitschrift für Katholische Theologie* 78 (1956), 169-93 and 257-305. Also, J. Roloff, *Apostolat-Verkündigung—Kirche* (1965), pp. 23-27. The implications of eschatology for the Church's continuity with the apostles have been recently emphasized by W. Pannenberg, "La signification de l'eschatologie pour la compréhension de l'apostolicité et de la catholicité de l'Eglise," *Istina* 14 (1969), 154-170; Engl. trans. in *One in Christ* 6 (1970), 410-429. See also

and schemes used to describe the apostles are quite different from the ones used in the case I have called "historical." This difference applies to the apostles themselves as well as to their relation to Christ and the Church. Thus instead of being understood as individuals dispersed throughout the world for mission, the apostles are understood as a *college*. The difference is considerable and corresponds to that between mission and eschatology. Mission requires *sending* to the ends of the earth, whereas the eschata imply the *convocation* of the dispersed people of God from the ends of the earth to one place.[11] The apostles in their eschatological function are inconceivable as individuals; they form an indivisible college. For this reason they are basically and primarily represented by the college of *the Twelve* whenever their eschatological function is mentioned.[12] In this case the apostles' relation both to Christ and to the Church is expressed in a way different from that of the historical approach. Here the apostles are not those who follow Christ but who *surround* Him.[13]

L. Cerfaux, "La mission apostolique des Douze et sa portée eschatologique," in *Mélanges E. Tisserant* I (1964), pp. 43-66, and Y. Congar, "Composantes et idée de la Succession Apostolique," in *Oecumenica* (1966), pp. 61-80, esp. pp. 75-76.

[11]*Didache* 9:4; 10:5. Cf. Matt. 25:32; John 11:52 etc. In stressing the difference between the "missionary" and the "eschatological" images of the apostolate, I do not wish to deny the eschatological character of the apostolic mission as it appears especially in Paul (see on this works mentioned in previous note, esp. Pannenberg and Congar). But I maintain the view that there is a difference between eschatology conceived as *orientation*, and eschatology conceived as a *state* of existence which reveals itself here and now. As orientation, eschatology appears to be the *result of historical process* as the climax of mission (e.g. in the above mentioned authors), whereas as a state of existence it confronts history already now with *a presence from beyond history*. In the latter case an "iconic" and liturgical approach to eschatology is necessary more than it is in the former. It is the understanding of eschatology as this kind of *presence* of the Kingdom here and now that requires convocation of the dispersed people of God and of the apostles. As such this image *presupposes the end of mission*. This proleptic experience of the presence of the eschata here and now—and not simply the orientation towards this end—was there from the beginning (Acts 2:17) and was realised mainly in the eucharist (*Didache*). It is with *this* kind of eschatology that I wish to relate my subject here.

[12]See e.g. Matt. 19:28; Luke 22:30. Cf. Acts 1:12-26 (for its eschatological connections cf. 2:17).

[13]This image, based on the Last Supper (note again the eschatological

And they do not stand as a link between Christ and the Church in a historical process but are the *foundations* of the Church in a presence of the Kingdom of God here and now.[14]

These two approaches to the idea of apostolic continuity should not, of course, be oversimplified, for, as I said earlier, the New Testament picture of the concept of apostolate is a complex one. One has to account, for example, for the place of Paul or the other "apostles" in the eschatological image which is based primarily on the Twelve.[15] But the fact that Paul himself—and Luke on his behalf—had to find a way of relating his apostleship to that of the Twelve and the Jerusalem Church,[16] indicates that the two approaches I have mentioned here were clearly reflected in the consciousness of the primitive Church.

3. The survival of these two approaches in post-apostolic

context), became the standard form of reference to the apostles in the eucharistic liturgies ever since the Apocalypse and Ignatius of Antioch.

[14]Apoc. 21:14. In Ephesians (2:20) we have the use of the image of the "apostles" as foundations of the Church in a historical sense. But in this case the reference to the "apostles" is probably not to the Twelve or the apostolic college, but to missionaries.

[15]For the present state of research on this subject see R. Schnackenburg, *op. cit.*, pp. 8ff.

[16]On Paul see the work of J. Munck, *Paulus und die Heilsgeschichte* (1954). Cf. the thesis concerning Paul's dependence on the Twelve by P. Gaechter, "Schranken im Apostolat des Paulus," in *Petrus und seine Zeit* (1958), pp. 338-450. On the importance of the Twelve for overcoming the tension ("dualism"?) between "institutional" and "charismatic" Apostolate, see J. L. Leuba, *L'institution et l'événement* (1950), pp. 47ff. The rise of the position of James is very instructive for the argument of this paper concerning our eschatological approach to apostolicity in terms of permanent Church structures. With the disappearance of the Twelve from the Jerusalem Church (dispersion for mission?) the scheme "apostles and presbyters" is replaced with that of "James and the presbyters" (Acts 21:18). The significance of this scheme lies in the eschatological nature of the Jerusalem Church as the center of the earth, where all mission converges in its final consummation (Rom. 15:19). Paul must be reconciled with "James and the presbyters" precisely because the latter represent the eschatological court of the Church. Thus we have from the beginning *a structure emerging from the eschatological state of the Church's convocation.* It is more than significant to notice how this model is transferred to the eucharist and through that to the episcopacy after the fall of Jerusalem. It is not possible to discuss this here (cf. n. 87 below; also my book *The Unity of the Church in the Eucharist and the Bishop in the First Three Centuries* [1965—in Greek]). But it is interesting to note the relation of this development to the eschatological approach to apostolicity.

times is very instructive for our subject. With the gradual disappearance of the apostles, the Church had to face the problem of apostolic continuity and work out a way of solving it. The existing sources indicate that both the historical and the eschatological approaches to continuity were preserved at that time.

The historical approach is clearly expressed by *I Clement*. The scheme "God sends Christ—Christ sends the apostles" becomes the basis for the notion of continuity in terms of historical process: "The apostles have announced to us the good news from Jesus Christ. Jesus Christ was sent by God. Thus Christ comes from God and the apostles from Christ. This double mission, therefore, with its order comes from the will of God."[17] This is precisely the New Testament scheme as I expounded it earlier on, and on its basis *I Clement* elaborates its theory of continuity: "Following the instructions of our Lord Jesus Christ, fully convinced by His resurrection and firm in their faith in the word of God, the apostles went with the assurance of the Holy Spirit to announce everywhere the good news of the coming of the Kingdom of heaven. In the various villages and cities they proclaimed the word and thus made their premises and . . . established ἐπισκόπους καὶ διακόνους for the future believers."[18] This is an elaborate theory of continuity based on the historical approach. Hence this text has been widely used in connection with the idea of apostolic succession.

Things are different, however, in the case of another source of the same period, namely the letters of St Ignatius of Antioch. Here we have an example of the eschatological approach to apostolic continuity, as I described it earlier. Ignatius' image of the Church is borrowed not from history but from the eschatological state of the Church's convocation "in the same place"[19] to partake of the eternal life of God as it is offered to the world at the eucharistic table. Here the image is very much like the one we find in the Apocalypse,[20]

17I Clement 42:1-2.
18*Ibid.* 42:2-4, cf. 44:1-4.
19This expression is used by Ignatius frequently and usually in connection with the eucharist, e.g. *Eph.* 5:2-3, 13:1; *Polyc.* 4:2; *Magn.* 7:12 etc.
20Apoc. 4-5.

and the implications for the relation of the Church to the apostles are clearly different from those we find in *I Clement:* the apostles are a united college and they surround Christ in His Kingdom. For this reason it is the *college of presbyters* surrounding the bishop, who sits "in the place of God" or is the image of Christ,[21] that Ignatius sees the image of the apostles.[22] Continuity here is guaranteed and expressed not by way of succession from generation to generation and from individual to individual, but in and through the convocation of the Church in one place, i.e. through its *eucharistic structure*. It is a *continuity of communities* and *Churches* that constitutes and expresses apostolic succession in this approach. If apostolic succession is understood simply in terms of history, the evidence of St Ignatius becomes embarassing—and it has been so precisely insofar as the eschatological approach to continuity has almost disappeared from our considerations.[23]

The subsequent history of these two approaches to apostolic continuity is extremely interesting, but does not concern us here. References to it will be made later on in this study by way of historical illustrations of some theological points. What has been said so far is enough to make clear the point that in the very beginnings of the Church's consciousness of continuity with the apostles—and this applies both to the Eastern and to the Western Churches—there are hidden the seeds of

[21]Ignatius, *Magn.* 6:1, 3:1-2; *Tral.* 3:1. The idea that the bishop is the image of Christ survived at least until the fourth century (e.g. in Pseudo-Clem. *Homil.* 3:62). Cf. O. Perler, "L'Evêque, représentant du Christ . . ." in *L'Episcopat et l'Eglise universelle,* ed. Y. Congar and B.-D. Dupuy, *Unam Sanctam* 39 (1962), pp. 31-66.

[22]Ignatius, *Magn.* 6:1. The image we get in Ignatius corresponds to that of Christ surrounded by the apostles in the eschatological—and eucharistic—convocation of the people of God (cf. above n. 11).

[23]The conviction underlying this article is that we are not allowed to form our view of apostolic continuity without taking Ignatius into account. Ignatius is by no means an exception in the early Church with regard to his view of apostolic continuity. He is preceeded by such sources as the book of the Apocalypse (chs. 4-5) and followed by a long tradition represented by the Syriac *Didascalia Apostolorum* (ch. 9), the *Constitutiones Apost.* (II, 24) etc. The iconological and eschatological approach of this tradition survived to a large extent in Byzantium and the Orthodox Churches. Disregarding all this tradition would mean depriving our view of apostolic continuity of an essential part of the most primitive approach to our subject.

two approaches to this continuity, of an "historical" and an "eschatological" approach.

4. If we now try to penetrate deeply into the theological and ecclesiological nature of these two approaches as they relate to the notion of apostolic continuity, the following points can be made.

The first observation has to do with the notion of continuity itself. What does continuity mean in each of these approaches? In the historical approach the main components of continuity are the following: In the first place continuity means succession or survival in time, i.e. from the past to the present into the future. This succession or survival of the Church's apostolic origins can take place in different ways. It can take place by way of *transmission* of certain powers, authority, etc.[24] It can also take place by way of normativeness, i.e. in the form of an example to be copied.[25] In any case the historical approach creates the basis of a *retrospective* continuity with the past. The anamnetic function of the Church is employed here in a psychological way, and this leads to the creation of a *consciousness of continuity* with the past. The Church recalls a time called "apostolic"; whether she relates to it through various media or by way of copying as faithfully as possible this normative period, the fact remains that in this approach *her apostolicity* comes *from the side of the past.* On the other hand the eschatological approach implies no sense of transmission or normativity. Here apostolicity comes to the Church from the side of the future. It is the anticipation of the end, the final nature of the Church that reveals her apostolic character. This anticipation should not be misunderstood as psychological; it is not a feeling of expectation and hope that is offered through it, but a real

---

[24]Such views developed in the West in the Middle Ages. See Y. *Congar L'Eglise de s. Augustin à l'époque moderne* (*Histoire des Dogmas* III. 3, 1970), *passim*, and esp. 173 ff. Also *ibid.*, "Quelques problèmes touchant les ministères," *Nouvelle Revue Théologique* 93 (1971), 785-800.

[25]This idea is inherent in the Reformation principle of *sola Scriptura*. Recently H. Küng,*Die Kirche* (1967), esp. pp. 421 f., in describing continuity with the Apostles in terms of "imitation" (*Nachfolge*) has basically adopted the approach to the Apostles as the example and paradigm to be copied.

presence of the eschata here and now. "*Now* is the judgment of the world,"[26] and now, this simple moment of the Johannine νῦν, all of history is consummated. The finality or ultimacy of things is what the eschatological approach to apostolicity brings forth. It is the *Risen Christ* that is related to apostolicity, i.e. the final and ultimate destiny of all that exists.[27]

All this affects the notion of continuity in a deeper way: it affects especially Christology and Pneumatology in their relation to the apostolic origins of the Church.

In the historical approach, Christology is inevitably the primary thing that provides the structure of continuity.[28] The Holy Spirit is the one that is *transmitted* and He is transmitted *by Christ*. He is the divine power which enables the apostles in their mission. He is also the one who creates the response to this mission. He is the animator of a basically *pre-conceived structure*.[29] In such an approach Pneumatology indicates an *agency;* the Spirit is the *agent of Christ* and is dependent on Him.[30] Here Christology indicates a self-defined event and so does the notion of the apostolate. In this his-

<hr/>

[26]John 12:31.

[27]On the importance of the Resurrection for the eschatological approach to apostolicity see W. Pannenberg, *op. cit.*, p. 158f. It must be noted that in the Johannine concept of "now" (νῦν) the finality of the risen Christ does not evolve from a historical process but comes to us as a *visit* and a tabernacle from outside (cf. John 1:14).

[28]For such a view see e.g. Y. Congar, "Pneumatologie et théologie de l'histoire," *Archivio di Filosofia* (1971), p. 63.

[29]The ecclesiology of Vatican II gives the impression that Pneumatology is used *after* the structure of the Church is established with the help of Christology Cf. ch. III above.

[30]The connection between what we call here the "historical" approach and this type of Pneumatology can be illustrated by the issue of *Filioque*. It is interesting that both the East and the West admit the dependence of the Holy Spirit upon the Son on the level of *historical mission*. The differences arise only when the metahistorical or iconological approach to the divine mystery becomes predominent. The problem can be traced back to the fourth century: St Basil in his *De Spiritu Sancto* replaces the formula of the Alexandrian theologians "from the Father—through the Son—in the Spirit" with that of "The Father with the Son and with the Spirit" precisely because his argument is taken from the realm of worship and not from historical revelation. It is worth looking at the *Filioque* problem from the angle of the fate of the iconological approach to God—and to reality in general—in Western thought.

torical approach to continuity, the Holy Spirit vivifies *pre-existing* and *self-defined events* and relates them to different times and circumstances.

In the eschatological approach, however, things are again different. Here the Spirit is the one who brings the eschata into history.[31] He confronts the process of history with its consummation, with its transformation and transfiguration. By bringing the eschata into history, the Spirit does not vivify a pre-existing structure; He *creates* one; He changes linear historicity into a *presence*. It is no longer possible to understand history simply as "past," i.e. to apply to it the psychological and experiential notion of *anamnesis* in the sense of the retrospective faculty of the human soul. When the eschata visit us, the Church's *anamnesis* acquires the eucharistic paradox which no historical consciousness can ever comprehend, i.e. the *memory of the future,* as we find it in the anaphora of the Liturgy of St John Chrysostom: "Remembering the cross, the resurrection, the ascension *and the second coming,* Thine own of Thine own we offer Thee." Unless the Church lets Pneumatology so condition Christology that the sequence of "yesterday-today-tomorrow" is transcended, she will not do full justice to Pneumatology; she will enslave the Spirit in a linear *Heilsgeschichte.* Yet the Spirit is "the Lord" who transcends linear history and turns historical continuity into a presence.[32]

All this shows how profoundly all of theology ties up with the notion of apostolic continuity. In the historical approach the apostles are significant for the Church because they are connected with a crucial historical event of the past. In the eschatological approach the apostles unveil and present to us not the words of the kerygma of Christ but the reality and the content of the event of Christ. In the historical approach the apostles are the *creators* of history whereas in the eschatological approach they are the *judges* of history. Correspondingly, in the first case the Church is apostolic when

---

[31]Acts 2:17.
[32]A more detailed discussion of this appears in my "Die Pneumatologische Dimension der Kirche," *Internationale Katholische Zeitschrift* 2 (1973), 133-147.

she faithfully *transmits* the apostolic kerygma; in the second case she is apostolic when she *applies* it to a particular historical context and then *judges* this context in a prophetic way through the vision of the eschata which she is supposed to maintain. Therefore, if the Church is to be truly apostolic, she must be both historically and eschatologically oriented; she must both transmit history and judge history by placing it in the light of the eschata.

II. *Towards a Synthesis of the "Historical"*
and the "Eschatological" Approach

All that has been said thus far leads to the necessity of a theological synthesis between the historical and the eschatological approaches to the Church's continuity with the apostles. If one studies the history of theology in the West, one sees how problematic this synthesis has been. Individualistic and psychological notions of continuity have determined Western theology in various forms.[33] Thus whenever historical continuity was found to be problematic (e.g. when the problem of the quest for the historical Jesus arose), the alternative was a more or less Neoplatonic dismissal of history, a resort into the eschatology of the meaning of events.[34] In the East, on the other hand, the eschatological approach very often took the same form of the search for meaning at the expense of history,[35] while a satisfaction with the vision of the eschatological image of the Church as it is expressed in her worship

[33]This is particularly true with regard to the sacraments, the ministry (problem of "character") etc.

[34]E.g. R. Bultmann's school clearly has tended in this direction. The current problem of reconciling the "charismatic" with the "institutional" aspects of the Church illustrates this further.

[35]One can see this is the East as early as Origen. His emphasis on the eschatological meaning of the Gospel at the expense of the historical is well known. See e.g. *In Jo.* 1:24, 6:6 etc. Cf. G. Florovsky, "Origen, Eusebius and the Iconoclastic Controversy," *Church History* 19, (1950) 77-96. Origen's views on apostolic succession are deeply influenced by this approach: apostolic succession is essentially a continuity of the *teaching* of Christ (*De Princ.* 4:9; *In Luk.* 34 etc.), a succession of Gnostics in the Spirit (*De Orat.* 28:9, cf. *Comm. Rom.* 7:5) rather than a succession through

has tended to paralyze missionary activity to an alarming degree.[36] How can the synthesis be achieved?

Speaking as I do here from the viewpoint of Orthodox tradition, I see a possibility of synthesis along the following lines.

1. The event of Christ must be regarded as *constituted* pneumatologically. I stress the word "constituted" because my intention is to say that Christ is not Christ unless He is an existence in the Spirit, which means an *eschatological existence.* Such a pneumatological constitution of Christology implies, from the viewpoint of ontology, the understanding of Christ not in terms of individuality which affirms itself by distancing itself from other individualities, but in terms of personhood which implies a particularity established in and through *communion.*[37] The implications of this for the notion of continuity are clear. In a pneumatologically constituted Christology an event can never be defined by itself, but only as a relational reality. It is this that allows the Biblical notion of "corporate personality" to be applied to Christ:[38] *Christ without His body is not Christ but an individual of the worst type.* Our continuity, therefore, with the Christ event is not determined by sequence or response based on distance; it is rather a continuity in terms of *inclusiveness:* we are *in* Christ, and this is what makes Him be *before* us, our "first-born brother" in the Pauline sense.[39] This is paradoxical but fundamental

historical institutions. The tendency to stress the "charismatic" at the expense of the "institutional" continuity of the Church reappeared in Orthodoxy through various pietistic movements and tendencies in modern times.

[36]This must be admitted in spite of any historical reasons that may be offered as explanations.

[37]It is noteworthy that it is the function of the Holy Spirit to open up being so that it may become relational. Without Pneumatology, ontology becomes substantialistic and individualistic. The Spirit was understood as "communion" both by the Greek (e.g. St Basil) and the Latin (e.g. St Augustine) Fathers—especially by the latter. But the importance of Pneumatology for ontology has never been a decisive one in Western thought.

[38]On "corporate personality" cf. S. Pedersen, *Israel, Its Life and Culture* (1926); H. Wheeler Robinson, *The Hebrew Conception of Corporate Personality* (1936); A. R. Johnson, *The One and the Many in the Israelite Conception of God* (1942); J. de Fraine, *Adam et son lignage: Etudes sur la "personalité corporative" dans la Bible* (1959).

[39]Rom. 8:29; Col. 1:15-18 etc. In a linear type of "Heilsgeschichte"

for understanding the new existence created in Christ. Christ's priority over us[40] is not a priority like the one created by our individualized existence and characterised by temporal sequence; it is a priority of inclusiveness: the including one being prior to the included. This is so precisely because the included is already in the including. God as the Spirit, i.e. as communion, is precisely the all-embracing existence which is participated without participating.[41] In the same Spirit of God, Christ contains us in Himself, by His very constitution as Christ in the Spirit. He thus in the Spirit contains by definition the eschata, our final destiny, ourselves as we shall be; He is the eschatological Man—yet, let me repeat, not as an individual but as Church, i.e. because of our being included in Him. It is in this sense that historical existence becomes in Christ and in the Spirit a continuity which comes to us from the future and not through the channels of a divided time sequence like the one we experience in our fallen state of existence. Thus when the eschata enter into history in the Spirit, time is redeemed from fragmentation, and history acquires a different sense.

2. Obviously this affects the notion of apostolicity in a decisive way. If Christ Himself is the eschatological man and our continuity with Him is not determined by the time sequence which implies distance, but by a concept of time determined by an event of communion, the apostles themselves cannot be enclosed in a self-defined event, in a closed past. Their uniqueness is not to be defined in terms of individualized temporal existence, even if this existence graciously,

the "before" indicates *a part* of history—a period preceding another one—just as it happens with historical consciousness as it is known especially in modern times. But if the historical consciousness is decisively determined by eschatology, the "before" is comprehensible only in terms of the "last," the final. Such is the Pauline understanding of the "first-born": Christ is "before" us (our πρωτότοκος brother and our ἀρχηγὸς) precisely in His being the "last" (ἔσχατος) Adam (I Cor. 15:45), the realization and consummation of history. It is obvious that all this makes no sense in terms of linear "Heilsgeschichte."

[40]Eph. 1:3; Col. 1:16-18; II Thes. 2:13 etc.

[41]Cf. the notion of κοινωνία in the Greek Fathers as discussed by A. Houssiau, "Incarnation et communion selon les Pères grecs," *Irénikon* 45 (1972), 457-68.

as it were, gives us something of this event which it exclusively possesses. It has done a lot of damage to the notion of apostolicity to think of it in terms of historical prerogatives, be it in the form of the Petrine keys or in that of the apostolic kerygma. For the keys are those *of the Kingdom*,[42] and the kerygma is not an objectifiable norm but the Risen Christ, i.e. a living person; in both cases historical prerogatives are eschatologized. The apostles continue to speak and proclaim Christ in the Church only because the Church is by her very existence the living presence of the Word of God as person. Thus the Church, in listening to the word of the apostles, listens as it were to her own voice, to the voice which comes from her very eschatological nature, echoing her own eschatological destiny. This makes the history of the Church identical with that of the world and of creation as a whole. Thus to recall that the Church is founded on the apostles in an eschatological sense makes the Church acquire her ultimate existential significance as the sign of a redeemed and saved creation. This makes the Church, in the words of St Paul, "the judge of the world,"[43] i.e. makes her acquire a prerogative strictly applied to the apostles and especially to the Twelve in their eschatological function.

3.   If the Christ event and history in general are pneuma-

---

[42]The power to "bind and loose" which is given to St Peter (Matt. 16:18-19) is incomprehensible without eschatology, since the nature of this power is eschatological: it concerns eternal finality. If this eschatological nature of the power given to Peter in Matt. 16:18 is taken into consideration, granting of this power to all the Apostles in John 20:23 or even to the entire community in Matt. 18:18 does not lead to irreconcilable alternatives. The fact that the primitive Church could accept all of these three possibilities at once (two of them appear even in the same Gospel!) points to the fact that primitive eschatology implied inevitably the image of the *convoked* Church and of the apostolic *college* (cf. above n. 11). If this perspective is recovered, any application of this authority would require the context of the *convoked* Church. In fact there is good historical reason to believe that the early Church applied this power to "bind and loose" from the beginning precisely in and through her convocation in the eucharistic gatherings. (The evidence on this point is considerable. Cf. my article "The Development of Conciliar Structures to the Time of the First Ecumenical Council" in *Councils and the Ecumenical Movement* [= World Council Studies 5, 1968] pp. 34-51, esp. 34-39). Cf. below on the implications of this approach for the Petrine role in the Church, and esp. n 115.

[43]I Cor. 6:2. Cf. previous note.

tologically conditioned, the fears that may be created by such an identification of the Church with the Kingdom disappear. Such fears, which were to some extent behind the reaction of the Reformation against the medieval Church, are justified only if this identification is derived simply from what we have called here the historical approach to apostolicity (which seems to have been the approach of the medieval Church). But in a pneumatological conditioning of history by eschatology this identification does not present any dangers. The reason is that it takes place *epicletically*. The epicletic aspect of continuity represents a fundamental point in what I am trying to say here, and its implications must be stressed. In an epicletical context, history ceases to be in itself a guarantee for security. The *epiclesis* means ecclesiologically that the Church *asks to receive from God what she has already received historically in Christ as if she had not received it at all,* i.e. as if history did not count in itself. This includes her continuity with the apostles in all its forms. Just as in the eucharist the words of institution cannot be a guarantee in themselves without the Spirit, although what the Spirit does is nothing but prove true the words of Christ. "This is my body," i.e. affirm history, so in her apostolicity, too, the Church needs the Pentecostal scene to be set again and again, each time she wants to affirm her apostolicity. The apostles had received the Spirit from the risen Christ and were baptized in Him in the Pentecost and yet when they elected the seven[44] they invoked Him again.[45] Any one who thinks in terms of historical continuity must seriously ask the question: What meaning does this repeated invocation of the Spirit have, if the historical approach to apostolic continuity is purely and simply to be accepted? The epicletic life of the Church shows only one thing: That there is no security for her to be found in any historical guarantee as such—be it ministry or word or sacrament or even the historical Christ Himself. Her constant dependence on the Spirit proves that

[44]Acts 6:1-6.
[45]That every ordination—especially that of a bishop—requires the Pentecostal event as its context is indicated in Orthodox liturgical tradition by the fact that in every episcopal ordination the feast of Pentecost is celebrated.

her history is to be constantly eschatological. At the same time
the fact that the Spirit points to Christ shows equally well
that history is not to be denied. "The Spirit blows where He
wills,"[46] but we know that He wills to blow towards Christ.[47]
Eschatology and history are thus not incompatible with each
other.

4. The epicletic conditioning, therefore, of the Church's
continuity with the apostles points to the possibility of a synthesis of the historical with the eschatological notion of continuity in a way which overcomes any Neoplatonic form of
dualism. To be sure, there is a tension between the "already"
and the "not yet" also in the existence "in the Spirit." But
this tension is not dualistic in any sense that would imply an
incompatibility between time and eternity, history and eschatology in a Neoplatonic fashion. The incarnation of God in
Christ makes it possible to say against Neoplatonic dualism
that history is a real bearer of the ultimate, of the very life
of God. History as existence in space and time offers in Christ
the possibility for communion with the *eschata*. The tension
therefore between history and Kingdom is not one of ontological dualism. The way we can describe it is as longing for
a *change of form,* for transfiguration. In the expression of
St Paul, we are anxious to exchange the present form for the
eschatological one[48] not because the present one is less real
or less "ontological" in its nature—it is the very same body
we have now that will be resurrected, according to Paul—but
because the presence and activity of the Antichrist in history
makes the present form of the Church's existence fragile and
a cause of suffering.[49] The *arrabon* of the Kingdom which
is the presence of the Spirit[50] in history, signifies precisely the
synthesis of the historical with the eschatological. This *arrabon*
does not imply—as it is often presented by New Testament
theologians—the absence of the eschatological from the historical, i.e. a hope and an expectation on the basis of a word

[46]John 3:8.
[47]John 16:14.
[48]II Cor. 5:1-5. Cf. I Cor. 15:53-54.
[49]II Thes. 2:7-9; II Cor. 4:7 etc.
[50]II Cor. 1:22; 5:5; Eph. 1:14.

of promise. On the contrary, it signifies a real presence of the eschatological on the basis of the fact that God is present in the historical and risen Christ. The ecclesiological significance of this can be illustrated by the ideas of the book of the Apocalypse, in which the Church lives in an intense epicletic atmosphere containing a synthesis of two elements: on the one hand, the assurance of Christ's presence on the eucharistic table and, on the other, the Church's cry: "Come Lord, come."[51] When the Church lives epicletically, she cannot but long for what she already is. The synthesis of the historical with the eschatological in this epicletical conditioning of history constitutes what we may properly—and not in the distorted sense—call the *sacramental* nature of the Church.

5. This leads to a consideration of the practical question: How can the Church *in fact* unite the two approaches into one synthesis? Is there any way in the Church's life in which the synthesis of the historical with the eschatological approaches is realized?

The early Church seems to offer the answer to this question by pointing towards the *eucharist*. There is, indeed, no other experience in the Church's life in which the synthesis of the historical with the eschatological can be realized more fully than in the eucharist. The eucharist is, on the one hand, a "tradition" (παράδοσις)[52] and a "remembrance" (ἀνάμνησις).[53] As such it activates the historical consciousness of the Church in a retrospective way. At the same time, however, the eucharist is the eschatological moment of the Church *par excellence,* a remembrance of the Kingdom, as it sets the scene for the convocation of the dispersed people of God from the ends of the earth in one place,[54] uniting the "many" in

---

[51]Apoc. 4-5 and 22:17.
[52]I Cor. 11:23.
[53]Luke 22:19; I Cor. 11:24-25.
[54]*Didache* 9:4, 10:5. Cf. the description of the eucharist as a σύναξις ἐπὶ τὸ αὐτὸ by Paul and Ignatius (cf. n. 11 above). It is also noteworthy that the celebration of the eucharist came to be associated very early with Sunday (Apoc. 1:10; on the evidence of the early sources see W. Rordorf, *Sunday: The History of the Day of Rest and Worship in the Earliest Centuries of the Christian Church* [1968] pp. 177ff. and 238ff.). The significance of the celebration of the eucharist on Sunday lies in the fact that Sunday is the eschatological day *par excellence.* If the eucharist was

the "one"[55] and offering the taste of the eternal life of God here and now.[56] In and through the same experience, therefore, *at one and the same moment,* the Church unites in the eucharist the two dimensions, past and future, simultaneously as one indivisible reality. This happens "sacramentally," i.e. in and through historical and material forms, while the existential tension between the "already" and the "not yet" is preserved.[57] In the consciousness of the ancient Church this is further emphasized through the use of the epiclesis in the eucharist: the "words of institution" and the entire anamnetic dimension of the Church are placed at the disposal of the Spirit, as if they could not constitute in themselves a sufficient assurance of God's presence in history. This makes the eucharist the moment in which the Church realizes that her roots are to be found *simultaneously* in the past and in the future, in history and in the eschata.

The result of the recognition of this unique function of the eucharist in the Early Church was to make the eucharist the milieu and the context in which the basic concrete manifestation of apostolic continuity would take place.[58] This centrality of the eucharist has been preserved in the liturgical and canonical tradition of the Orthodox Churches, but Orthodox theology has very often disregarded it, thus making the synthesis between "historical" and "eschatological" problematic.

---

to be understood primarily as an anamnesis in historical terms, the natural day of its celebration would be the day of its institution before the crucifixion, and not the day of the resurrection.

[55]I Cor. 10:16-17; Mark 14:24 and parallels. For the ecclesiological implications of this idea cf. chapter 4 above: "Eucharist and Catholicity."

[56]See especially the Fourth Gospel (6:27-51) and Ignatius (*Eph.* 20:2; *Magn.* 6:2 etc.). On Ignatius see J. Romanides, *The Ecclesiology of St Ignatius of Antioch,* (1956).

[57]Cf. above n. 51.

[58]I Cor. 14 shows that already in the first apostolic communities the eucharistic gatherings were the context of charismatic manifestations. The liturgical evidence of the early Church, since Hippolytus, shows that ordination into the ministry ought to be placed in the same context.

III. *Concrete Consequences for the Life of the Church*

With these observations in mind we may now look at some
concrete implications of this synthesis for the life and structure of the Church. The relation of the Church to the apostles
has traditionally included the following main elements:

1. *Continuity through the apostolic kerygma.*[59] The kerygmatic nature of the apostolic function can be understood in
both historical and eschatological terms, but it is the synthesis
of these two "in the Spirit" that offers the theological perspective for the application of the notion of continuity to the
apostolic kerygma. In the New Testament itself we can find
an idea of *paradosis* or *logia* which are historically transmitted
from place to place and time to time. And yet, it is the Spirit
that vivifies the words,[60] and it is only in the Spirit that the
kerygma of Christ can make sense.[61] The apostolic kerygma
needs to be constantly placed in the Spirit in order to be life
and not just words. It cannot be an objectified norm in itself,
something that judges the community of the Church from
above or from outside.[62] It is in the context of the *koinonia*
of the Spirit, which implies the concrete continuity of the
Church, that the kerygma of the apostles can be "continued"
in a living way.

In the course of the second century and mainly through St
Irenaeus and his defence against Gnosticism, the apostolic
kerygma, as Irenaeus approaches it in his *Epideixis,* implies
some kind of objectification in the sense of an historically
transmitted norm.[63] Thus this historical approach to apostolic
continuity threatens in a way to overcome the eschatological

[59]The term *kerygma* is used here in the broad sense which includes both
the act of proclamation of important news to the public (original sense;
cf. Luke 12:3; Acts 10:42; Col. 1:23; I Tim. 3:16; Apoc. 5:2) and the
content of the *kerygma,* the *didache,* together with its interpretation through
doctrine, dogma, etc., as it came to be understood especially from the second
century onwards with Irenaeus' *Epideixis.*

[60]John 6:63. Cf. Rom. 2:29.

[61]I Cor. 12:3.

[62]Cf. Y. Congar, *Ministères et Communion ecclésiale* (1971), p. 90.

[63]Apart from Irenaeus' *Epideixis* as a whole, see his *Haer.* III 3:1; IV
26:2; 38:8 etc.

one. This danger, however, is overcome in Irenaeus' theology thanks to two factors which survive so strongly in his theology: Pneumatology and the centrality of the eucharist. The Church is to be found only where the Spirit is[64] and the apostolic tradition comes to the Church not just through history but as a *charisma*.[65] At the same time, true and orthodox doctrine is to be synthesized with the eucharist: "our doctrine agrees with the eucharist and our eucharist with our doctrine."[66] This synthesis safeguarded the apostolic kerygma from objectification in its transmission through history.

Although the needs of the Church at that time made it imperative to objectify, in a certain sense, the word of God, to create the Scriptural canon, etc.,[67] and thus strengthen the historical approach to the idea of apostolic continuity, the eschatological perspective was not lost. But how could the eschatological perspective be preserved under such circumstances?

In the first place, already in the theology of the Greek Fathers, especially St Athanasius and St Cyril of Alexandria, the idea of the Logos of God as person qualified decisively the idea of the Logos of God as word—spoken or written.[68] In a eucharistic approach to this idea, which characterized both of these Fathers and the Church of that time as a whole,[69] this meant that the spoken or written word of God,

[64]Irenaeus, *Haer.* III 24:1.

[65]*Ibid.* IV 26:2.

[66]*Ibid.* IV 18:5.

[67]Cf. A. Benoît, "L'apostolicité au IIe siècle," *Verbum Caro* 58 (1961), 173-84.

[68]The problems which the use of the term *logos* as "word" for Christ created in the early Church show how dangerous the application to Christology of the notion of the "word" as spoken or written can be. As a reaction against Sabellianism and Arianism, the Fathers were forced to deny entirely any association of these two senses of *logos* and thus replace definitely the connotation of spoken or written word with that of *person* exclusively. See e.g. Eusebius, *Dem. evang.* 5:5 and especially Athanasius *Contra Ar.* 2:35 and Cyril of Alexandria, *De recta fide ad Theod.* 6. The symbol of Sirmium (351) even anathematizes those who call the *logos* of God ἐνδιάθετος or προφορικός.

[69]It is interesting to note how the Christological controversies of the early Church related to the eucharist. See e.g. H. Chadwick, "Eucharist and Christology in the Nestorian Controversy," *Journal of Theological Studies* 2 (1951), 145-64.

as it is historically formulated and transmitted, becomes life and divine presence only in the context of the eschatological community of the eucharist. By developing the "liturgy of the word" as an integral part of the eucharistic liturgy, the Church did nothing but eschatologize the historical, i.e. make the apostolic kerygma come to the Church not simply from the side of the past but simultaneously from the side of the future.[70] Only when the preached word becomes identical with the eucharistic flesh does the synthesis of the historical with the eschatological continuity of the kerygma take place. Then the Johannine mentality of the "word made flesh" unites with the Irenaean view that orthodox doctrine and eucharist form an indivisible unity.

Orthodox theology has not fully drawn its conclusions from this. There is a prevailing view among the so-called "conservative" Orthodox theologians that the doctrines of the Church constitute something "untouchable." This turns dogmas into petrified relics from the past and widens the chasm between the historical and the eschatological perspectives of the continuity of the apostolic kerygma. A study of the early Church and an appreciation of the eucharistic basis of doctrine, however, show that it is better to understand dogmas as doxological statements of the community,[71] as the "faith transmitted *to the saints*,"[72] constantly received and re-received by the consciousness of "the community of the saints" in new

[70]In the Orthodox Liturgy this is indicated by the fact that the readings from the Bible are placed in the doxological context of the *Trisagion* which is sung before them. This is clearly meant to indicate that the word of God comes to the Church not simply from the past as a book and a fixed canon, but mainly from the eschatological reality of the Kingdom, from the throne of God which is at that moment of the Liturgy occupied by the bishop. This is why the reading is traditionally *sung* and not just read didactically. (Some Orthodox priests today, apparently not realizing this, do not sing the Gospel readings but read them like prose in order to make them more understandable and thus edifying!)

[71]E. Schlink, *Der kommende Christus und die kirchliche Traditionen* (1961) has worked out a remarkable appreciation of the doxological nature of doctrine. The contrast between the "kerygmatic" and the "doxological" kinds of theological statements, which is found in this book, points precisely to the necessity of a synthesis between the "historical" and the "eschatological" approaches to apostolic continuity.

[72]Jude 3.

forms of experience and with a constant openness to the
future.

2. *Continuity through the apostolic ministry.* Perhaps no
other aspect of apostolic continuity has suffered so much from
the lack of the synthesis we are discussing here, as that of
continuity through the ministry. Already in *I Clement*[73] the
missionary or historical scheme of continuity implies the
idea of apostolic succession through an instituted ministry.
Irenaeus once more makes the ministry a norm of some kind
for the Church's continuity with the apostles.[74]

(a) The question that this raises in the first place is the
more general one concerning the place that any form of
ministry may have in a proper synthesis of the historical with
the eschatological perspective of continuity. The most serious
problem which the absence of such a synthesis creates is
whether any ministry is necessary at all for apostolic continuity, i.e. whether in fact the eschatological and the historical aspects of continuity are not finally irreconcilable. The
dilemma: "institutional" versus "charismatic" which is so
widespread today is a genuine product of the lack of such a
synthesis.

One of the greatest and historically most inexplicable mis-
fortunes for the Church came when, I do not know how, the
most charismatic of all acts, namely ordination into the ministry, came to be regarded as a non- or even anti-charismatic
notion. One can suspect on this point a hidden interference
of Neoplatonism in Christian theology, perhaps quite early
in history.[75] But the historical question does not concern us
directly here. The point I wish to make is this: If ordination
is a charismatic event, then it must take place in an eschatological context. It is not enough to think of ordination as an
historical transmission of apostolicity. Ordination must also
be a movement coming from the side of the eschatological

[73]See above n. 17 and 18.
[74]Irenaeus, *Haer.* III 3:1-4; IV 26:2. Also Tertullian, *De Praescr.* 32 and
Hippolytus, *Philos.* 1, *proem.*
[75]This is, for example, noticeable in Origen's distinction between the actual
fact and its meaning, which leads to a contrast between charisma and ministry
—a consequence which is already present in Origen's thought, as his views on
apostolic succession show. See above n. 35.

finality, from the convoked and not just from the dispersed people of God. Hence all ordinations would have to take place in an epicletic context and, more than that, in the context of the community of the Church gathered ἐπὶ τὸ αὐτὸ, with the apostles not as individual originators of ministry but as a presiding college. It is for this reason that not only all charismatic manifestations in the primitive Pauline Churches took place during the eucharistic gatherings,[76] but also, as is implied in the *Didache*[77] and clearly evidenced by Hippolytus' *Apostolic Tradition*,[78] ordination to the ministry in the early Church took place in the same context. The significance of placing ordination in the eucharistic context lies in that in this way the so-called "institutional" does not constitute a self-defined norm. If the epiclesis of the Spirit is constantly required in the context of the eschatological community for ordination, it follows that it is not the institution as such that signifies and actualizes the continuity with the apostles. The fact that each ordination has to take place within the eucharistic context—and not in the private study of a bishop—shows clearly that the historical or institutional continuity must be conditioned by the eschatological community gathered together. This implies that in fact all the orders of the Church are partakers of the apostolic continuity which is realized through an act of ordination. Whereas the historical scheme of continuity can lead to a sacramentalism in ordination by limiting apostolic continuity to the so-called ordained ministry, the eschatological approach leads to the conclusion that, for apostolic continuity to take place, the order of the baptized layman is indispensable. The Church, therefore, relates to the apostles not only through ordination but also through baptism.[79]

[76]See I Cor. 14.

[77]*Didache* 15 (on ordination) is joined with 14 (on the Sunday eucharist) with the word "therefore."

[78]Hippolytus, *Apost. Trad.* 2.

[79]Cf. B.-D. Dupuy, *op. cit.* p. 348: "C'est le peuple fidèle en son entier qui porte conjointement avec les ministres la succession apostolique." It is usually forgotten that baptism itself is an ordination in that it comprises two elements: (a) laying on of hands with invocation of the Spirit (hence confirmation is inseparable from baptism), and (b) assignment to a particular *ordo* (τάγμα or τάξις in Greek) in the Church. On the latter—which is

(b) With these remarks in mind we may now consider
the meaning that episcopal apostolic succession can have for
Orthodox theology. In the case of what we have called here
an historical approach to continuity, the bishop can be singled
out from the Church as an individual possessing the plenitude
of apostolicity which he then transmits to others through
ordination. Thus one can talk of an "essential" ministry from
which the rest of the ministry is derived. It is interesting that
when a group of Anglican theologians published such a thesis
some years ago,[80] the idea which was found suitable to support this thesis (from the New Testament) was that of apostolicity in terms of *shaliach*. This supports further my argument that the missionary scheme leads to an individualization
of the apostolate. As A. Ehrhardt[81] has argued, however, the
shaliach idea is of no value for the purpose of establishing
episcopal succession in the early Church. Instead, he puts
forth the thesis that the first episcopal lists were inspired by
the lists of Jewish highpriests and notes that Eusebius' lists of
succession begin not with a particular apostle but with *James*.[82]
If this thesis is accepted, the indication is clear that what we
have called here the eschatological model of the Jerusalem
Church structure has been decisive in the rise of episcopal
apostolic succession. We can describe then episcopal succession as a continuity of the Church not with an individual
apostle but with the apostolic college as a whole[83] and the

usually overlooked under the influence of Tertullian and later Latin writers—
see, for example, *I Clement* 40:3-41 where *tagma* applies also to the laity.
A fuller discussion appears in my "Some Reflections on Baptism, Confirmation and Eucharist," *Sobornost* 5 (1969), 644-52.

[80]K. E. Kirk, ed., *The Apostolic Ministry: Essays on the History and the
Doctrine of Episcopacy* (1946, second edit. 1957).

[81]A. Ehrhardt, *The Apostolic Succession in the First Two Centuries of the
Church* (1953).

[82]*Ibid.* pp. 35-61.

[83]Cf. F. Dvornik, *The Idea of Apostolicity in Byzantium and the Legend
of St. Andrew* (1958), pp. 39f. Cf. Y. Congar, *L'Eglise une, sainte, catholique
et apostolique* (Mysterium Salutis 15, 1970), p. 196. N. Afanasiev, in spite
of his eucharistic ecclesiology, failed to appreciate the indivisibility of the
apostolic college in succession and put forth the view which is incompatible
with the eschatological image of the Church that "l'évêque devient par son
Eglise, le successeur de tel on tel apôtre, et non pas des apôtres en général,"
in "Réflexions d'un Orthodoxe sur la collégialité des évêques," *Le Messager
Orthodoxe* (1965), 7-15.

community of the Church in its eschatological setting.[84]

Now, if in addition to Ehrhardt's argument we take into account other pieces of evidence from the early Church, we may illustrate this thesis even further.

In spite of the obscurity which surrounds the origins and early development of the episcopal office, it seems possible to discern two different ways of understanding the bishop's function at that time. On the one hand he was understood as a "co-presbyter," i.e. as one—presumably the first one—of the college of the presbyterium.[85] On the other hand he was looked upon as the type of James the brother of Christ,[86] i.e. as the image of Christ—an idea found in Ignatius and other documents of that time.[87] This resulted naturally into the double image we encounter for the first time clearly in Hippolytus: the bishop as *alter Christus* and *alter apostolus.*

It is worthwhile stopping for a moment at the evidence of Hippolytus, for, in my view, he seems to be the first one to offer a synthesis of the images of episcopate which I have just mentioned. This Hippolytan synthesis acquires special importance for our subject, as it seems to correspond to the synthesis of the historical and the eschatological perspectives

[84]The performance of every episcopal ordination within the context of the Pentecostal event (cf. above n. 45) implies the existence of the eschatological community here and now with the Twelve as its head. Cf. Acts 1-2 where the Pentecostal event is related to both of these elements (2:17: eschatological event; 1:13-23: the indivisible college of the Twelve) and finally the eucharist (3:42).

[85]This is clearly indicated by the use of the term *presbyters* for the bishop by Irenaeus (*Haer.* IV 26:2). This should be taken as a survival of an old usage in the West, as it can be inferred from *I Clement* 44, I Peter 5:1, etc.

[86]This is the case in the early succession lists as they appear in the canon of Eusebius-Jerome. See A. Ehrhardt, *op. cit.,* pp. 35ff.

[87]See above n. 21. The way I interpret and classify the historical evidence with regard to the eschatological image of succession implies the following scheme: "James with the presbyters" (Acts) = "Christ with the presbyters" (Apocalypse) = "bishop (image of Christ) with the presbyters" (Ignatius, *Didascalia, Constitutiones* etc.) = "bishop as successor of James" (Eusebius-Jerome succession lists). Obviously this article is not the place for a detailed demonstration of this (this appears in another forthcoming publication). It suffices to show here that the eschatological model of the Jerusalem Church was transferred to the eucharistic structure of each local Church and influenced decisively the idea of apostolic continuity. It is most unfortunate that the classical notion of apostolic succession has been formed without taking this development into account.

of apostolic continuity. An analysis of the views of episcopacy implied in the *Apostolic Tradition* leads to the following observations:

(i)   The bishop is simultaneously the image of Christ and the image of the apostles.[88] This combination of the two images is decisive for the history of the concept of apostolic succession in terms of the synthesis between the historical and the eschatological perspectives.

(ii)   The presbyterium is understood as a *college* and is related to the functions of counseling and governing.[89] This means that the christological image is reserved for the bishop, who alone like Christ can *give* the ministry,[90] while the presbyters surround and accompany him in this "giving."[91] The implication of this is that apostolic continuity is realized through the bishop, not as an individual, but in his being surrounded by the college of the presbyterium. This is a way of preserving the balance between the *alter Christus* and the *alter apostolus* images of episcopacy.

(iii)   Furthermore, all this presupposes the convocation of the entire community ἐπὶ τὸ αὐτὸ for all the functions of episcopacy (e.g. ordination) which relate to the continuation of the apostolic ministry.[92] The context must be that of the synthesis between history and eschatology provided by the eucharist. It is for this reason that the eucharist is the indispensible context of ordination.

The conclusion which emerges from this Hippolytan syn-

[88]Hippolytus, *Apost. Trad.* 3 (prayer for the ordination of a bishop).
[89]*Ibid.* 8 (prayer for the ordination of a presbyter).
[90]Such is the argument of Hippolytus concerning the laying on of hands by the presbyters on the candidate for ordination into the order of the presbyters: "Presbyter enim solius habet potestatem ut accipiat, *dare autem non habet potestatem.* Quapropter clerum non ordinat; super presbyteri vero ordinatione consignat episcopo ordinante" (*ibid.* 9; text in B. Botte, *Hippolyte de Rome, La Tradition Apostolique* [= Sources chrétiennes 11, 1946] p. 40).
[91]Cf. the problem concerning the blessing of the eucharist by the presbyters in the same text, and Botte's interpretation (*ibid.*, p. 30), to which N. Afanasiev (*Trapeza Gospodnia* [1952], p. 3) objects by referring to Hippolytus' argument quoted in the previous note.
[92]This is indicated by the provision of the *Apost. Trad.* that the ordination should take place during the eucharistic gathering. Cf. the acclamation *"axios"* in the Orthodox services of ordination. For an early source of this practice see *I Clem.* 45:3.

thesis is to be noted and underlined most emphatically. *Apostolic succession through episcopacy is essentially a succession of Church structure.* The concrete implications of this are clear: in adhering to episcopal succession the Church does not isolate episcopacy from the rest of the Church orders (including the laity) but, on the contrary, she makes it absolutely dependent on them, just as they are absolutely dependent on it. It is a false idea of succession to break down this interdependence of orders, for without the complete structure of the community the eschatological perspective, i.e. the convocation of the dispersed people of God, disappears entirely. We are then left with the purely historical approach to continuity accompanied with notions of sacramentalism, juridical *potestas* and all the problems they entail. In a full synthesis of the historical with the eschatological perspectives, episopal succession becomes indispensible only because through it, it becomes clear that it is the entire community of the Church that embodies apostolic continuity.

That the bishop is to be understood as part of the structure of the community and not as an individual is to be seen in the way his ordination and power of jurisdiction are conditioned liturgically and canonically up to now, at least in the East. Thus: (i) no bishop can be ordained without reference to the name of his community *in the very prayer of ordination.*[93] This applies today even to the ordination of titular bishops.[94] This is especially significant for the East,

[93]For the sources see "L'évêque d'après les prières d'ordination," in *L'Episcopat et l'Eglise universelle* (above n. 21), pp. 739-780. The prohibition of ordinations in *absoluto* (canon 15 of I Nicaea; canon 6 of Chalcedon etc.) is related to the same principle.

[94]The existence of titular bishops in the Orthodox Churches points to a grave anomaly. If a bishop is ordained for a certain community, he must be free to exercise fully his ministry in this community. Only if he is separated from his flock because of historical circumstances can he be regarded as a canonical bishop in spite of his absence from his community. But the ordination of bishops with the intention of using them as bishops with a dependent authority (assistant bishops etc.) is a violation of basic ecclesiological principles under the influence of a false notion of sacramentalism as a transmission of episcopacy from one individual to another. Cf. the problem of *episcopi vagantes*. See Y. Congar, *L'Eglise une . . .*, p. 205f.: *"Ce que la succession apostolique n'est pas"* and the strong but justifiable remarks of C. Vogel, "An Alienated Liturgy," *Concilium* 28 (Feb. 1972), 11-25, esp. p. 18f.

which has never understood the power of jurisdiction as being independent of the prayer of ordination.[95] (ii) This is underlined by a significant canonical provision surviving up to today in the East, although without consciousness of its meaning, namely that only bishops who are heads of actual communities can participate in a council. It is evident from this that the *charisma veritatis* of the bishop is not an individual possession transmitted through ordination but is tied up with the entire community.[96] In episcopal succession, therefore, we have essentially succession of communities. All this helps us answer the historical question which is full of important implications for ecclesiology: Why did the Church choose the bishop as the instrument of apostolic succession? Why were there, for example, no lists of presbyteral successions? If the concern of the Church was historically to transmit the apostolic doctrine, the natural thing would have been to see this transmission through the presbyters, who were in fact charged precisely with the task of teaching the faith at that time.[97] Indeed, every form of historical transmission of apostolic functions could be realized through other ministries outside the bishop.[98] It is only when apostolic continuity is understood as a continuity of *structure* and as a succession of *communities* that the episcopal character of apostolic succession acquires its uniqueness. But the element of "structure" and "community" emerges only when the eschatological perspective, as we have described it here, influences our understanding of apostolic continuity in a decisive way.

[95]See below at n. 110.

[96]Cf. the remarkable work of V. Fuchs, *Der Ordinationstitel von seiner Entstehung bis auf Innozenz III* (1930), *passim*, esp. pp. 61ff.

[97]The evidence is abundant, although usually unnoticed by historians. E.g. *Shepherd of Hermas*, Vis. 3:4; Tertullian, *De Praescr.* 2; Origen, *In Ezekiel* 2:2 and Hippolytus, *Apost. Trad.* 8 (as reconstructed by G. Dix, *The Treatise on the Apostolic Tradition of Saint Hippolytus of Rome* [1937], p. 13). This is further supported by the existence of famous presbyters known as teachers (Clement of Alexandria, Origen etc.). For further evidence and a detailed discussion cf. my book *The Unity . . .* pp. 160f. All this shows that the Church of the first centuries did not understand apostolic succession as a succession of teaching. She in fact detested the idea that the Church could be conceived as a "school." See Hippolytus, *Philos.* 9:12:21.

[98]Why not, for example, recognize a succession of charismata etc? This question is posed especially today.

(c)   If we arrive at the importance of the episcopal succession via the idea of continuity of *structure*, we can appreciate the traditional assignment to the bishop of the role of the sole ordainer.[99] Because of his place in the structure of the community, especially in its eucharistic form, the bishop is the one through whom all charismatic manifestations of the Church must pass, so that they may be manifestations not of individualism but of the *koinonia* of the Spirit and of the community created by it. Extraordinary or (as they are called today) "charismatic" ministries have their place in the Church and must be encouraged. But it is only if they are parts of the structure of the community that they are not in danger of becoming the kind of individualistic manifestations which St Paul fought so vigorously in Corinth. All these extraordinary ministries, therefore, become integral parts of the apostolic continuity in the synthesis I am expounding here, if they go through the bishop, in whom the entire structure converges and the "many" become "one" in a particular existential milieu.

(d)   We can now consider the question of the Church's relation with the apostles on another level, broader than that of the local community. One of the natural consequences of the historical approach to apostolic continuity is that through it the *founding of churches* acquires special significance. This, as we have noticed, forms an integral part of the theory of continuity elaborated by *I Clement* and is tied up with the idea of mission and of transmission of the apostolic kerygma. This leads naturally to the importance of the Churches which can claim apostolic foundation and origin. If an apostle preached or even died in a particular Church, this Church could claim special authority with regard to apostolic continuity.

The argument of the special authority of apostolic sees was used very frequently in the course of the second century[100]

---

[99]See Hippolytus (n. 90 above). Even after the bishop lost his exclusive right to offer the eucharist (on this right see Hippolytus, *Apost. Trad.* 3 cf. 8), his exclusive right to ordain was not questioned. E.g. Jerome, *Ep.* 146 (PL 22: 1194) and John Chrysostom, *In I Tim.* 11 (PG 62: 553).

[100]E.g. Tertullian, *De Praescr.* 20:4-7, 9; 32; 36:1; *Scorp.* 9; Irenaeus, *Haer.* I 10:1-2 etc.

and afterwards.[101] The point that interests us here is that this argument can make sense only if the apostles are understood as individuals, dispersed in the world as missionaries—which is precisely what the historical approach is about, as I have expounded it here.[102] But what happens when the eschatological perspective enters into the picture and the apostles are understood as a college surrounding Christ?

The first theologian I know of who altered decisively the Ignatian scheme as well as the Hippolytan synthesis so as to respond to this problem seems to have been St Cyprian. With Cyprian the eschatological image of the apostolic college surrounding Christ—an image which was applied to the structure of the local Church by Ignatius and Hippolytus (the bishop surrounded by the presbyterium)—is changed to become an image of the apostolic college surrounding its head, *St Peter.* Thus for him each episcopal throne is not, as it is for Ignatius, the "place of God" or Christ, but the *cathedra Petri.*[103] The significance of this alteration is that we can now talk of *unus episcopatus* dispersed over the earth with Peter as its head.[104] This leads to the concept of episcopal collegiality, as it has been expounded today in Roman Catholic theology.

The implications of this Cyprianic view are so important that they require serious reflection. How could this view be understood in a synthesis of the historical with the eschatological perspectives of apostolic continuity?

In the first place it must be noted that for St Cyprian *each* episcopal throne is a *cathedra Petri.*[105] This is significant because it implies that the Ignatian view of the indivisibility of the apostolic college in its eschatological nature, as it is manifested in the eucharist, is preserved fully for each episcopal Church.[106] It is, therefore, wrong to read universalistic ideas

[101]E.g. Augustine, *Ep.* 232:3 (PL 33: 1028) etc. Cf. F. Dvornik, *op. cit.*
[102]Thus Tertullian thinks consistently in terms of the missionary—historical approach: *De Praescr.* 21:4; 37:1 etc. In such an approach certain sees become "models" for the others. Thus, with regard to Rome, Y. Congar, *Ministères* . . . p. 98f.
[103]Cyprian, *Ep* 69(66):5; 43(40):5; *De unit.* 4.
[104]*Ibid., De unit.* 5.
[105]See n. 103 above.
[106]This implies also the principle that each bishop is independent and

into the ecclesiology of Cyprian.[107] There are, however, two basic elements in this view which decisively affect the synthesis we are concerned with here. In the first place this view leads to the disappearance of the Christological image of episcopacy. Thus it leads away from both Ignatius and Hippolytus. The bishop becomes *alter apostolus*[108] (Peter) but not *alter Christus*.[109] In the second place, and as a consequence of this, the structure of the local Church ceases to reflect the Kingdom of God with Christ surrounded by the apostles. The eschatological perspective, therefore, is in danger of disappearing from ecclesiology. We are getting very near to an idea of apostolic succession understood in strictly historical terms and regardless of the eschatological structure of the community.

Nevertheless, if we wish to do justice to the intention of St Cyprian, we must make sure at least that in understanding the bishop as *alter Petrus* we do not dissolve the apostolic college. This means that we must take seriously his application of the image of the apostolic college in its entirety to each episcopal Church. This would preserve an essential part of the eschatological image of apostolicity in the Church structure. In speaking, therefore, of *unus episcopatus* we should not speak of *a structure outside or above or independent of the concrete community* to which each bishop is attached through ordination.

This leads us to a point which is essential to the Orthodox view of apostolic continuity through the episcopal college. For Orthodox theology—or rather for Orthodox tradition—the decisive link between the apostolic college and the episcopal college lies, structurally speaking, in the *ordination* of the bishop.[110] There is a double conditioning of each episcopal

directly responsible to God for his community. Thus Cyprian, *Ep.* 55 (52): 21. For a discussion of the implications of this principle see E. Lanne, "Pluralisme et Unité," *Istina* 14 (1969), 178f.

[107]As it was done, for example, by N. Afanasiev, "La doctrine de la primauté à la lumière de l'ecclésiologie," *Istina* 2 (1957), 401-20.

[108]*Ep.* 3:3 (Hartel, 471): "apostolus, id est episcopus."

[109]This seems to me to be a *crucial* moment in the history of the concept of apostolic succession and of episcopacy in general. It is at *this* point that I suggest that we should begin our reconsideration of these concepts.

[110]The roots of the synodal institution are to be found precisely in the *ordination* of each bishop. Hence *every* bishop (with a community) has

ordination which is significant in this respect: on the one
hand, as I have already said, the bishop is attached to a
particular community; on the other hand, he is ordained by
at least two other bishops.[111] He is thus linked simultaneously
with the apostolic college as it is expressed in his own Church
and in other Churches. This simultaneity of the two dimensions, local and universal,[112] protects the idea of apostolic
college from a historization which would make impossible
the "theophanic" revelation and existential realization of the
eschatological structure of the Church in each local eucharistic community.

The Petrine role, therefore, in apostolic succession through
episcopacy is not irrelevant to, but can be integrated in the
synthesis which I am expounding here. This would require a
theological appreciation of the proper relation between the
apostolic college in its local and in its universal manifestations. Such a realtion can only be one of *identity*, so that
neither of these manifestations may have priority over the
other.[113] This would, I think, do justice to the intention of

the right to participate in the synodical activity of the Church by virtue of
his ordination. The practice which has prevailed in some Orthodox Churches
in modern times to be governed by "permanent synods" based on a selection
of certain bishops and the exclusion of others constitutes a direct violation
of this important ecclesiological principle.

[111]Hippolytus, *Apost. Trad.* 2; Council of Arles c. 20; I Nicaea cc. 4
and 6 etc. For a full discussion of the sources see L. Mortari, *Consacrazione
episcopale e Collegialitá. La testimonianza della Chiesa antica* (1969).

[112]J. Meyendorff, *Orthodoxie et Catholicité* (1965), p. 147, and other
Orthodox theologians tend to give priority to the bishop's place in his own
local Church and make this the basis for episcopal collegiality on a broader
level. I think this approach, although aiming at emphasizing the right point
that the bishop should be related to a particular Church, helps perpetuate the
false dilemma "local versus universal"—a dilemma transcended by the very
nature of the Eucharist (cf. chapter 4 above). Only through a *simultaneity*
of these two dimensions—a simultaneity inherent in episcopal ordination itself
—can we arrive at the proper perspective. Cf. next note.

[113]In Roman Catholic theology the tendency has often been to give priority
to the bishop's attachment to the universal college over his attachment to a
particular local Church. Thus, for example, earlier A. Gréa, *L'Eglise et sa
divine constitution* (1884, re-ed. 1965) and more recently E. Schillebeeckx,
L'Eglise du Christ et l'homme d'aujourd'hui selon Vatican II (1965), pp.
99ff.; J. Colson, *Les fonctions ecclésiales* (1956), p. 341; K. Rahner, "De
l'épiscopat" in *Eglises chrétiennes et Episcopat* (1966), p. 209 etc. H. de
Lubac, *Les églises particulières dans l'Eglise universelle* (1971), p. 82, regards

St Cyprian and in spite of the defects of the Cyprianic view itself[114] may offer significant ecumenical possibilities today.[115]

One of the points that become clear in any case, when we place the universal dimensions of apostolic continuity in the light of the synthesis I am expounding here, is that we cannot argue from the standpoint of *special apostolic sees* without destroying this synthesis. Special apostolic character can and must be recognized in all those Churches which happen to have historical links with one or more of the great apostles. But this is not to be confused with the deeper and fundamental notion of apostolic continuity which passes through the very nature and structure of each Church and relates not just to the historical but also to the eschatological perspective of apostolic continuity. In the Orthodox Churches such sees have been honored and given primacy (e.g. as patriarchates and otherwise), but they have never been distinguished from the rest of the episcopal sees from the point of view of the essential apostolic continuity in which both the historical and the

the question as open. However other Roman Catholic theologians insist that the priority of the universal college over the local Church is to be rejected and replaced by a synthesis of the two. Thus, H.-M. Legrand, "Nature de l'Eglise particulière et rôle de l'évêque dans l'Eglise," in *La Charge pastoral des évêques . . . Décret "Christus Dominus"* (1969), pp. 118f. and especially Y. Congar, *Ministères . . .,* pp. 123-140. Needless to say, the question is of great importance to the Orthodox. Cf. E. Lanne, "To What Extent is Roman Primacy unacceptable to the Eastern Church?" *Concilium* 47 (April 1971), 62-67, esp. p. 66.

[114]The main defect, in my view, is that the christological discussion of episcopacy (cf. Ignatius, Hippolytus etc.) disappears and is replaced by an apostolic college from which, in fact, Christ is absent. This not only destroys the view of the Church as the image of the Kingdom—a view so essential to both eucharist and eschatology—but it also leads to the search for a "vicarius Christi" outside or above the apostolic—and the episcopal—college. On the problems that this has created in medieval ecclesiology see Y. Congar, *Ministères . . .,* pp. 112f.

[115]Cf. J.-J. von Allmen, "L'Eglise locale parmi les autres Eglises locales," *Irénikon* 43 (1970), 512-37. I should like to note especially his observation (p. 529f.) that the words of Christ to Peter concerning his particular task in the Church are situated in Luke—and perhaps in the rest of the Gospels— in the context of the Last Supper. This point has many important implications for placing the Petrine task in a perspective similar to the one of the present study and perhaps making it ultimately acceptable to those who hold a eucharistic as well as a historical approach to the continuity of the Church. But this requires further elaboration.

eschatological perspectives merge into a synthesis.[116] This observation may serve to illustrate further how deeply this synthesis is rooted in the consciousness of the Orthodox Church.

IV. *Conclusions for the Ecumenical Debate*

The classical concept of apostolic succession has been formed in an one-sided way. It has virtually ignored the fundamental Biblical image of the apostles as an indivisible college surrounding Christ in His Kingdom. As a consequence of this, it has ignored entirely a long tradition, well established in the early Church, especially in Syria and Palestine (Ignatius of Antioch, *Didascalia, Apostolic Constitutions,* Eusebius' succession lists, etc.), which applied this image of the apostolate to the notion of apostolic continuity.

As a result of this, the classical concept of apostolic succession has presented continuity in terms of historical process. Ideas of transmission, normativeness, etc. have become keynotes in this concept. Continuity with the apostles became inconceivable apart from the notion of a linear history. The problems that this one-sided approach has created hardly need to be mentioned. They are still with us today in the ecumenical dialogue.

My attempt in this brief study has been to do some justice to the traditionally overlooked approach which I have called "eschatological"—with the necessary qualifications to which I have referred. I have done this because I believe that no research into the theological consciousness of the Orthodox Churches can be done properly without this approach which,

---

[116]The principle of the *essential equality of all bishops*—and local Churches —stems precisely from the eschatological image of the apostolic college *as an indivisible whole,* which is realized and expressed *in its totality* through each bishop in each Church. Hence the importance of this principle in the early Church (e.g. Cyprian: n. 106 above) and in Orthodox Canon Law. This should not be obscured by any historical cases pointing to the contrary. On this principle in the context of Vatican II see H.-M. Legrand, *op. cit.* p. 122, where a distinction is made between an ecclesiologically justifiable "égalité fondamentale entre toutes les Eglises particulières" and "une hiérarchie réelle" for the sake of "le bien commun."

although practically absent from theological manuals, nevertheless survives vividly in the iconological and liturgical approaches to the mystery of the Church. I have, therefore, done this in the first place because Orthodox theology needs badly to be reminded of it. At the same time, I hope that the ecumenical dialogue as a whole can profit something from doing justice to this traditionally ignored approach.

At first sight the eschatological image of the apostles, to which I have referred in this study, seems to have little to do with *continuity:* can we talk about the eschatological realities in terms of continuity? The answer is of course negative. The Kingdom comes to us as a *visit* and a *presence;* it does not come "by observation" (Luke 17:20). The synthesis, therefore, between the "historical" and the "eschatological" perspectives of apostolicity cannot remove the tension between history and the eschata. Nevertheless "presence" and "continuity" *can* be related in a synthesis. In fact they *have* been related in the early Church. The synthesis of the two perspectives is not just a theoretical construction; it is a practical possibility.

What makes this synthesis possible is that the Kingdom of God is always present *with a structure.* Those who operate with the dilemma "institution or event" may revolt against such a thesis, but they must think twice before they do so. The reason is twofold. In the first place there is no Kingdom of God outside the work of the Holy Spirit, who is by definition *communion.* This means that the Kingdom of God is a community and this implies a structure, for it implies both a convocation and a basic line of demarcation, a judgment (Matt. 25). In the second place there is no Kingdom of God which is not centered on Christ surrounded by the apostles. And this implies again a structure, a *specificity of relations,* a situation in which the relations within the community are *definable,* and they are definable not arbitrarily but *in accordance with the eschatological nature of the community.* All this means that any reference to the presence of the eschata in history (Acts 2:17) implies automatically a communion structured in a certain manner (Acts 1:12-26 and 2:42). This is

already a synthesis between the historical and the eschatological realities.

How can this structure which emerges from the eschata be
translated into concrete historical terms? And how can this
translation take place without turning the Kingdom into sheer
history? It is at this point that institutions appear to be
threatening he nature of the Church.

The way the Church faced this problem from the beginning is, and I think will always be, the only way to face it.
Our Lord, before He left His disciples, offered them a sort
of "diagram" of the Kingdom when He gathered them
together in the Upper Room. It was not one "sacrament" out
of "two" or "seven" that He offered them, nor simply a
memorial of Himself, but a real image of the Kingdom. At
least this is how the Church saw it from the beginning. In
the eucharist, therefore, the Church found *the structure of
the Kingdom,* and it was this structure that she transferred to
her own structure. In the eucharist the "many" become "one"
(I Cor. 10:17), the people of God become the Church by
being called from their dispersion (*ek-klesia*) to one place
(ἐπὶ τὸ αὐτό). Through her communion in the eternal life
of the Trinity, the Church becomes "the body of Christ,"
that body in which death has been conquered and by virtue of
which the eschatological unity of all is offered as a promise
to the entire world. The historical Jesus and the eschatological
Christ in this way become one reality, and thus a real
synthesis of history with eschatology takes place.

It is not, therefore, an accident that the eucharist provided
the early Church from the beginning with (a) the basic
concept and framework of her structure, and (b) the context
for the perpetuation of this structure in history. This leads to
a real synthesis between the historical and the eschatological
dimensions of the Church's existence without the danger of
"institutionalization." For the eucharist is perhaps the only
reality in the Church which is *at once an institution and an
event;* it is the uniquely privileged moment of the Church's
existence in which the Kingdom comes epicletically, i.e. *without emerging as an expression of the historical process, although it is manifested through historical forms.* In this

context the Church relates to the apostles simultaneously by looking backward and forward, to the past and to the future —always, however, by letting the eschaton determine history and its structures.

If this synthesis is applied to the problems faced by the Churches today, some fundamental reconsiderations will inevitably emerge. In the first place, the Churches will have to reconsider any notions that they may have of a *derived* ministry. Continuity of apostolic ministry will cease to be identical with canalization. The same would apply to the continuity of faith or doctrine. Tradition is not just passed on from one generation to another; it is constantly re-enacted and re-received in the Spirit. This will bring out the importance of the Church as a *community*—the community which results from the communion of the Spirit—and of the basic *structure* of this community—the structure which emerges from the vision of the eschatological community as the complex of the specific relations (ministries) in and through which the Spirit constitutes this community.

Thus the structure which provides the historical form of the Church's continuity with the apostles will be determined not just by history but also—or rather ultimately—by the eschatological vision of the Church. The historical heritage of the past—on which the Churches have insisted for so long —as well as the historical needs of the present (concern with social problems, etc.)—which seem to preoccupy the ecumenical movement in our days—will both have to be judged by this ultimate, *final judgment* provided by the vision of the *eschata,* without which no real unity of the Church can exist.

For a long time now the Churches have been using criteria of unity by singling out various *norms* (this or that ministry, this or that doctrine, etc.). And yet every such norm taken in itself cannot but be a false criterion. The Church relates to the apostles in and through the presence of the eschatological community in history. This is not a denial of history, for it is through historical forms that this presence takes place. But the ultimate criterion for unity is to be found in the question to what extent the actual form of the Church's ministry and message today—or at any given time—reflect the presence of this eschatological community.

6.

Ministry and Communion

I. *The Theological Perspective*

Discussions about ministry and ordination have usually been dominated by a certain problematic inherent in scholastic theology. Some of the characteristics of this theology[1] are worthy to be mentioned, for they form basic components of the theological perspective in which the ministry is usually placed. In the first place, both ministry and ordination are approached as *autonomous* subjects: they are treated quite apart from Christology or Trinitarian theology. Secondly, Christology itself is treated as an autonomous subject and not as an integral part of both Trinitarian theology and ecclesiology. This gives rise both to Christomonistic tendancies in understanding the person and ministry of Christ, and—what is more significant for us here—to great difficulties in relating the Church's ministry to that of Christ. Finally, and because of all this, ministry and ordination are not basically approached from the angle of the *concrete ecclesial community* but of the individual person (his "ontology" or his "function").

The theological perspective in which the Church at the time of the Greek Fathers would place her ministry does not leave any room for approaching it as an autonomous subject. This is to be seen in the way this ministry is to be related to the ministry and person of Christ. Here the follow-

[1]For an examination of these characteristics see Y. Congar, *L'Eglise de s. Augustin à l'époque moderne* (Histoire des Dogmes III/3, 1970), especially pp. 173 ff.

ing principles, typical of the Greek patristic tradition, may
be mentioned briefly:

(a)   There is no ministry in the Church other than Christ's
ministry. This assertion, which seems to go back to the New
Testament Church,[2] is understood by the Fathers so realistically that not only the dilemma of choosing between an *opus
operantis* and an *ex opere operato* is avoided but also any
other question implying a *distance* between the Church's and
Christ's ministry becomes irrelevant and misleading. This
identification of the Church's ministry with that of Christ has
gone beyond the theology of the Fathers and entered the
liturgical life of the ancient Church in a decisive way: in the
eucharist, Christ is not only the one who is offered and who
receives but also the one *who offers*.[3] This identification lends
itself to "mystical-monophysitic" interpretations, but the fact
that it is to be found in theologians such as St John Chrysostom, who shares the Antiochene "down-to-earth" mentality,
indicates that it is along lines other than those of monophysitic
mysticism that we should try to understand its meaning.[4]

(b)   The identification of the Church's ministry with that
of Christ is possible only if we let our *Christology* be *conditioned pneumatologically*.[5] This can happen if we see the

[2]There is hardly any ministerial title in the New Testament, which is not
attributed to the person of Christ by the primitive Church. Thus, Christ is
the "apostle" (Heb. 3:1), the "prophet" (Matt. 23:8; John 13:13), the
"priest" (Heb. 5:6, 8:4, 10:21, 2:17), the "bishop" (ἐπίσκοπος: I Pet.
2:25, 5:4; Heb. 13:13), the "deacon" (Rom. 15:8; Luke 22:27, cf. Phil.
2:7) etc.

[3]Thus in the Liturgy of St John Chrysostom, prayer before the "Great
Entrance": "Thou art the offerer and the offered, the acceptor and the
distributed, Christ our God." The references to Chrysostom's writings on
this point are numerous. See, e.g., *Hom. on. Hebr.* 12-14, PG 63:95-116;
Hom. on I Cor. 8, 1, PG 61:69; *Hom. on John* 86.4 PG 59:472. For other
Fathers see, e.g., Gregory Naz. on *Baptism*, 40, 26, PG 36:396; and Ps.
Dionysius Areop., *Eccl. Hier.* 5, 5, PG 3:513.

[4]Monophysitism is usually attributed to Ps. Dionysius Areop. for his views
on the ministry. Yet cf. the following expressions of St John Chrysostom:
"οὐδὲν γὰρ ἄνθρωπος εἰς τὰ προκείμενα (i.e. sacraments) εἰσάγει
ἀλλὰ τὸ πᾶν τῆς τοῦ Θεοῦ δυνάμεως ἔργον ἐστί, κἀκεῖνος ὑμᾶς
ἐστιν ὁ μυσταγωγῶν."

[5]Christology for Eastern theology is not a self-existent and self-explained
domain of theology. Cf. N. Nissiotis, "La Pneumatologie ecclésiologique au
service de l'unité de l'Eglise," *Instina* 12 (1967), pp. 322-340. The insistance
on Pneumatology was so evident in Byzantine theology that Thomas Aquinas

mystery of Christ as being *initiated* by the Father who actually
sends the Son in order to fulfill and realize the eternal design
of the Holy Trinity to draw man and creation to participation
in God's very life. In this understanding of Christology, Christ
cannot be isolated from the Holy Spirit in whom he was born
of the Virgin;[6] in whom he became able to minister on earth,[7]
in whom finally, and most significantly for our subject, he can
now minister to this pre-eternal plan of God for creation *in*
or rather *as* the Church. What, therefore, the Spirit does
through the ministry is to constitute the Body of Christ *here
and now* by *realizing* Christ's ministry *as* the Church's
ministry.

The implications of this include the following: (i) the
ministry of the Church does not represent an "interim" period
in the stages of *Heilsgeschichte,* but it exists as an expression
of the *totality* of the Economy. We cannot, therefore, understand the nature of the ministry by seeing it simply in terms
of a *past* (Christ's ministry in Palestine) or a *present* (ministry as service to the needs of today) but of the *future* as well,[8]
namely as sustaining for creation the hope of the *eschata,* of
sharing God's very life, by offering a *taste* of that here and
now; (ii) the identification of the Church's ministry with
that of Christ is to be seen in existential *soteriological* terms
which have profound anthropological and cosmological implications. If soteriology means, as it was the case in the
patristic period, not so much a juridical reality by means of
which forgiveness is granted for an act of disobedience, but
rather a realization of *theosis,* as communion of man—and
through him of creation—in the very life of the Trinity, then
this identification acquires existential importance: the Church's
ministry realizes here and now the very saving work of Christ,

accused the Greeks that for the sake of Pneumatology they minimized the
dignity of Christ. See Y. Congar, *op. cit.,* p. 267.

[6]Matt. 1:20; Luke 1:35.

[7]Luke 4:13.

[8]The importance of eschatology for understanding the Church's ministry is
rightly stressed by W. Pannenberg, "Die Bedeutung der Eschatologie für das
Verständnis der Apostolizität und Katholizität der Kirche," *Katholizität
und Apostolizität* (Beiheft zu *Kergyma und Dogma* 2, 1971), pp. 92-109.
Cf. notes 106 and 107 below.

which involves the *very personal life* and presence of the
one who saves.[9]

(c) But by establishing this approach to the relation
between the ministry of Christ and that of the Church we
have done something fundamental to our Pneumatological
understanding of the ministry: instead of *first* establishing
in our minds the scheme "Christ—ministry" and *then* trying
to fill this with the work of the Holy Spirit, we have made
the Spirit *constitutive of the very relation between Christ and
the ministry.* The implications of this for our theology of the
ministry are of paramount importance, as will be seen throughout this study. At the moment, as we try to set the general
theological perspective, this means that there is a fundamental
*interdependence between the ministry and the concrete com-
munity of the Church* as the latter is brought about by the
koinonia of the Spirit. Methodologically, this means that we
possess no other way of knowing what the nature of the
ministry is apart from the concrete community and that, equally,
we cannot establish first our idea of the concrete community
and then look at the ministry. The paradox which emerges
from an attentive study of I Corinthians 12 is precisely that
Paul there offers a "definition" of the Body of Christ, the
Church, *only in terms of ministry* (membership of the Body
equals charismata and vice-versa). Our understanding of the
ministry, therefore, can only depart from the *community*
created by the Spirit.

If we bear this in mind, we can understand better certain
liturgical and practical elements in ordination, which theologians tend to bypass in constructing their views on the ministry.
Thus, according to the ancient tradition common to both East
and West, (i) all ordinations must be *related* to a *concrete com-*

---

[9]This accounts for the fact that in the East, we find neither the notion of
"created grace" which was developed by medieval Western theologians nor
an abstraction of Christ's "acts" or "influence" from his person, as it developed later in Protestant theology. Cf. the criticism of the latter in D.
Bonhoeffer's "Christology" (*Gesamelte Schriften,* Vol. III, 1960), pp. 166-
242, especially pp. 176 ff. God's *direct* personal involvement in salvation
represented a basic issue in the controversies of the fourteenth century between
Gregory Palamas and Barlaam, and it forms part of the Greek patristic view
of grace as direct *participation* and *communion.* Cf. J. Meyendorff, *Christ in
Eastern Christian Thought* (1969), pp. 85 ff.

munity,[10] and (ii) all ordinations must take place *within the context of the eucharistic assembly*.[11] Both of these, to which other similar cases may be added,[12] point to the close relation between ministry and community. But it is mainly the second of these two that is extremely revealing from the point of view of the theology of the ministry. Why the *eucharistic* community and not any other assembly of the local Church is made the exclusive context of ordination? No theologian, especially of the patristic tradition, can bypass this question without making it *decisive* for his views on the ministry.[13] In the following paragraphs of this study, this question will always play implicitly a basic role. As far as the general theological perspective is concerned, it must be observed that, in fact, no community except the eucharistic one realizes and portrays simultaneously all the principles of the theological perspective we have just outlined. It is in the eucharist, understood properly as a community and not as a "thing,"[14] that Christ is present here and now as the one who realizes God's self-communication to creation as communion with His life,

[10]The prohibition of ordinations *in absoluto* by the canons of the early Church (e.g. canon 6 of Chalcedon) should not be regarded as a mere "canonical" matter without deep ecclesiological implications.

[11]This is clearly stated already in Hippolytus' *Apostolic Tradition,* but essentially it can be traced back to the primitive association of charismatic manifestations with the eucharistic gatherings (cf. J. Zizioulas, J.M.R. Tillard, J. J. Von Allmen, *L'Eucharistie* ("Eglises en Dialogue" no. 12, 1970), pp. 45ff. For the connection between ordination and the Last Supper from another viewpoint cf. the remarks of T. F. Torrance, "Consecration and Ordination," *Scottish Journal of Theology* 11 (1958), 241.

[12]For example, the interesting resemblance between the rite of ordination and that of matrimony in the actual liturgical service of the Orthodox Church must be related to the same idea of the bond which ordination creates between the ordained and the Church.

[13]This organic connection between eucharist and ministry is not simply a demand of theology but also of history, at least for the first three centuries, as it seems to result from a study of the sources. Cf. J. D. Zizioulas, *The Unity of the Church in the Eucharist and the Bishop during The First Three Centuries* (in Greek—1965), especially pages 29-148.

[14]In Orthodox spirituality, too, the understanding of the eucharist as a "community," a gathering ἐπὶ τὸ αὐτό, tends to be overshadowed by individual pietism. The works of O. Casel and G. Dix in the West have contributed decisively to the rediscovery of this fundamental aspect of the eucharist. Cf. also W. Elert, *Abendmahl und Kirchengemeinschaft in der alten Kirche hauptsächlich des Ostens* (1954).

and in the existential form of a concrete community created by the Spirit. Thus the eucharistic assembly becomes, theologically speaking, the natural milieu for the birth of ministry understood in this broader soteriological perspective. We shall now try to see what this means with regard to specific aspects of ministry and ordination.

II. *The Relational Character of the Ministry*

In discussions of the subject of the ministry, the questions very often raised have to do with the way the ministry *originates* and is *transmitted* in the Church. These questions imply an understanding of ordination as a transmission of *potestas* either with or without a transmission or bestowal of a certain *charisma* or *grace*. In the former case, grace is again objectified and understood as some*thing* that can be *possessed* by an individual and transmitted.[15]

The response to which such questions may lead theology are inevitably characterized by the notion of causality. Tradi-

[15]This objectification of grace may be traced back to the Augustinian distinction between grace as such and its efficacy or fruits, the former being something that can be "possessed" and "transmitted" regardless of the latter (e.g. *Ep.* 98, PL 33:363. Cf. note 28 below). In the Middle Ages and the Council of Trent the sacraments were understood as "instrumental causes," "containing" grace and representing an "instrumental production" of grace. See R. Schulte, "Sacraments: I. The Sacraments in general," in *Sacramentum Mundi,* V (1970), pp. 379 f. After Vatican II, the theology of the sacraments is placed in the context of "life" in general or the Church as sacrament. See *ibid.* pp. 380 ff. In the writings of K. Rahner the notion of causality, although maintained and used, is removed from the Aristotelian idea of cause and effect with the help of a theology of symbolism. (See his *The Church and the Sacraments* [1963], especially pp. 34 f. 38 and 96.) This approach resembles very much the theology of symbolism of the Greek Fathers (e.g. Cyril of Jerusalem, Ps. Dionysius Areop. and Maximus the Confessor) provided that it is put in the context of Pneumatology which would protect us from turning an "intrinsic symbolism" into a law operating almost by necessity. It is for this reason that the notion of causality, being, in some way or other, always connected with the idea of necessity, becomes difficult to apply to a pneumatologically conditioned ecclesiology. With regard to the idea of *potestas,* it seems that this has disappeared from the new rite of ordinations of the Roman Catholic Church, according to A. Houssiau, "La signification théologique du nouveau rituel des ordinations," in *Mélanges G. Philips* (1970), pp. 271, 279.

tionally, theology has been divided mainly into the following two lines which form two options of a dilemma also lying behind contemporary theological discussions. The dilemma consists in the choice between (i) a transmission of the ministerial *potestas* or grace through the ordaining minister as part of the linear historical line of apostolic succession, and (ii) an understanding of the *community* as possessing and transmitting the charismatic life, or *delegating authority*, to the ordained person. Historically the first option represents the line usually taken by the so-called "catholic" theology of the ministry, whereas the second one is related to the idea of the "priesthood of all believers" as it is traditionally understood in Protestantism. The revival of Biblical studies in our days, with its critical approach to the sources and its stress on the absence of the "bishop" from the writings of the New Testament, has inevitably pushed theology towards the choice of the second option of this dilemma.[16] But the sources give answers only to questions we put to them, and this makes it imperative to check whether the dilemma we impose on these sources is as inevitable as traditionally theology has made us believe.

Whichever pole of the above mentioned dilemma we may choose, we still work in it with the notion of causality, and it is this very notion that becomes questionable in the light of the theological perspective of the present study. Thus the question to be raised fundamentally is this: *is there anything that may be understood as preceding and causing ordination in the Church? Is there a depository or a source of ministry? Is there a generic principle of the ministry* (be it the power of the ordaining bishop or a "priestly" nature of the community)? *How does the ministry come about?*

(a) In the first place, it must be stated emphatically, that there is no such a thing as "non-ordained" persons in the

---

[16]We have in mind works such as H. Küng, *The Church* (1968), and reactions to that work by Y. Congar, in *Revue des sciences philosophiques et théologiques* 53 (1969), 693-706 (Cf. the response by H. Küng, *ibid.* 55 (1971) 193 ff.); E. Cothenet, in *Esprit et Vie*, 24 July 1969, pp. 490-496; P. Grelot, "La structure ministérielle de l'Eglise d'après S. Paul," in *Istina* 15 (1970), pp. 389-424. On the whole discussion see H. Härling—J. Nolte, *Diskussion um Hans Küng "Die Kirche"* (1971).

Church. Baptism and especially confirmation (or chrismation) as an inseparable aspect of the mystery of Christian initiation involves a "laying on of hands" ("chrismation" in this respect is another form of the same thing). The East has kept these two aspects (baptism—confirmation) not only inseparably linked with one another but also with what follows, namely *the eucharist*. The theological significance of this[17] lies in the fact that *it reveals the nature of baptism and confirmation as being essentially an ordination*, while it helps us understand better what *ordination itself* means. As we can see already in Hippolytus' *Apostolic Tradition*,[18] the immediate and inevitable result of baptism and confirmation was that the newly baptized would *take his particular "place" in the eucharistic assembly*, i.e. *that he would become a layman*. That this implies ordination is clear from the fact that the baptized person does not simply become a "Christian," as we tend to think, but he becomes a *member of a particular "ordo"* in the eucharistic community. Once this is forgotten, it is easy to speak of the laity as "non-ordained" and thus arrive at the possibility—witnessed to by the history of the Church in a dramatic way—of either making the layman an unneccessary element in the eucharistic community (hence the "private mass" and the entire issue of clericalism) or of making him the basis of all "orders," as if he were not himself a specifically defined order[19] but a generic source or principle (hence the prevailing view of "the priesthood of all believers" in all its variations).

The theological implication of all this is that ordination, i.e. *assignment to a particular "ordo" in the community*, appears to be paradoxically enough not something that *follows* a pre-existing community but an act *constitutive* of the community. Being used to individualism in ontology, we find it hard to think of a community which does not *first* exist

---

[17]For details cf. J. D. Zizioulas, "Some Reflections on Baptism, Confirmation and Eucharist," in *Sobornost* 5 (1969), 644-652.

[18]*Apost. Trad.* 21 (ed. *Botte*, p. 54).

[19]Cf. *I Clem.* 40.3—41.7: no confusion of "orders" or transgression from one "order" to another is permissible. This implies that the "layman" is also an "order" (τάγμα or τάξις).

itself and then *produce* or *sustain* or *possess ministry.*[20] In this way of thinking, we find it natural to speak of the community *first as a unity and then as a diversity* of ministries. But in a pneumatologically conditioned ontology the fact is that *the Holy Spirit unites only by dividing* (I Cor. 12:11). The conclusion of this is that ordination, as it is seen in the case of baptism, is the act that *creates the community* which thus becomes understood as *the existential "locus" of the convergence of the charismata* (I Cor. 12).[21]

(b) Following these remarks, which illustrate how in a pneumatologically understood ecclesiology ordination does not represent an act of progression and causality, we can understand better the "one-sided" and almost "monophysitic" view expressed for example in the writings attributed to Dionysius the Areopagite, that in ordination the bishop ordains "not by his own movement (gesture) but by the divine movement. . . ."[22] This view has nothing to do with the

[20]Thus the expression: "the ministry *of* the Church" is not to be understood in the sense of a possessive genitive. The being of the Church does not precede her actions or ministries. Charismatic life (i.e. concrete ministries) is constitutive of and not derivative from the Church's being. The question whether "essence" precedes "existence" or not should not be introduced into ecclesiology; it is rather along the lines of a *simultaneity* of the two that we must understand the Church. Cf. K. Rahner's view that "the Church is the visible outward expression of grace *not in the sense that she subsequently announces* as it were the presence of something already there . . ." (our underlining); also his insistence that the Church as a local event is not to be understood as something subsequent to the universal Church (*Episcopat und Primat* [1962], p. 26 and 34). Yet in spite of this Rahner seems to hold the idea of an "essence" or "potentiality" of the Church leading to an "actuality" or "event" and hence to the subordination of the local to the universal Church (*ibid.*). Cf. Part IV and note 105 below.

[21]This stress on the existential and charismatic nature of the Church should not be taken to imply an undermining of the *historical* nature of the Church. But the acceptance on the other hand of the historical nature of the Church should not imply an ecclesiological ontologism according to which the Church's being is presupposed as the intrinsic source of her actions. Such an implication results from the view that the Church's historical existence (e.g. apostolic succession) is *something* else than her constant charismatic reconstitution. On the contrary, the view we are presenting here is that the two, i.e. historical existence (succession, etc.) and charismatic event, *coincide with each other.* It is in this sense that we should try to understand, for example, apostolic succession (see Part IV below). In this way the existential-charismatic approach to ecclesiology does not threaten the historical basis of the Church, but implies it.

[22]*Eccl. Hier.* 5, 5, PG 3:513: "τὸν θεῖον ἱεράρχην οὐκ αὐτοκινήτως

monophysitic tendencies usually attributed to this writer by
scholars, but it is simply typical of the *epicletic* approach of
the Greek Fathers. The liturgical formula of ordination itself
reveals the same approach in (i) making God the subject of
the verb "ordain" ("The divine grace . . . ordains"), and (ii)
requiring that the eucharistic assembly sing the "Kyrie eleison"
during the moment of ordination. The meaning of all this is
that ordination depends essentially on *prayer* and not simply
on an objective transmission of grace. This is to be conceived
not in the usual understanding of prayer as *assisting* us in
something *we* do, but as attributing *the very action* to God
Himself.[23]

In the light of these remarks, we can understand the proper
meaning of two other parts of the procedure of ordination,
namely *election* by the people and acclamation of approval
(in the East by crying "axios") by the congregation. The fact
that the early Church could dispense with the part of the
election by the laymen[24] (a practice which was perhaps not to
be found in all regions, anyway) shows that in spite of its
importance this part could not be made a *condition* for ordination, as if the charisma depended on the decision of the
people *outside* the eucharistic community. The case, however,
was different with the approval of the people within the
eucharistic assembly. The "axios," as another form of the
liturgical "amen"[25] of the congregation, signified the participation of the entire community in ordination, just like the
singing of the "Kyrie eleision" to which we have already
referred. To be sure, this is not a satisfactory interpreation
for those who are looking for a "democratic" view of the

χρὴ τὰς ἱερατικὰς ποιεῖσθαι τελεσιουργίας, ἀλλ' ὑπὸ κινοῦντι
ταύτας."

[23]Cf. from a reformed point of view the remarks of T. F. Torrance, *op. cit.*
p. 251. For Eastern theology, this "epicletic" approach is a fundamental consequence of the pneumatological conditioning of Christology and ecclesiology.
Cf. the meaning of the "epiclesis" in the eucharist.

[24]See e.g. canon 13 of Laodicea.

[25]The liturgical "amen" as a sign of the indispensability of the order of
the layman for the eucharist is very important. Cf. P. Rouget, *Amen: Acclamation du peuple sacerdotal* (1947) ,and G. H. Williams, "The role of the layman in the Ancient Church," in *Greek, Roman, and Byzantine Studies* 1
(1958), 9-42.

Church. But a "democracy" which makes the community a *condition* for divine action conditions the very charismatic nature of the ministry.

This *immediacy* of divine action in ordination is what safeguards the charismatic nature of the ministry. The same immediacy expresses also the identification of the Church's ministry with that of Christ—a basic theological component of the perspective we discussed in the first part of this study. All this could have become sheer monophysitism had it not been for the fact that it is all expressed in a "eucharistic" way, i.e. in and through the concrete local community, which however, is to be understood as something constituted by the very event it constitutes. The organic link of ordination with this community is thus a key for all theology of the ministry: it points to divine action, fully incarnating itself in creation yet without depending ontologically on it.[26] Without the community, or rather the *eucharistic* community, creaturely being (be it man or nature or even community of men) tends to become a condition for divine grace. In the eucharistic community, creaturely being achieves its full affiliation, not by becoming a condition for God's grace but by being deified in giving itself up to God's love. It is this that makes the ministry belong to the *new*, and not to the old, *creation*, i.e. to a creaturely being which affirms itself not by becoming a condition for God's love (this is the "old" sinful being) but by ceasing to be such a condition.[27] And it is this that makes the Church differ essentially from a human "democracy."

If ordination is approached in this way, ministry ceases to be understood in terms of *what it gives* to the ordained and

[26]Cf. K. Rahner's speaking of "an incarnational tendency" of grace ("Personal and Sacramental Piety," in *Theological Investigations* II [1967], p. 119).

[27]A basic theological implication in what is said here is that in allowing for a creaturely "being" we must in no way make it a condition for God's life and love. Adam's sin consists in man's self-affirmation independently of God. An understanding of human nature in itself, i.e. apart from its communion with God, makes man a "partner" of God on equal terms and as such it sanctions his fallen state, by transforming him into a necessary condition in God's exercise of His grace. The sacraments and the ministry in particular represent theological areas in which this problem reveals itself in a crucial way.

becomes describable only in terms of *the particular relation-ship* into which it places the ordained. If ordination is under-stood as constitutive of the community and if the community being the *koinonia* of the Spirit is by its nature a *relational entity,* ministry *as a whole* can be describable as a complexity of relationships within the Church and in its relation to the world. In fact, without the notion of "relationship" the minis-try loses its character both as a charisma of the Spirit, i.e. part of His *koinonia,* and as service (*diakonia*).

In employing the term "relationship" in order to describe the nature of the ministry, we do not take it in the sense of an abstract and logical *relatio*[28] but as having a deeply ontolo-gical and soteriological meaning. In Greek patristic tradition, this would include two aspects with regard to the ministry: (i) A relational reality which unites the community itself in and by dividing it into ministries. St Maximus the Confessor coins the remarkable term "co-divided" (συνδιαιρουμένη) in order to indicate this character of ordination.[29] And (ii) an act by which the Church and, through her, mankind and creation are brought into the reconciling and saving relation-ship with God which has been realized in Christ. In this sense, ministry is understood as "ambassadorship" (πρε-σβεία) mainly in the tradition of the Antiochene Fathers.[30]

Thus it is the ministry that more than anything else renders the Church a *relational* reality, i.e. a mystery of love, reflecting here and now the very life of the trinitarian God. Because this reality is realized within the world and historical exist-ence which still bears the Cross in its heart and has to contend with the presence and work of the Devil, this *relational* nature of the Church is constantly revealed by way of a *double*

[28]It must be made clear that our view of "relationship," on which we base our approach here, is not to be reduced to something that has no ontological content, like e.g. in the scholastic *oppositio relationis.* For St Augustine, too, relational context is indispensable for the sacramental grace. Grace according to him appears only in *caritas* and *unitas* (cf. Y. Congar, *op. cit.* pp. 11-24), though with the help of a distinction, unfamiliar to the Eastern tradition, he would restrict this condition to the fruits of grace and not to the grace itself. Cf. note 15 above.

[29]*Myst,* 2, PG 91:668C-669A.

[30]E.g. John Chrysostom, *Hom. on. II Cor. 11,* PG 61:477-478; *On the Priest* 4, 4, PG 48:680.

movement: (i) as a baptismal movement which renders the Church a community existentially "dead to the world" and hence separated from it, and (ii) as a eucharistic movement which relates the world to God by "referring" it to God as *anaphora*[31] and by bringing to it the blessings of God's life and the taste of the Kingdom to come. It is this double movement of the Church's relational nature that makes the ministry realize its relational character as a movement of the Church both *ad intra* and *ad extra*.

If we look at the history of the birth and establishment of the various orders and ministries we shall see how quickly the Church concentrated ordination almost exclusively on her ministries *ad intra*. This development begins so early—certainly it is already there with St Ignatius of Antioch[32]—and it is to be evaluated in a positive and not in a negative way. For the main theological implication of this is connected with the fact that ordination is related to the eucharistic community, and for this reason the ministries or "orders" that are suggested by the structure of this community become the *decisive* ones for all ministries. By reserving ordination to these ministries, the Church has at least preserved the correct visible point of reference for its ministry.

Thus the particular ministries of (i) the laity, (ii) the deacons, (iii) the presbyters and (iv) the bishop, clearly evidenced with St Ignatius, became the indispensable ministries of the Church in her relation *ad intra* during the entire history of the Church until and perhaps including the Reformation.[33] The tragedy with regard to this development lies

---

[31]This "anaphoric" quality of the Church, expressed *par excellence* in the eucharist, is the main manifestation of the priestly character of the Church and her ministry. Thus the latter must be related to the eucharist in order to find its fulfilment.

[32]*Tral.* 3, 1: "χωρὶς τούτων (i.e. bishop, presbyters, deacons) ἐκκλησία οὐ καλεῖται."

[33]Cf. J.-J. Von Allmen, *Le saint ministère selon la conviction et la volonté des Réformés du XVie siècle* (1968), especially pp. 213 ff. The issue is not whether we have the name of "bishop" but the reality of his office. For an application of this principle to the problem of the ministry in the primitive Church, see G. Konidaris, "Warum die Urkirche von Antiochia den *proestota presbyteron* als *ho Episkopos* bezeichnete," *Münchener theologische Zeitschrift*, 1961, pp. 269-284.

in the fact that theology rather soon lost the proper perspective which is suggested by the organic link of these ministries with the structure of the eucharistic assembly, and thus, given other historical[34] and theological[35] factors, the view of these orders as relational realities making sense only in their *interdependence in the community* was replaced by an approach to them as *individual offices,* with all the well-known consequences for the history of the Church and of theology.

If the relational character of these orders is recaptured in the light of the eucharistic community to which they naturally belong, perhaps many of the existing problems will disappear. This will affect mainly two areas in the theology of the ministry:

(a) The area of the ecclesiological justification of each one of the basic orders. By regarding them as parts of a relational whole we can affirm and justify their distinctiveness and specificity, and hence their *indispensability.* The laity will thus become the *laos* who is gathered from the world to realize in the community of the Church the eschatological unity and salvation of the world in Christ. The deacons, whose existence causes so much embarrassment to the theology of the ministry[36] precisely because their eucharistic role has been lost, will regain their profound significance as bearers of the world (in the form of the gifts and petitions of the faithful) to the head of the eucharistic community in order to bring them back again to the world (in the form of the Holy Communion) as a sign of the new creation which is realized in the communion with God's life. The presbyters will become again the *synedrion* of the community portraying

---

[34]The most important historical factor is the appearance of the parish as a eucharistic gathering distinct from the episcopal eucharistic assembly. This development led to the dissociation of the presbyter from the bishop as well as to the disintegration of the originally collegial *presbyterium,* itself, and hence to the idea that a eucharistic community does not necessarily involve *all orders.* Cf. J. D. Zizioulas, *The Unity* . . ., pp. 151-188 and ch. VIII below.

[35]Such theological factors are to be found, for example, in the development of an individualistic approach to the eucharist, the association of the ministry with an individually possessed *potestas,* etc.

[36]For the difficulties in defining the proper meaning of the office of the deacon in the Church, cf. E. Lanne, "L''Eglise locale et l'Eglise universelle," *Irénikon* 43 (1970), 489.

in liturgical as well as in actual terms the important and lost dimension of judgment with which the Church relates both *ad intra* and with the world. Finally, the bishop will cease to be everything and become the head of the community that unites it in itself and with the other communities in time and space—a prerogative important enough to give him the place of the unique ordainer and all the high honor it implies, yet always and only because of his *relation to the community* and in interdependance with the rest of the orders.

(b)   With regard to the *authority* which is implied in the ministry, a recovery of the relational nature of the ministry in the light of the eucharistic community will prove pointless the fight against "institution"—an issue about which one hears so much today—since it will make "institution" not only meaningful but also *relational*. Authority being tied up with a ministry understood as an objectified *office* and as *potestas* naturally becomes oppressive and provokes revolutionary reactions.[37] On the other hand, in a relational view of the ministry, authority establishes itself as a demand of the relationship itself. Thus the Church becomes *hierarchical* in the sense in which the Holy Trinity itself is hierarchical: by reason of the *specificity of relationship*.[38] The ministry, viewed in this way, creates degree[39] of honor, respect and true authority precisely in the way we see this in trinitarian theology. Being a reflection of the very love of God in the world,

---

[37]The opposition between *Amt* and *Geist* with which theology has been operating since Harnack and Hatch (cf. a similar assumption in our days: E. Käsemann, *Exegetische Versuche*, I, p. 128 f.: ordination implies "monopolizing" the Spirit by an individual) is based on the conception of office and institution as objectified things. Things change, however, if the office or institution is placed in the context of Pneumatology and is understood in *relational* terms.

[38]The notion of "specificity" is fundamental in trinitarian theology: the Son has everything in common with the Father and the Spirit except being Father or Spirit and the Spirit possesses everything the Father and the Son possess except being Father or Son (Gregory of Nazianzos, *Or.* 34, 10, PG 36:252 A).

[39]The notion of βαθμός (degree) is applied to the ministry by the canonical and patristic writings (e.g. *Can. Apost.* 82; Basil, *Ep.* 188, *canon* 1 etc.), but it is not meant to introduce a classification into the ministry. Cf. note 56 below. In Ps. Dion. Areop. (*Eccl. Hier.* 5, PG 3:500-516) the terms τάξις and τάγμα are preferred.

the Church reflects precisely this kind of authority through and in her ministry. Hierarchy and authority are thus born out of relationship and not of power (*auctoritas* or *potestas*) —be it an "ontological" or a "moral" kind of power.

This leads us to a consideration of the Church's ministry *ad extra*. In a relational notion of the ministry, such as it is revealed in the light of the eucharistic community, the Church's "ontology" becomes conditioned existentially through her ministry. This happens precisely in the Church's missionary existence in the world, and it means more specifically the following things:

(a)   The ministry relates the Church to the world in an existential way, so that any separation between the Church and the world in the form of a *dichotomy* becomes impossible. As it is revealed in the eucharistic nature of the Church, the world is *assumed* by the community and referred back to the Creator.[40] In a eucharistic approach it is by being *assumed* that the world is judged, and not otherwise.

(b)   The mission of the Church in the world is, therefore, inconceivable in terms of an attitude *vis-à-vis* the world.[41] The relational character of the ministry implies that the only acceptable method of mission for the Church is the *incarnational* one: the Church relates to the world through and in her ministry by being involved existentially in the world. The nature of mission is not to be found in the Church's *addressing* the world but in its being fully in *com-passion* with it.[42]

[40]Cf. note 31 above.

[41]Cf. the view that "the Church is *in the world*" expressed in the constitution *Gaudium et spes*. That such a view excludes the conception of the Church as a society *vis-à-vis* other societies in the world is stressed by G. Thils, *Une "Loi fondamentale de l'Eglise"?* (1971), p. 15.

[42]Thus the so-called "ministry of the word" is not to be understood in terms of the Church's "addressing" the world, but in terms of her being involved in the world with com-passion, since the Word of God is not to be isolated from his *incarnation*. This means that, for example, preaching as such cannot be understood as a ministry in itself. The Word of God permeates the entire ministry: every minister in some way or other *proclaims* (cf. Paul's understanding of the eucharist as "proclamation" in I Cor. 11:26, and Ignatius in *Eph.* 19, 1); equally, however, the Word of God itself is permeated by the ministry. This is the result of the fact that for the Church the Word of God is no longer simply a prophetic utterance, as it was in the Old Testament, but "flesh" (John 1:14).

(c)   But precisely all this shows that the ministry of the Church *ad extra* must be an organic part of the concrete local community and not of a vague "mission" of the "Church" in general. The significance of this for our understanding of the *ad extra* ministry is fundamental: no form of such a ministry can exist without being organically related to the concrete *eucharistic* community. It is, therefore, precisely this relational nature of the Church that makes it imperative that all ministries *ad extra* spring from the eucharistic community and thus go necessarily through the hands of its president (bishop). They thus become themselves eucharistic or *para-eucharistic* forms of ministry.

(d)   Finally, all this means that the Church must always have a *variety* of such ministries *ad extra,* according to the needs of the time and the place in which she exists. Such ministries will always be necessary to a Church that has not become unrelated to the world, but they cannot acquire permanent forms, being always dependent upon the needs of the particular place and time in which the Church finds herself. From this point of view the ministries *ad extra* differ from those *ad intra,* in that the latter are essentially permanent,[43] dictated by the Church's eucharistic structure as the community gathers together in its baptismal distinctiveness from the world.

III.   *The "Sacramental" Character of the Ministry*

Discussions about the ministry have for many centuries centered on the question whether ordination confers upon the ordained person something "ontological" or simply "functional." In the broader context of a sacramental theology understood mainly in terms of "natural" versus "supernatural" and of grace as something "given," "transmitted," and

[43]In this particular sense the distinction between "permanent" and "movable" ministers can be a valid one. But it would be a mistake to call only the "moving" ministers "charismatic," as it was done by Harnack and many historians after him. A ministry, whether "permanent" or not, which is not charismatic is not a ministry of the Church. Cf. note 37 above.

"possessed,"[44] the question was what ordination *does* to the ordained individual. Here again the same ontology of objectification is implied: man is defined as an *individual;* he either "possesses" some*thing* or he does not—in the latter case, he simply *functions* or *serves.*

If, however, we bear in mind the relational character of the ministry which we discussed in the previous part of this study, our understanding of ordination will be also affected from the *anthropological* point of view. Just as the Church becomes through the ministry a relational entity both in itself and in its relation to the world, so also the ordained man becomes, through his ordination, a *relational entity.* In this context, looking at the ordained person as an *individual* defeats the very end of ordination. For ordination, to use a most valuable distinction offered by modern philosophy,[45] aims precisely at making man not an individual but a *person,* i.e. an *ek-static* being, that can be looked upon not from the angle of his "limits" but of his *overcoming his "selfhood"* and becoming a related being. This shows that the very question of whether ordination is to be understood in "ontological" or in "functional" terms[46] is not only misleading but absolutely impossible to raise in the context of our theological perspective in this study. In the light of the *koinonia* of the Holy Spirit, ordination relates the ordained man so profoundly and so existentially to the community that in his new state after ordination he cannot be any longer, as a minister, conceived in himself. In this state, existence is determined by *communion* which qualifies and defines both "ontology" and "function." Thus it becomes impossible in this state to say that one simply "functions" without implying that his being is deeply and decisively affected by what he does. In the same way, it becomes impossible to imply in this state that one

[44]Cf. note 15 above.
[45]Cf. M. Buber, *I and Thou* (1958), p. 62, and N. Berdyaev, *Solitude and Society* (1938), p. 168.
[46]Thus N. Afanasiev ("L'Eglise de Dieu dans le Christ," in *La Pensée Orthodoxe,* 13 [1968], 19) and N. Nissiotis ("The Importance of the Doctrine of the Trinity for Chuch Life and Theology," in *The Orthodox Ethos,* ed by A. J. Philippou [1964], p. 64) speak of ordination in terms of "functional," while others of "ontological" (e.g. P. Trembelas, *Dogmatique,* III (1968), p. 329 f.).

"possesses" anything as an individual. Could one ever isolate and objectify the state created by love and speak of some*thing* given by it? Or could one say that in a state of love one simply "functions"?[47] Ordination and ministry as communion are precisely and *only* describable in terms of love. This is what St Paul seems to do when he is faced with an impasse in trying to explain the mystery of the Church's charismatic nature.[48]

If we free ourselves from the dilemma "ontological" versus "functional," what categories can we use to indicate the new state into which ordination brings the ordained person? In view of what we have said earlier, any categories we may employ must belong to the type of relational language, i.e. they must allow for the ordained individual to be conceived and spoken of not in himself but as a relational being. The categories used by the Greek Fathers seem to be precisely of this kind. We may look at them briefly.[49]

(a) We have already mentioned the Antiochene understanding of the ministry in terms of "ambassadorship" (πρεσβεία).[50] This term points clearly beyond any objectification of the charisma of ordination. As Theodore of Mopsuestia puts it, the grace received by the minister in his ordination is "for those who need it,"[51] i.e. as a gift *for* the

[47]These are crucial questions pointing to the fact that it is quite inadequate to speak of the ministry as a choice between "ontological" or "functional," and thus to the need of working out some new way of expressing the effect of ordination upon the ordained. This may underline the importance of the ontology of the person discussed in chapter 1 of this book.

[48]I Cor. 13, with its famous hymn to love is usually abused and misused for homiletical purposes, as if its meaning could be understood apart from what is said by Paul in chapter 12. A right exegesis of this "hymn" demands placing it in the context of Paul's attempt to express his theology of the charismata in the previous chapter. His reference to love in chapter 13, therefore, represents Paul's attempt to clarify the paradox of the Church' unity in and through the "divisions" of the charismata. The conclusion that follows such an exegetical approach is that only in terms of love can one understand the mystery of charismatic life and therefore of ministry.

[49]A very helpful investigation of the sources is offered in J. M. Garrigues, M. J. Le Guillou and A. Riou, "Le caractère sacerdotal dans la tradition des Pères grecs," *Nouvelle revue théologique* 8 (1971), 801-820.

[50]See note 30 above.

[51]"The grace of the Spirit (is) conferred upon him (the priest) *for this service* . . ." *Liber ad Baptizandos* II, 6 (ed. and transl. by A. Mingana,

others. This does not imply that the minister himself is not
in need of that grace. The point is that he needs it precisely
because he does not "possess" it but gets it himself *as a
member of the community.* This category of "ambassadorship," a favorite term of St John Chrysoston especially,[52] is
so loaded with soteriological and existential connotations that
leaves no room either for objectification of the charisma or for
its reduction to the level of mere "function."

(b)   Another kind of language which may be easily misunderstood in an "ontologistic" way is that used mainly by
theologians of the Cappadocian and the Alexandrian traditions. Thus Gregory of Nyssa speaks of ordination as "transfiguration" (μεταμόρφωσις)[53] and Cyril of Alexandria as
"transmutation" (μεταστοιχείωσις)[54] of the ordained. Yet
in both of these cases these terms are used in the sense
always of *participation*: the priest receives the grace "as part
of" the eucharistic community[55] and the change that takes
place is described in terms of *honor, glory, dignity* etc.,[56] i.e.

Woodbrooke Studies, VI [1933], p. 120). It must be noted that Theodore,
in accordance with the extreme Antiochene tendency to keep separate the divine
from the human nature, understands the priest as an "intermediary" (*ibid.* p.
119) between man and God. He thus seems to follow a line different from
the Alexandrian tradition, and even from that of Chrysostom, who would
attribute all sacramental action to Christ or to God Himself. Nevertheless it
is noteworthy that Theodore, too, conceives the priesthood in strictly relational terms, as it is seen from his comments on the congregation's reply
"And unto thy spirit" to the priest's blessing: "They (the congregation)
requite him (the priest) with an identical prayer so that it may be made
manifest to the priest and also to all of them that it is not only they that
are in need of the benediction and the prayers of the priest, but that he
also is in need of the prayer of all of them . . . indeed all of us are one
body of Christ, our Lord, and all of us are members one of another, and the
priest only fills the *rôle of a member* that is higher than the other members
of the body, *such as the eye or the tongue"* (*ibid.* p. 90 f.).

[52]See note 30 above.
[53]*In Bapt Christi,* PG 46:581D-584A. Cf. note 49 above.
[54]*In Joh.* 12, 1 (ed. P. E. Pusey, vol. 3, 131 f.).
[55]Gregory of Nyssa, *loc. cit.*: the ordained priest is singled out of the
community to become *its* ("leader" and "president"). It should be noted
that the term "president" (προεστώς, cf. Justin, *I Apol.* 67) is a relational
term.
[56]Gregory of Nyssa (*ibid.*) sees this change in the priest's becoming
σεμνός and τίμιος by way of inner change πρὸς τὸ βέλτιστον. Cyril of
Alex. understands this change in terms of Paul's words: "not I, but the grace
of God which is in me" (I Cor. 15:10), which he goes on to explain in

in terms of an anthropology of *theosis,* typical to the Alexandrian tradition, which implies no "natural" change although it affects man in his being.[57] As St Maximus the Confessor, in his remarkable perception of the dynamism of being, puts it, ordination to the ministry is to be seen as part of the broader christological movement between the Creator and creation—a movement which affects being, yet not statically but precisely as a *movement* and in the framework of a "cosmic liturgy."[58]

(c) Another kind of language used in early patristic literature in connection with the ministry is what we may call a *typological* one. This language is again significantly pointing in the same direction of a relational understanding of the minister. We encounter this kind of language as early as St Ignatius of Antioch in his way of speaking of the various orders in the Church in terms of *typos* or *topos*: e.g. the bishop is the "type" or "in the place" of God, etc. It is significant to note that this kind of language becomes possible only when one has in view the concrete eucharistic community.[59] Ordination thus becomes what we tried to describe in the previous part of this paper, an assignment to a particular *place* in the community, and the ordained is defined after his ordination precisely by his "place" in the community which in its eucharistic nature portrays the very Kingdom of God here and now.[60] It is for this reason that this typological language

terms of "communion" in Christ's own (divine) nature through "participation" (μετουσία) in the Holy Spirit. This amounts, for Cyril, to an elevation of the ordained to a "glory" above human nature, i.e. to the "dignity" which befits "divine nature alone" (*In Joh.* 12, 1, *ibid.,* pp. 132, 133 and 140).

[57]Without a proper idea of *theosis* the "change" in ordination, as described e.g. by Cyril of Alexandria (see previous note), cannot be understood. In the tradition of the Greek Fathers, "deification" of human nature does not mean "divinization" in a sense of a "natural" change. It is to be understood in terms of an elevation of human nature to the glory and life of God by "participation" (μετοχῆ). Without this idea of "participation" and "communion" the language employed by the Greek Fathers in connection with the ministry can be easily misunderstood. Cf. ch. II § 5.

[58]Maximus the Confessor, *Myst.* 2, PG 91:669A.

[59]Ignatius, *Magn.* 6, 1; 3, 1-2; *Tral.* 3, 1. There is no doubt that Ignatius had the image of the eucharistic community in mind when speaking of the bishop as being the "type" of God or sitting "in the place of God."

[60]This is why Ignatius would regard the local Church united around the

of Ignatius could find its way so easily into the early liturgical
documents, such as the Syriac *Didascalia Apostolorum* and
the *Apostolic Constitutions*.[61]

In order to understand this better, we must combine it
with the more obviously soteriological notion of ἀντί (= in
the place of) used for the relation between, e.g., bishops or
priests and Christ by Chrysostom.[62] This way of speaking
lends itself unfortunately to the idea of "vicar" in a juridical
sense, i.e. as a *representation of someone who is absent*. But
its correct meaning is to be found only in the idea of *representation by participation,* as implied in the Biblical image
of the "corporate personality"[63] (e.g. in the "Servant of God"
or the "Son of Man") and used so significantly in the narra-
tives of the Lord's Supper in the Gospels.[64] Thus the ordained
person becomes a "mediator" between man and God not by
presupposing or establishing a distance between these two
but by *relating* himself to both in the context of the community of which he himself is part. It is in this way that the
gradual application of the term *priest* was extended from the
person of Christ, for whom alone it is used in the New
Testament,[65] to the bishop, for whom again alone it was used
until about the fourth century. In being the head of the

bishop as identical with the whole or "catholic" Church united in Christ
(*Smyr.* 8). The word ὥσπερ which connects the local with the "catholic"
Church in this well-known passage, does not imply a *contrast*, as many scholars
have taken it to imply, but an *identity* between the two, local and "catholic."
Ignatius sees no difference between unity in Christ and unity in the bishop.
Thus *Eph.* 5, 1; *Magn.* 3, 1-2; cf. *Polyc. inscr.* Cf. ch. IV above.

[61]*Didascalia* 9 (ed. and transl. R. H. Connolly [1929], p. 86 f.). For the
Const. Apost. (II, PG 1:668) the bishop is "God on earth after God," the
presbyters "a type of the apostles" etc. On this typology cf. Ignatius, *Magn.*
6, 1 and previous note.

[62]E.g. *In II Cor.* 11, PG 61:477. Chrysostom's understanding of the ministry as being exercised "ἀντ᾽ αὐτοῦ (Christ) καὶ τοῦ πατρός" reminds one
of Ignatius (notes 59-61 above). That this ἀντί does not introduce distance
but identity is explained by Chrysostom himself: "Christ Himself appeals,
Christ's Father Himself through us" (*ibid.,* 478).

[63]On this image cf. S. Pedersen, *Israel: Its Life and Culture* (1926); H.
Wheeler Robinson, *The Hebrew Conception of Corporate Personality* (1936),
pp. 49 ff.; A. R. Johnson, *The One and the Many in the Israelite Conception
of God* (1942); and J. de Fraine, *Adam et son lignag: Etudes sur la "personalité corporative" dans la Bible* (1959).

[64]Cf. O. Cullmann, *Die Christologie des Neuen Testaments* (1958), p. 63f.

[65]Heb. 5:6, 8:4, 10:21, 2:17.

eucharistic community and offering in his hands the eucharist —a task of the episcopate *par excellence* in the first four centuries[66]—the bishop, and later on the presbyter precisely and significantly enough when he started offering the eucharist himself, acquired the title of *priest*. But, as the history of the extention of the term "priest" to the presbyter shows,[67] it is the particular place in the eucharistic community and *no other reason* that accounted for the use of the term "priest" in both cases. The fundamental implication of this is that there is no *priesthood* as a *general and vague* term, as it was to become later on in theology under the name of *sacerdotium* —a term which acquired almost the meaning of a generic principle pre-existing and transmitted in ordination from the ordainer to the ordained or from "all believers" to a particular one. The true and historically original meaning of the term is this: as Christ (the only priest) becomes in the Holy Spirit a community (His body, the Church), His priesthood is realized and portrayed in historical existence here and now as a eucharistic community in which His "image" is the head of this community[68] offering *with and on behalf* of the community the eucharistic gifts. Thus the community itself becomes priestly in the sense of I Peter 2:5,9, yet—and this must be stressed in view of what we said in the previous part of this paper—neither in the sense that the priestly character of the community precedes the ordained *sacerdos,* nor in the sense that it derives from him, but of the togetherness and simultaneous gathering ἐπὶ τὸ αὐτὸ of *all the orders* of the community. By understanding priesthood in this way we can see both how the order of the priest becomes relational (= a

[66]This is evident in the prayer of ordination of the bishop in Hippolytus' *Apostolic Tradition* (ch. 3, ed. Botte, p. 8) as contrasted to that of the presbyter (cf. 7, *ibid.* p. 20 f.) which does not mention the offering of the eucharist.

[67]The presbyter acquires the title of "priest" in the sources only after the (orginally) one episcopo-centric eucharistic community is divided into smaller presbytero-centric units (parishes) in the fourth century. This is shown from a comparative examination of the sources. On this see my book *The Unity* . . . pp. 153-176.

[68]The idea that the bishop is the "image of Christ" lasted at least until the fourth century (cf. Ps. Clem. *Hom.* 3, 62). Cf. O. Perler, "L'evêque, représentant du Christ . . ." in *L'Episcopat et l'Eglise universelle* (ed. Y. Congar *et al., Unam Sanctam* 39, 1962), pp. 31-66.

place *in* the community) and at the same time strictly *specific* and personal (no eucharistic community without this *particular* order and *no confusion of orders*).[69]

In stressing the relational character of the minister we must in no way imply that ordination means nothing for *the ordained person himself*. Of course—and this is basic in the perspective of this study—any *isolation* of the ordained person from the rest of the members of the Body amounts to his death: so fundamental is the relational character of Church membership, that individuals disappear as such and become sharers of the eternal and true life only as members one of another. The eschatological fate, therefore, of any Christian is deeply dependent on his relational existence in the community of the saints. And if the resurrection of the Christians is not the resurrection of individuals but of a community, a body (I Thess. 4), the same is true about the eschatological fate of the charismata: they will all be in the end determined by love, i.e. by their relational existence in the Body of Christ (I Cor. 12-13). If, therefore, it is at all possible to speak of the ordained person in himself, it is again only in the light of his position in the Body that we can do so.

The question whether the ministry is only of the "cultus *praesentis* ecclesiae"[70] or not, was never raised in the East. This was so precisely because of the relational and the "typological" approach we discussed earlier here: what happens in the community of the Church, especially in its eucharistic structure, has no meaning in itself apart from its being a reflection—not in a Platonic but a *real* sense[71]—of the com-

---

[69]Cf. note 19 above. An illustration of this is to be found in the issue of concelebration. With regard to this, one must distinguish carefully between (a) a concelebration which means that all orders do the same thing (this is illustrated, for example, by the practice of the common citation of the eucharistic canon); and (b) that each order participates in the eucharist in its own proper quality, i.e. by occupying its own "place." It is in the sense of (b) that concelebration is implied in our approach in this study and not in the sense of (a), which in fact essentially contradicts (b) and represents a very late development (thirteenth century in the West[?], never so far recognized in the East. Cf. J. Hanssens, "De concelebratione eucharistica," in *Periodica* 17 [1927], 143-21; 22 [1932], 219).

[70]Thomas Aquinas IIIa *pars* 63.1 ad 1; 3 ad 3.

[71]The Platonic and Philonian (cf. Philo, *De opif.* 16-19) relation

munity of the Kingdom of God. This mentality is so fundamental that there is no room for the slightest distinction between the worshipping eucharistic community on
earth and the actual worship in front of God's throne.[72] What
does this imply for the ordained person himself? The answer
to this question involves two extremely delicate observations
which, due to our being philosophically conditioned by an
ontology of objectification, become very difficult to express
without the risk of being misunderstood.

The first remark to be made is that because of the relational
nature of ordination, no ordained person realizes his *ordo*
in himself but in the community. Thus if he is isolated from
the community he ceases to be an ordained person (no
anathematized or excommunicated[73] minister can be regarded
as a minister).[74] The fact that in the case of his rehabilitation
this person is not re-ordained does not imply a recognition
that he was still a minister during his excommunication[75]—
such an ontologism would be inconceivable, as the case
of an anthematized person would clearly show. The

between the intelligible prototype and its concrete sensible antitype presupposes that the latter exists really only in so far as it reflects the former. But
for the Fathers (e.g. Ignatius of Antioch) the local Church is in itself a
reality in which the "catholic" Church is fully present and real.

[72]John Chrysostom, *In Heb.* 14, PG 63:111-112: "the Church (in its eucharistic gathering) is heavenly and nothing else but heaven." Also, Maximus
the Confessor, *Myst.* 1, PG 91:664D-668C. The eucharistic liturgy actually
in use in the Orthodox Church repeatedly makes this point. The same view
is portrayed in the architecture and iconography of the Byzantine churches.
Cf. Y. Congar, *L'Eglise . . .*, pp. 68 ff.

[73]We use "excommunication" here not in the sense of a mere disciplinary
action but in that of a real cutting off of someone from the life of the
community.

[74]It would be inconceivable in this approach to think, for example, of Arius
as being still in any way a priest!

[75]Cf. H. Alivisatos, *Economy According to Canon Law of the Orthodox
Church* (1949 in Greek), p. 80 f. Alivisatos rejects the notion of "character."
Ch. Androutsos, *Dogmatics of the Orthodox Eastern Church* (1907—in Greek)
p. 314 f., rejects it too, but in fact he adopts it in another form in his
Symbolics, 2nd edition, p. 381. P. Trembelas, *op. cit.,* p. 329 f. seems to
accept it. Earlier on the "Orthodox Confession" of Dositheus had clearly
adopted the theory of indelible character (see ed. by J. Karmiris, II, p. 760).
With regard to re-ordination it is noteworthy that Apostolic Canon 68, although forbidding it, states that this cannot apply to the rehabilitation of a
heretic.

practice of avoiding re-ordination is rather to be seen from the angle of the community again and not the individual: the community having once ordained someone *recognizes* his position in re-admitting him, and thus does not repeat the service of ordination. That avoiding re-ordination is not to be regarded as a matter of ontological "possession" of the charisma is to be seen in the fact that the Church may *degrade* a rehabilitated minister, as was the case in the early Church[76] —something that would be unacceptable to a theology that looks at the minister as an individual regardless of his place in the community.

The second remark to be made is a more positive one. Precisely because of the identification of the eucharistic community, into which one is ordained, with the worshipping community before the throne of God, ordination is not something of a *temporal nature* but of *eschatological decisiveness.* The eschatological character of ordination is expressed in the Greek patristic tradition with the term "perfection" (τελείωσις).[77] This has again nothing to do with a "natural" or moral perfection as such. It is to be understood rather in the light of the "typological" language of St Ignatius, which we have already mentioned, and especially that of "term" or "end" (πέρας) used by St Maximus the Confessor in connection with ordination. In the understanding of St Maximus, the Ignatian liturgical typology becomes, as it is usual with this Church Father, dynamic: ordination (baptism being included) realizes the movement of creation towards its eschatological end; the eucharistic altar expresses here and now the eschatological nature, the πέρας, of the community and, through and in it, of creation.[78]

It is this sense of eschatological significance and decisiveness that allows for the application of the term "seal" (σφραγὶς) to ordination. Did the East use this term in the

---

[76]E.g. canon 8 of I Nicaea states that a rehabilitated bishop may be placed in the rank of the presbyter, and canon 10 of Neocaesaria that a deacon may become a subdeacon.

[77]Ps. Dionysius Areop. *Eccl. Hier.* I-V, PG 3:372-513; cf. Cyril of Alexandria, *In Joh.* 12, 1, ed. Pusey, III, p. 133.

[78]Maximus Conf., *Myst.* 2, PG 91:669A-D.

same sense as St Augustine[79] did? It is difficult to answer this question, especially in view of the fact that a whole sacerdotal ontologism in the West based itself on St Augustine's notion of "seal." What seems to be true about the Greek Fathers is that they certainly used this term to indicate chrismation as ordination in an eschatological sense: the baptized person, *after* his baptism in the water, is "sealed with the Holy Spirit,"[80] "for the day of redemption" (Eph. 4:30). This eschatological finality makes this a σφραγὶς ἀκατάλυτος[81] or ἀνεπιχείρητος[82] in this sense very much like the Augustinian notion of a sign by which God will recognize His own in the last days.[83] But the term σφραγὶς would never acquire in the Greek Fathers a strictly ontological meaning in the sense of πρᾶγμα; it would be understood rather as σχέσις, which is usually *contrasted* by them with πρᾶγμα. If, for example, we study carefully the application of σφραγὶς or *character* to the person of Christ (cf. Heb. 1:3) by the Greek Fathers, we shall notice clearly this distinction: e.g. for St Basil, the Son in the "character" and σφραγὶς of the Father,[84] but the names "Father" and "Son," at least for Cappadocian theology, are not names of πρᾶγμα but of σχέσις.[85] It would take us very far to explain here what σχέσις means for the Greek Fathers. In order to avoid misunderstanding, however, it should be stated that this notion is not to be taken in the sense of a logical

[79]*Sermo ad Caes, eccl. pl.* 2, PL 43:691.

[80]Cyril of Jerusalem, *Catech. Myst.* 3, PG 33:1088 f.

[81]Cyril of Jerusalem, *Procat.* 16, PG 33:360.

[82]Basil, *Hom* (*in s. Bapt.*) 13, 5, PG 31:433.

[83]On the notion of σφραγὶς in the patristic period cf. J. Gallot, *La nature du caractère sacramentel* (1957), especially pp. 35 ff.

[84]Basil, *De Spir. san.* 64, PG 32:185 C.

[85]Thus, Gregory Naz. *Or.* 29, 16, PG 36:96: "οὔτε οὐσίας ὄνομα ὁ πατὴρ οὔτε ἐνεργείας σχέσεως δέ." Also for Maximus the Confessor σχέσις and πρᾶγμα are to be clearly distinguished (*Pyr.*, PG 91:340D-341A). The insistence upon the distinction between a strictly ontological (πρᾶγμα or οὐσία) and a relational (σχέσις) approach to reality characterizes Greek patristic thought in general. It would take us too far to examine here what σχέσις means for the Greek Fathers. In case, however, that this may be misunderstood as meaning a simply logical *relatio*, it must be noted that σχέσις does not exclude but, on the contrary, includes in itself or carries with it the notion of "being"; it is precisely, as the Cappadocians put it, a *mode of being* (τρόπος ὑπάρξεως), yet not in the sense of

abstraction, but means a *particular existential state of being* (a "mode of existence") in which being both *is itself* and at the same time cannot be spoken of in itself, but only as it "relates to." If we apply this to ministry, the σφραγὶς of ordination becomes a matter of σχέσις, yet not without significance for the being of the ordained person. In this sense no ordained person can appear before God in the last days pretending, as it were, that he had never been ordained. If love will survive as the eschatological quintessence of the charismata (I Cor. 13), ordination will emerge even more clear and decisive, precisely because it is relational.[86]

IV. *Ministry and Unity*

. The ministry is what makes the ecclesial community and the ordained person relational not only to each other and the world but also with regard to the *other communities that exist or have existed in the world.* The sin of individualism which is overcome in the *koinonia* of the Spirit is not less serious if applied to a community than it is when applied to individual christians. Just as *unus christianus nullus christianus,* to remember an old Latin saying, in the same way a eucharistic community which deliberately lives in isolation from the rest of the communities is not an ecclesial community. This is what renders the Church "catholic" not only on the level of "here and now" but also on that of "everywhere and always."[87] The ministry of the Church must reflect this catholicity by being a unifying ministry both in time and in

objectified "being" that can be understood in itself, but of "being" *as it relates to.* The implications of this distinction are of fundamental significance for theology and especially for the doctrine of grace and the ministry. The thesis of the present study, as the reader will have realized, depends very much on this. Cf. ch. I.

[86]This means that the sacramental character of the ministry in its implications for the ordained is not to be determined by either "ontologism" or "functionalism" but by the notion of *koinoia,* i.e. communion and love, and by its *eschatological* decisiveness. Cf. J.D. Zizioulas, "Ordination et Communion" *Istina* 16 (1971), 5-12.

[87]Cf. Cyril of Jerusalem, *Catech.* 18, 23, PG 33:1044; and Vincent of Lerins, *Com.* 2, PL 50:640.

space. The eucharistic nature of the ecclesial community points
inevitably in this direction by opening up a particular community so that it relates to all other communities in spite of
divisions caused by space and time. Thus the eucharist is
offered not just on earth but before the very throne of God
and with the company of all the saints, living and departed,
as well as in the name of "the catholic Church in the world."[88]

Now, the realization of this relation and unity in time and
space must take place in such a way as to not destroy the
unity of the local community. The reason for this is that once
this unity is destroyed individualism makes again its appearance. Thus, if we say for example that the various communities in the world can simply unite through the love or faith
of their *individual members,* we not only make unity an
abstract matter on the level of subjective emotion or belief,
but—what is more important—we allow for the Christian to
be conceived in himself and not as part of his existential
milieu here and now, i.e. as part of the local eucharistic
community. It is precisely for this profound reason that the
eucharistic community must both always be *local* and always
have the priority over against a universal unity in our ecclesiological thinking.[89]

If we admit that the *ek-static* and relational nature of the
local community must be realized while this community retains its unity and not through its individual members independently and directly, this leads us inevitably to the special

[88]Cf. Liturgy of St John Chrysostom, prayer of the anaphora: "Again we
offer unto Thee this reasonable service for those who have fallen asleep in
the faith . . . for the world, for the holy, catholic and apostolic Church."

[89]Cf. K. Rahner, *Episcopat und Primat,* where it is stressed that the Church
as an "event" acquires necessarily a *local* character. The insistence of Eastern
theology on the priority of the local Church must be seen in the light of the
pneumatological approach of this theology to the mystery of the Church. A
pneumatological approach inevitably brings forth the *existential* aspect of the
Church. The proper relation between the pneumatological and the christological approaches to ecclesiology seems to constitute a crucial problem in the
relation between the "Eastern" and the "Western" views of the Church. The
theology of the institutions of the Church will have to take into account both
of these approaches, the right aim being, in our view, to establish the meaning
of these institutions in the *simultaneity* and mutual *interpenetration* (cf. notes
20 and 21 above) of Christology and Pneumatology. Cf. ch. III above.

importance of the head of each local community, the bishop.[90]
The role of the bishop as the visible center of the unity of
the eucharistic community is precisely what has made him so
vital for the unity of the Churches both in space and time.
This has happened under two forms: *apostolic succession* and
conciliarity.

Apostolic succession has again become a problem in theology because of an approach to the ministry in terms of
causality and objectified ontology. The bishop having acquired
the status of an office, regardless of his position in the community, became in the theology of apostolic succession an
individual who is linked with the apostles through a chain
of individual ordinations, and who is thus transmitting to the
other ministers below him grace and authority out of what
he has received and possesses. This view was found by the
Reformation tradition to involve a formalization and institutionalization of the ministry which was incompatible with the
freedom of the Spirit. Thus either the "baby was thrown away
with the bath-water" and the issue became one of "having"
or "not having" apostolic succession, or else it was given
meaning by making apostolic succession a matter of faithfulness to the truth.[91]

In the light of the Greek Fathers and of the perspective of
this study, our approach to this issue must be again through
the local community and the relational character of the ministry. On this basis the following observations could be made:
(a)   The bishop succeeds the apostles not in himself, i.e.
as an individual, but as the head of his community. That this
is the understanding of the early Church is to be seen in the
following facts: (i) Every episcopal ordination was conditioned by the naming of the community to which the bishop

[90]Related to this is the provision of the canons of the ancient Church that
every bishop must be ordained in the presence of at least two other bishops.
Cf. Hippolytus' *Apost. Trad.* 2. (ed. Botte, p. 4 f.), I Nicaea, canon 4, etc.
For a more detailed discussion see C. Vogel, "Unité de l'Eglise et pluralité
des formes historiques . . ." in *L'Episcopat et l'Eglise universelle* (ed. Y.
Congar et al., *Unam Sanctam* 39, 1962), pp. 601 ff., and L. Mortari, *Consacrazione episcopale e collegialità* (1969), pp. 33 ff.

[91]For a discussion of these problems cf. the symposium of Roman Catholic,
Protestant and Orthodox theologians: *Katholizität* (Beiheft zu *Kerygma und
Dogma* 2, 1971).

was assigned, and could not be *in absoluto*. The important thing is that this naming of the community appears in *the very prayer of ordination*,[92] which means that the bishop is *not first* made a bishop in a general sense and *then* assigned to a community, but that this assignment is inherent in the ordination itself. It is for this reason that the East could never distinguish the right of administration or jurisdiction from ordination itself.[93] (ii) Apostolic succession was from the beginning related to attempts at reconstructing episcopal lists. The fact that these lists were exclusively episcopal and never, for example, presbyteral is significant in that they point to the bishop's capacity as the head of his community and not as *depositum* of truth in himself. It is interesting to note that for the first three centuries, when these lists were diligently composed, the presbyters were regarded as the teachers of the people[94] while the bishop could even be a "silent" person in the community.[95] It is of course true that from the middle

[92]We should like to stress this point particularly because its implications are important in connection with note 89 above. It is noteworthy that even when the institution of the so-called "titular bishops"—who are essentially bishops without a flock—was introduced, provision was made that the name of the diocese, even from among those which no longer existed, would be mentioned in the prayer of ordination. This, of course, amounts to a contradiction between theory and practice in ecclesiology, but it nevertheless reveals that the Church has never admitted in her consciousness an episcopate which is not conditioned by a community *in its very roots* (prayer of ordination). If this is taken seriously into account, it becomes clear that a bishop is not *first* ordained as bishop of the universal Church and *then* "assigned" to a place within it, but he is a bishop of the universal Church only in and by becoming a bishop of a concrete community. Hence the perplexity of the Orthodox with regard to the "missio canonica." On this point, cf. P. Duprey, "The synodical structure of the Church in Eastern Orthodox Theology," *One in Christ* 7 (1971), 173 n. 60 and 176 f.

[93]With regard to Roman Catholic theology, cf. K. Rahner, *Church and Sacraments,* p. 103, n. 11. A certain departure from this distinction between sacramental order and jurisdiction is indicated in the new rite of ordination of the Roman Catholic Church, according to A. Houssiau, *op. cit.* p. 270. On the origination of this distinction in the West see G. Alberigo, *Lo Sviluppo della dottrina sui poteri nella Chiesa Universale* (1964), pp. 69 ff.

[94]See, for example, the prayer of ordination of the presbyter in Hippolytus *Apost. Trad.* 7 (ed. Botte, p. 20 f.). For more sources cf. J. D. Zizioulas in *Katholizität und Apostolizität* (see note 88 above), pp. 48 ff.

[95]Ignatius, *Philad.* 1, 2. Cf. *Katholizität* . . ., p. 48, n. 91. Also, H. Chadwick, "The silence of bishops in Ignatius," *The Harvard Theological Review,* 43 (1950), 169-172.

of the second century onwards the emphasis on the didactic function of the bishop becomes stronger,[96] but it was nevertheless felt always deeply that the Church is not a "school"[97] and that the successors of the apostles were not perpetuators of ideas like the heads of philosophical schools nor teachers in the same sense that the presbyters were. Being ordained to be the heads of their eucharistic communities, they were successors of the apostles precisely as spokesmen of these communities.

All this means that apostolic succession is essentially a matter of charismatic identification of the various communities in time. The *retrospective* dimension which is inevitably implied in this (= identity with the original apostolic Church) is not, therefore, to be isolated either from the *existential* (= the community here and now) or from the *prospective* one (= the future communities and the "last days" themselves). Linear historicism, like objectified ontology, becomes conditioned by the Spirit. The *anamnetic* faculty of the eucharistic community involves precisely a "remembrance" not only of the past but also of the future in the present.[98]

Similar observations must be made with regard to conciliarity, i.e. the unity of the Church in space. Here again our starting point is the local community, for the same existentially significant ecclesiological reasons. As we tried to show on another occasion,[99] the phenomenon of the "councils" cannot be historically understood apart from a primitive conciliarity which existed on the local level and which was not unrelated to the eucharistic community. Most of the early

[96]This is seen, for example, in the *Martyrium Polycarpi* 16, 2, in Irenaeus, etc.

[97]Hippolytus, *Philos.* 9, 12, 21, PG 15:3386: the "catholic Church" is not a "school" (*didaskaleion*).

[98]Cf. Liturgy of St John Chrysostom, prayer of the anaphora: *"Commemorating this command of our Savior and all that was endured for our sake, the cross, the grave, the resurrection after three days, the ascension into heaven, the enthronement at the right hand of the Father, and the second and glorious coming again, thine own of thine own we offer to Thee . . ."*

[99]J. D. Zizioulas, "The Development of Conciliar Structures to the Time of the First Ecumenical Council," in *Councils and the Ecumenical Movement* (World Council of Churches Studies 5, 1968), pp. 34-51.

councils, if not all of them, were concerned with eucharistic communion, mainly in the form of the problem of admitting persons excommunicated by one Church to communion in another.[100] or with the restoration of a broken eucharistic fellowship.[101] All this shows that no local Church could be a Church unless it was open to communion with the rest of the Churches. Schism between two or more Churches was as intolerable as divisions within one community, and conciliarity was concerned with that more than anything else.[102]

The fact that in this case again it was the bishop that became essentially the sole participant in the councils should be seen in the light of his position in the community and not in terms of individual authority. That this was so is to be seen in the following significant facts: (i) A tradition that survives up to now in the Eastern Orthodox Church—though unconsciously as to its rationale—provides that *only the diocesan bishops are allowed to vote in a synod*. This condition speaks loudly for the fact that a bishop is not a member of a council in himself but as the head of a community. To deprive of this right someone who is in all respects a "bishop" except in not heading a community,[103] would be absurd had it not been for the interpretation we are giving here, namely that a bishop participates in a council only as the head of his community. (ii) No decision of a council is authoritative in itself unless it is *received* by the communities. The question of "reception" of a council is extremely broad and complicated and it would fall beyond our present scope to discuss it here in detail.[104] It must be noted, however, that in an "individualistic" under-

[100]This situation is reflected by canon 5 of I Nicaea.

[101]Cf. the paschal controversies in the second century, as described by Eusebius, *Eccl. Hist.* V, 16, 10 and 28, 9, 9.

[102]All doctrinal decisions of the ancient Church ended with anathemas, i.e. excommunications from the eucharist. Eucharistic communion was the ultimate aim of doctrine, and not doctrine itself.

[103]The case of bishops who have been deprived of their communities by force, being in a certain sense under persecution, could not apply to this rule, which refers only to the "retired" and the so-called "titular" and "assistant" bishops.

[104]For an Orthodox discussion of this problem, see: L. Stan "Concerning the Church's Acceptance of the Decisions of Ecumenical Synods," in *Councils and the Ecumenical Movement* (see note 96 above), pp. 68-75. Cf. W. Küppers, "Reception, Prolegomena to a Systematic Study," *Ibid.* pp. 76-98.

standing of apostolic succession and the episcopate in general, "reception" as a condition for conciliarity can make no logical sense: if the bishops decide on the grounds that they possess this authority as individuals then their decisions do not in any sense depend on reception by the people, unless that is to say, the other extreme is followed and the theory is adopted that the bishops in council have an authority delegated by their flocks and are therefore accountable to them. In this latter case ordination as a charismatic thing (Irenaeus' *charisma veritatis*) would have nothing to do with conciliarity. Reception, on the other hand, organically related to conciliarity is inevitable when we think in terms of conciliarity as identity of the communities expressed in charismatic terms. It is thus not a juridical thing but a matter of charismatic *recognition*. It is for this reason that a true council becomes such only *a posteriori;* it is not an institution but an *event* in which the entire community participates and which shows whether or not its bishop has acted according to his *charisma veritatis*. From the point of view of the ministry of episcopate, this shows again how relational remains always what is given or rather realized in ordination.[105]

105We should like to emphasize the distinction between forms of ministry requiring ordination and institutions which are not based directly on ordination. Those among the Orthodox who speak of the synod as the "highest authority" in the Church must explain how there could be an authority which is not rooted in ordination. Only if we accept a distinction between *Amt* and *Geist*, or between *potestas ordinis* and *iurisdictionis*, can we speak of an authority which does not necessarily stem directly from ordination. But neither of these distinctions can be easily accepted by Eastern Orthodox theology. If there have been cases in the history of the Orthodox Church which make it difficult to avoid operating with these distinctions (see e.g. P. Duprey, *op. cit.,* p. 176), this does not mean that we should get our theological norms from these cases or that we should not at least try to understand these particular historical cases in the light of the main stream of the tradition. A study of this tradition as a whole shows that, at least in the East, a distinction was always made between "the dignity of honor or *taxis*" and that of "the power of the Spirit," i.e. of authority based on ordination. (This formulation of the distinction is made by Athanasius the Greek in a text of the year 1357 which is regarded as significant for the theology of communion by Y. Congar, *L'Eglise* . . ., p. 265). In the same spirit the Byzantine canonists interpreted the famous canon 34 of the "Apostolic Canons" (cf. P. Duprey, *op. cit.,* p. 154 f.). This is not the place for a discussion of the proper theological significance of the synodical system. Such a significance is not to be denied, but it should be properly integrated into the theology of ordination. Needless

V. *The "Validity" of the Ministry*

All that has been said so far leads to the question whether it is at all proper to speak of the "validity" of a certain ministry. "Validity" is basically a juridical term, and it implies that the ministry can be isolated from the rest of ecclesiology and be judged in itself. This notion implies, furthermore, that there can be objective criteria, such as "faith" or "historical apostolic succession" etc., that can form the norms for such a judgment. Such an approach would tend to undermine the fact that all these "criteria" originally formed an integral and organic part of the concrete community, especially in its eucharistic form. Their meaning, therefore, depends constantly on their natural context, which is the community. We have seen, for example, how this is the case with apostolic succession. The same must be remembered with regard to "faith": the "symbols" or "confessions" of faith were not in the early Church autonomous statements, as they are today in dogmatic manuals, but integral parts of the life and especially the worship of the community; they started as baptismal creeds and were adopted and used again as confessions for baptismal and eucharistic use. The great methodological error in the classical theories of "validity" therefore is that they tend to go to the unity of the community via these criteria, as if the latter could be conceived before and regardless of the community itself.

If, as we have insisted in this paper, we do not isolate the ministry from the reality of the community created by the *koinonia* of the Holy Spirit, what "validates" a certain ministry is to be found not in isolated and objectified "norms" but in *the community* to which this ministry belongs. It may be argued that the community is something we cannot grasp and deal with and we shall therefore sooner or later arrive at the procedure of "criteria." But to arrive at a certain judgment by considering the community first is essentially different from looking at the community through the spectacles of isolated "criteria."

to say that this subject is of extreme importance in the theological discussions between Roman Catholics and Orthodox.

The first and fundamental consequence of the method of
looking at the community first and then at the criteria is
that the recognition of ministries becomes in fact a *recognition
of communities* in an existential sense. Thus one's primary
question in facing another ministry would be a question concerning *the entire structure of the community* to which it
belongs. When we say "structure" we do not mean a certain
institution as such but the way in which a community relates
itself to God, to the world and to the other communities.
Baptism, for example, is to be seen as a prerequisite for
recognition of a ministry because it determines the entire
structure of the community and the way it relates both to
God and the world. Thus it is obvious, at least from the point
of view of the theological perspective we are using in this
study, that a fundamentally different way of a community's
relating to God and the world amounts to making this community "unrecognizable" by other communities, not juridically
but existentially. This is due to the fact that Church structure
and the ministry are not simply matters of convenient and
efficient arrangements, but "modes of being," *ways of relating*
between God, the Church and the world. The various forms
of ministry may differ at times and at places provided that
they do not introduce or imply a fundamentally different way
of the Church's relating herself to God and the world. This
means that a difference in ministerial form *as such* cannot
determine the recognition of a ministry: the history of the
Church has plenty of such examples to offer. At the same
time, however, this means that not every form of ministry
would do for the expression of the Church's right relation
with God and the world. Plurality and diversity of ministerial
forms cannot be made a necessary implication of the existential and eschatological conditioning of the past structures,[106]
a conditioning on which we have insisted in this study. Just
as the baptismal *structure* of the community is not basically
changed by this conditioning, so in the same way the eucharistic *structure* must be understood as implying something
permanent, its permanence being dictated precisely by its

[106]As it seems to be the case with W. Pannenberg, *op. cit.*, p. 106 f.

existential and eschatological nature. Similarly, it is not possible to avoid structures that express in a relational existential and eschatological way the identity of each community with those of the past, especially with the original apostolic communities, and with those of the present, implying a constant openness to the future.[107] To take an example, the real issue between the episcopally and the non-episcopally structured communities of today would become in this approach whether or not episcopacy is essential to the Church's proper relation with God and the world, i.e. whether or not a community with episcopacy can feel an existential identity with a community which has no episcopacy.[108] It is in this sense that recognizing a ministry is a matter of recognizing a community.

If we follow this line, it is evident that the issue of "validity" of orders cannot be approached from the angle of "economy" (οἰκονομία), as it has often been done by Orthodox theologians. The entire idea of "economy" is itself extremely obscure[109] and its actual application in history so complex[110] that it becomes extremely difficult to use it as a principle in deciding for the "validity" of orders. But more important than that is the fact that "validity" is not something to be graciously, as it were, *granted* by one who "has" to one who "has not." Such an approach to the ministry will make it again an objectified thing and would imply the unacceptable principle that the Church may recognize a sacramental reality which does not in fact exist.[111] If, according to our approach in this study, recognition is not a juridical but an existential matter, and if the ministry is not a matter of "arrangement" but of the fundamental relational nature of the Church, then

---

[107]Cf. the significant remarks of W. Pannenberg, *ibid.,* concerning the three points "on which every contemporary claim to catholicity must prove itself."

[108]The study of J. J. von Allmen, *Le saint ministère . . ., passim* and especially pp. 213 ff. is most illuminating on this point.

[109]Cf. H. Alivisatos, *op. cit.*

[110]Cf. K. Duchatelez, "L'économie baptismale dans l'Eglise Orthodoxe," *Istina* 16 (1971), 13-36; also "La notion d'économie et ses richesses théologiques," in *Nouvelle revue théologique* 92 (1970), 267-292.

[111]H. Alivisatos, *op. cit.,* p. 77 and G. Florovsky, "The doctrine of the Church and the Ecumenical Problem," *The Ecumenical Review* 2 (1950), 159 f.

recognizing a ministry falls outside the scope of any dispensational approach. "Economy" is indeed a vital tool in pastoral care, especially for a Church such as the Orthodox that has to deal with canons of a past age, not adjusted to the present. But the recognition of orders is a matter not of strict canonical arrangements but of ecclesiology in its fullest sense.

It is not our purpose in this study to offer practical suggestions as to how the problem of "validity" of orders can be solved. Others might draw better than we could any practical implications that may exist in the approach to the ministry we have tried to establish here.[112] What is sufficient for the object of this study is to indicate where the problem should be placed and what theological issues it involves. From this point of view our inquiry in this study shows that a reconsideration of the approach to the problem of the ministry may be necessary. Instead of trying to recognize each other's "orders" as such, the divided communities of our time should rather try to recognize each other as ecclesial *communties* relating to God and the world through their ministries in the way that is implied in the mystery of Christ and the Spirit. This is not a matter of "confessional" agreements, but of a more existential *rapprochement* to which divided Christendom is called.

---

[112]Cf. for example, the remarks offered by Y. Congar, "Quelques problèmes touchant les ministères," in *Nouvelle revue théologiques* 93 (1971), 795 f., and G. Tavard, "The Function of the Minister in the Eucharistic celebration," *Journal of Ecumenical Studies* 4 (1967), 629-649, which appear to be of interest from the viewpoint of the present study.

7.

The Local Church
In a Perspective of Communion

I. *The Historical and Ecclesiological Background*

The basic ecclesiological principle applying to the notion of the local Church in the Orthodox tradition is that of the identification of the Church with the eucharistic community. Orthodox ecclesiology is based on the idea that wherever there is the eucharist there is the Church in its fulness as the Body of Christ. The concept of the local Church derives basically from the fact that the eucharist is celebrated at a given place and comprises by virtue of its catholicity *all* the members of the Church dwelling in that place. The local Church, therefore, derives its meaning from a combination of two basic ecclesiological principles:

(a) *The catholic nature of the eucharist.* This means that each eucharistic assembly should include *all* the members of the Church of a particular place, with no distinction whatsoever with regard to ages, professions, sexes, races, languages, etc.

(b) *The geographical nature of the eucharist,* which means that the eucharistic assembly—and through it the Church—is always a community of *some place* (e.g. the Church of Thessalonika, of Corinth, etc. in the Pauline letters).[1]

---

[1]The preposition "in" is also used in the Pauline letters in connection with the local Church. The significance of this way of speaking lies in the idea that the Church "dwells" in a geographical place as a "visitor" (πάροικος).

The combination of the above two ecclesiological principles results in the canonical provision that there should be only one eucharistic assembly in each place. But the geographical principle gives rise inevitably to the question of what we mean by a "place": how are we to define the limits of a particular place which should be the basis of only one eucharistic assembly and thus of one Church? This question receives particular significance when the complexities of the early historical developments are taken into account. Since the Orthodox tradition was formed, both ecclesiologically and canonically, on the basis of these early historical developments, we must examine them briefly.

Already in New Testament times there seems to be a tendency to identify ἐκκλησία or even the ἐκκλησία τοῦ Θεοῦ with the assembly of the Christians of a particular *city*. From a study especially of the Pauline letters we are led to the conclusion that almost without exception the word ἐκκλησία is used in the singular when applied to a city, whereas its use in the plural is always connected with geographic areas larger than the city. If this is not to be regarded as a mere accident, it becomes significant to ask: why does Paul *never* use the term Church in plural when referring to a city? Given the concreteness with which the word ἐκκλησία is used in Paul's writings, where it normally means the actual assembly of the faithful (see e.g. I Cor. 10-14), the conclusion is almost inevitable that there was only one such assembly which was named ἐκκλησία. In other words, we must conclude that the earliest form of local Church we know of is that of *the Church of a city,* and that the concrete form of this city Church is the assembly that comprises *all* the Christians of that geographical area. Christianity seems to have appeared first as a city Church and if we read rightly the existing sources, it must have remained such until at least the middle of the second century.[2]

This is closely connected with the *eschatological nature* of the eucharist to which we shall refer again.

[2] If Justin's evidence in his *I Apology* (ch. 65) means that the Christians of the villages outside Rome would go to the city for the Sunday eucharistic assembly, it would appear that in spite of practical difficulties even in a Church as large as that of Rome in the second century the principle which is

The first complication with regard to the principle: one Church—one eucharist—one city, arises historically with the concept of the κατ' οἶκον ἐκκλησία (household Church). If this term meant in fact the formation of an ἐκκλησία on the basis of the unit of the *family,* then we are confronted with a definition of the local Church in a non-geographic sense; we are in fact faced with a *sociological* conception of "locality." I have tried elsewhere[3] to examine this problem and I can only repeat here my conclusion that the term κατ' οἶκον ἐκκλησία in the New Testament does not point to a family-centered gathering but rather to the assembly of all the faithful of a city who meet as *guests of a particular house* (see Rom. 16:23, cf. the archeological evidence of churches named after house-owners in Rome, etc.). One could even claim that there seems to have been no more than one such "household Church" in each city at that time.[4] If these conclusions are right, we can explain why there is no evidence of any major difficulty in connection with the organization of the early Church stemming from the "household churches." Not only the fact but even the name of the household Church disappears very soon, leaving behind no trace of a situation which would suggest an alternative to the identification of the early local Church with the Church of a city.

Far more serious in its implications and consequences for the concept of the local Church has been another development in early Church organization, namely the emergence of the *parish,* both in its rural and in its urban form. The details of the historical developments with regard to this problem do not concern us here.[5] What is of crucial importance, however, for the understanding of the local Church in the Ortho-

emphasized by Ignatius of Antioch, that there should be only one eucharist under one bishop in each place, seems to be observed. This seems to be the case until the village Christians acquire their own bishops (the *chorepiscopoi*) which are witnessed for the first time in the second century.

[3]In my book *The Unity of the Church in the Eucharist and the Bishop in the First Three Centuries* (1965—in Greek).

[4]The existing evidence is rather obscure but it is noteworthy that there is not a single case where the term "household Church" would appear more than once with reference to the same city in the same text.

[5]For a detailed discussion of this complex historical problem, cf. my above mentioned book.

dox tradition is the question whether the parish could be called in fact a "local Church." The complication arises out of two basic considerations:

(i) *The ecclesiological principle of the identification of the Church with the eucharist,* or rather with the eucharistic community. Since the parish is precisely a eucharistic community, it becomes almost imperative to call the parish an ἐκκλησία.

(ii) *The episcopal ministry.* The office of the bishop in the early Church is essentially that of the president of the eucharistic assembly. All the liturgical and canonical elements in the ordination of the bishop presuppose the primitive situation whereby there was in each eucharistic assembly— and by extension in each city Church— *one* bishop (all bishops' names in the early Church, beginning with the times of Ignatius of Antioch, bear connection with a particular *city*), who was surrounded by the *college* of the presbyters (he was in fact one of the presbyters himself) and was called "presbyter" for a long time (cf. Irenaeus). What the emergence of the parish did was to destroy this structure, a destruction which affected not only the episcopal office but also that of the presbyter. For it meant that from then on the eucharist did not require the presence of the presbyters as a *college*— an essential aspect of the original significance of the presbyterium—in order to exist as local Church. An *individual* presbyter was thus enough to create and lead a eucharistic gathering—a parish. Could that gathering be called "Church"?

The answer to this question has been historically a negative one with regard to the Orthodox Church. I personally regard this as a fortunate thing for the following reason: the creation of the parish as a presbytero-centric unity, *not in the original and ecclesiologically correct form which we might describe as "presbyterium-centered,"* but in the sense of an *individual* presbyter acting as head of a eucharistic community, damaged ecclesiology seriously in two respects. On the one hand, it destroyed the image of the Church as a community in which *all* orders are necessary as *constitutive* elements. The parish as it finally prevailed in history made redundant both the deacon and the bishop. (Later, with the private mass, it made redundant even the laity.) On the other hand, and as a result of that, it led to an understanding of the bishop as an administrator rather than a eucharistic president, and the presbyter as a "mass-specialist," a "priest" —thus leading to the medieval ecclesiological decadence in the West, and to the well-known reactions of the Reformation, as well as to a grave confusion in the ecclesiological and canonical life of the Eastern Churches themselves.

It is for these reasons that we should regard the proper ecclesiological status of the parish as one of the most fundamental problems in ecclesiology—both in the West and in the East. The Orthodox Church, in my understanding at least, has opted for the view that the concept of the local Church is guaranteed *by the bishop* and not by the presbyter: the local Church as an entity with full ecclesiological status is the *episcopal diocese* and not the parish. By so doing the Orthodox Church has unconsciously brought about a rupture in its own eucharistic ecclesiology. For it is no longer possible to equate every eucharistic celebration with the local Church. But at the same time by so opting it has allowed for the hope to exist for the restoration of the communal nature of the local Church, according to which the local Church can be called ἐκκλησία only when it is truly catholic, i.e. when it includes (a) the laymen of all cultural, linguistic, social and other identities living in that place, and (b) all the other orders of the Church as parts of the same community. Thus one can hope that one day the bishop will find his proper place which is the eucharist, and the rupture in eucharistic ecclesiology caused by the problem "parish-diocese" will be healed in the right way.[6]

[6]In practical terms the only proper solution would be the creation of *small* episcopal dioceses. This would be an excellent thing from many points of view. For example: (a) it would enable bishops really to know their flocks and be known by them, which would automatically improve the pastoral quality of episcopacy; (b) it would reduce the load of administration which the bishops have at present, thus enabling them to function primarily as presidents of the eucharist which is their ministry *par excellence;* (c) it would make it possible for the *collegial* character of the presbyterium to reappear in the extremely significant ecclesiological sense it had in the ancient times (cf. the *synthronon* of the ancient cathedrals), which would strengthen the much weakened importance of the presbyter, especially in the Orthodox Church; (d) it would make it unnecessary to maintain the scandalously uncanonical institution of the

With the development of the metropolitan system and gradually of that of the patriarchates in the ancient Church the center of "local" unity was shifted from the episcopal diocese to larger geographical units comprising the dioceses of a province under the headship of the bishop of the metropolis of that province. This development, which survives only nominally today in Orthodoxy (cetrain bishops are called "metropolitans" but in fact the metropolis as an entity does not exist any longer, having disappeared together with the ancient Roman or Byzantine province), has not essentially altered the view of the local Church as identical with the episcopal diocese. The metropolitan system having developed in close connection with the synodal practice in the ancient Church represented an "occasional" or "casual" sort of Church "localization," coinciding with the meetings of the synods. As the principle of *the essential equality of all bishops* became a basic feature in Orthodox canon law, neither the metropolitans nor the patriarchs ever reached the position of heads of *particular ecclesial units* representing structures *above* or *besides* the episcopal diocese. Permanent synods do exist in the Orthodox Churches, but they are never understood as separate ecclesial "bodies" which could be called "local Churches." With the development of the famous theory of the *pentarchy* in Byzantium, a system emerged in Orthodoxy whereby the entire οἰκουμένη comprised five divisions (patriarchates). But in spite of efforts made by some modern Orthodox to give to the patriarchates the name of "local Church," the principle of the equality of all bishops from the point of view of ecclesiological status has made it again impossible to create a special *ecclesial* entity out of the patriarchate.[7]

assistant bishop, which is a modern western invasion into the Orthodox tradition. The existence of small episcopal dioceses is clearly evidenced by ancient tradition (when Gregory the Wonderworker became bishop of Neocaesarea he had only seventeen faithful in his diocese!).

[7]I maintain the view that the *ecclesial* status of any unit in the Orthodox Church other than the episcopal diocese does not derive from the unit itself but from the episcopal diocese or dioceses involved. This applies not only— as we have seen—to units smaller than the diocese (e.g. the parish), but also to larger ones. Thus, a metropolis, an archdiocese or a patriarchate cannot be called a *Church* in itself, but only *by extension,* i.e. by virtue of the fact

Finally, in this historical survey we must mention the idea of *autocephaly* by which the Orthodox Church is mainly known today. The principle of autocephaly is based on the modern concept of the nation, as it was developed mainly in the last century. According to this principle, the Orthodox Church in each nation is governed by its own synod without interference from any other Church and has its own head (patriarch, archbishop or metropolitan). In the present state of theological confusion in which Orthodoxy finds itself, it is customary to call these autocephalous churches "local Churches" and thus very often allow for the possibility to have the episcopal diocese so absorbed by the entity called "autocephalous Church" as to bypass it entirely through either a permanent synod or the head of the autocephalous Church, neither of which is always truly representative of all the dioceses—local Churches of that particular area.[8]

II.   *Questions Concerning the Theology of the Local Church Today*

1.   *Ecclesiality and Locality*

The term "local Church" comprises two aspects corresponding to the words of the term, neither of which should be taken without the other. The first aspect is that of *locality;* the other is that of *ecclesiality.* If these aspects are taken together, the question that must be constantly raised is the following twofold one: what makes a Church "local" and what makes a local body "Church"? For not every gathering

that it is based on one or more episcopal dioceses—local Churches which are the only ones on account of the episcopal eucharist properly called Churches. This also means that a metropolitan, patriarch etc. owes his ecclesiological status to the fact that he is the head of a particular local Church.

[8]In order to avoid turning the autocephalous Church into a unity deriving its ecclesiality from itself and not from the episcopal dioceses it involves (cf. previous note), it is necessary for the head of each autocephalous Church to be surrounded by a synod of bishops belonging to that area. However, this synod should be representative of all the episcopal dioceses of the area. Wherever circumstances permit it, all bishops either simultaneously or by way of rotation should be members of such a synod.

254 BEING AS COMMUNION

of Christians is automatically "Church" and not every Church is necessarily "local." If we apply the perspective of eucharistic ecclesiology to this question, we are led to the following remarks:

(a)   The Church is local when the saving event of Christ takes root in a particular local situation with all its natural, social, cultural and other characteristics which make up the life and thought of the people living in that place. Just as it happens in the eucharist where the people offer to God as the Body of Christ all that is "His own" (the fruits of the earth together with the products of their everyday labor), the same must apply to the Church's life, if it is to be truly local: it must absorb and use all the characteristics of a given local situation and not impose an alien culture on it.

(b)   But this absorption and use of local culture may make a Church local but not necessarily Church. For the saving event of Christ does not purely and simply affirm human culture; it is also critical of it.[9] What aspects of culture are to be excluded from absorption and use by the local church, if it is to be not just local, but also "Church"? The answer to this question depends on the theology one holds in general and on one's priorities as to what is essential or not in the Christian faith. If the eucharistic perspective is allowed to play a decisivie role in this case, the criteria of ecclesiality can be reduced to no more than the following one.

The eucharist is the moment in the Church's life where the anticipation of the *eschata* takes place. The *anamnesis* of Christ is realized not as a mere re-enactment of a past event but as an *anamnesis of the future*,[10] as an eschatological event. In the eucharist the Church becomes a reflection of the eschatological community of Christ, the Messiah, an image of the Trinitarian life of God. In terms of human existence this

---

[9]This is indicated by the fact that the eucharist is preceded by baptism. The world cannot become Church without some kind of purification.

[10]Cf. the thesis of J. Jeremias in his *The Eucharistic Words of Jesus* with regard to the New Testament. The ancient liturgies (e.g. those of John Chrysostom, Basil etc.) preserve exactly the same interpretation of *"anamnesis"* when they speak of "remembering" in the eucharist not only the past events of salvation history but also the *second coming*. This *remembering of the future* is an essential aspect of the eucharist.

mainly means one thing: the transcendence of all divisions, both natural and social, which keep the existence of the world in a state of disintegration, fragmentation, decomposition and hence of death. All cultures in one way or other share in this fallen and disintegrated world, and therefore all of them include elements which need to be transcended. If the Church in its localization fails to present an image of the Kingdom in this respect, it is not a Church. Equally, if the eucharistic gathering is not such an image, it is not the eucharist in a true sense.[11]

With such existential criteria in mind we can be more specific by asking the question: what concrete form should a local Church take in order to be both "local" and "Church"? Here the following structural elements become essential.

(a) If in a given locality there is more than one cultural element—as is the case, for example, in many of our modern pluralistic societies—the Church should make efforts to reach these elements through its missionary activity by making full use of such cultural elements in the preaching of the Gospel. In these efforts it may be necessary to form groups and assemblies of people sharing the same cultural elements for a further deepening of the understanding of the Gospel. The same can be true in cases where pastoral and not simply missionary purposes prevail. In order to meet the needs of people who work in places other than the ones they live in, similar assemblies can be formed to relate the Gospel to particular professional and intellectual or social conditions.

(b) These groups or assemblies formed on the basis of a particular culture, class, profession or age should learn to regard themselves *not* as Churches, and be taught to seek the experience of the *Church* only in gatherings where *all* ages, sexes, professions, cultures etc. meet, for this is what the Gospel promises us to be the Kingdom of God: a place where all the natural and cultural divisions are transcended. Insofar as the eucharist is regarded to be such—and only such—an

[11]A eucharist which discriminates between races, sexes, ages, professions, social classes etc. violates not certain ethical principles but its eschatological nature. For that reason such a eucharist is not a "bad"—i.e. morally deficient —eucharist but no eucharist at all. It cannot be said to be the body of the One who sums up all into Himself.

eschatologically inspired gathering, its celebration must be reserved for this kind of experience alone. And insofar as the Church reflects in her nature this eschatological destiny portrayed in the eucharist, only such gatherings should be named "Church." Other gatherings are not unrelated to the Church or eucharist; they are extensions of the reality of the Church. But they lack the element of catholicity which is suggested by the eschatological nature of both Church and eucharist and could not be called Churches.

(c) This kind of approach to the ecclesiality of the local Church puts the *geographical* aspect of locality in an advantageous position compared with other aspects of "locality," such as culture or profession. For the geographic "place" can serve as the common ground for the meeting of the various cultural and other elements ἐπὶ τὸ αὐτό, "in the same place"—an expression so significantly used for both Church and eucharist in the New Testament as an expression of *geographical* locality. In this kind of approach the geographical aspect of locality appears to be an indispensable element in the concept of the local Church.

(d) A ministry of such a local unity is necessary if this transcendence of natural and cultural divisions is to take place. Whether one calls this ministry episcopacy or otherwise is irrelevant for the theology of the local Church. What appears to be necessary in view of what we have just said is that the ministry should be tied up with (i) the eucharistic assembly as its head, and (ii) a particular geographic area. It is only if these two conditions are kept that the office of the bishop can make sense to ecclesiology.[12] Other ministries of local unity such as the presbyterium and the deacons become essential elements, depending on the "typology" of the eschatological community one regards as fundamental to one's theology.[13] But certainly the gathering of the *laos* in its en-

[12]These two conditions were faithfully kept in the ancient Church. They have been seriously obscured if not at times disregarded in later developments and practice in the Orthodox Churches themselves.

[13]It was, for example, an indispensable part of the ecclesiological consciousness of the early Church to have a ministry portraying the apostles surrounding Christ and "judging the twelve tribes" of the New Israel. This gave rise to the ministry of the presbyters (cf. Ignatius of Antioch etc.). To the extent

tirety—i.e. in all its "local" aspects—is an indispensable form of local Church structure. For it is this that proves the Church to be "catholic." Without some form of "congregationality" there is no local catholicity.

2. *Locality and Universality*

From what has just been said it follows that the "catholicity" of the Church is not to be juxtaposed to locality: it is rather an indispensable aspect *of the local Church,* the ultimate criterion of ecclesiality for any local body. Universality, however, is a different notion and can certainly be contrasted with locality. How does the concept of universality affect our understanding of the local Church?

It is in the nature of the eucharist to transcend not only divisions occurring within a local situation but also the very division which is inherent in the concept of geography: the division of the world into local places. Just as a eucharist which is not a transcendance of divisions within a certain locality is a false eucharist, equally a eucharist which takes place in conscious and intentional isolation and separation from other local communities in the world is not a true eucharist.[14] From that it follows inevitably that a local Church, in order to be not just local but also Church, must be in full communion with the rest of the local Churches in the world.

For a local Church to be in full communion with the rest of local Churches the following elements are involved:

(a)   That the problems and concerns of all local Churches should be the objects of prayer and active care by a particular local Church. If a local Church falls into indifference as to what is going on in the rest of the world, it is certainly not a Church.

(b)   That a certain common basis of the vision and understanding of the Gospel and the eschatological nature of the Church exist between a local Church and the rest of the local

that this consciousness survives in the Church, the institution of the presbyters acquires its indispensability in the structure of the local Church.

[14]For a detailed discussion see ch. 4 above.

Churches. This requires a constant vigilance concerning the true faith in all local Churches by every single local Church.

(c)   That certain structures be provided which will facilitate this communion. On this point some further explanations become necessary.

If the locality of the Church is not to be absorbed and in fact negated by the element of universality, the utmost care must be taken so that the structures of ministries which are aimed at facilitating communion among the local Churches do not become a superstructure over the local Church. It is extremely significant that in the entire course of church history there has never been an attempt at establishing a super-local eucharist or a super-local bishop. All eucharists and all bishops are local in character—at least in their primary sense. In a eucharistic view of the Church this means that the local Church, as defined earlier here, is the only form of ecclesial existence which can be properly called Church. All structures aiming at facilitating the universality of the Church create a *network of communion of Churches, not a new form of Church*.[15] This is not only supported by history, but rests also upon sound theological and existential ground. Any structural universalization of the Church to the point of creating an ecclesial entity called "universal Church" as something parallel to or above that of the local Church would inevitably introduce into the concept of the Church cultural and other dimensions which are foreign to a particular local context. Culture cannot be a monolithically universal phenomenon without some kind of demonic imposition of one culture over the rest of cultures. Nor is it possible to dream of a universal "Christian culture" without denying the dialectic between history and eschatology which is so central, among other things, to the eucharist itself. Thus, if there is a transcendence of cultural divisions on a universal level—which indeed must

[15]This is not to deny that there is only *one* Church in the world. But the oneness of the Church in the world does not constitute a structure besides or *above* the local churches. Any ecclesial communion on the universal level should draw its forms from the local Church reality. It is not an accident that the synods according to Orthodox canon law are composed only of *diocesan* bishops. All forms of ministry of universal ecclesial communion should have some local Church as its basis.

be constantly aimed at by the Church—it can only take place *via* the local situations expressed in and through the particular local Churches and not through universalistic structures which imply a universal Church. For a universal Church as an entity besides the local Church would be either a culturally dis-incarnated Church—since there is no such a thing as universal culture—or alternatively it would be culturally incarnated in a demonic way, if it either blesses or directly or indirectly imposes on the world a particular culture.

In conclusion, all church structures aiming at facilitating communion between local Churches (e.g. synods, councils of all forms etc.) do possess ecclesiological significance and must be always viewed in the light of ecclesiology. But they cannot be regarded as forms of *Church* without the serious dangers I have just referred to.

3. *The Local Church in a Context of Division*

Our actual situation in the Church is more seriously complicated by the fact that the local Church has to be conceived in a context of confessional division. The concept of the Church as a confessional entity (Orthodox, Anglican, Lutheran etc.) is historically a late phenomenon and has come to complicate the ecclesiological situation to an alarming degree. For in addition to a cultural pluralism we are now faced with a confessional pluralism on the local level. Can we draw a parallel and apply what we said about cultural transcendence also to confessional pluralism? Can we say that as the eucharist brings together Jew and Greek, male and female, black and white, it should also bring together Anglican and Lutheran and Orthodox etc. in a certain local area? In fact this is what the practice of intercommunion implies. The objections to this practice by the Orthodox are well-known and I do not wish to repeat the same arguments here. I should simply like to raise two questions bearing on the nature of the local Church.

(a)   Has a confessional body *per se* the right to be regarded as Church? If the condition of ecclesiality is to be inseparably linked with that of locality, the answer is definitely negative. A Church must incarnate people, not ideas or beliefs. A confessional Church is the most disincarnate entity there is; this is precisely why its content is usually borrowed from one or other of the existing cultures and is not a *locality* which critically embraces all cultures.

(b)   Can a local Church be regarded as truly local and truly Church if it is in a state of confessional division? This is an extremely difficult question. If the notion of the local Church with all the implications we have mentioned here is to be taken into account—if in other words the Church is a true Church only if it is a local event incarnating Christ and manifesting the Kingdom in a particular place—we must be prepared to question the ecclesial status of *confessional* churches as such, and begin to work on the basis of the nature of the local Church. This cannot be done overnight, for confessionalism is rooted deeply in our history. But we must be ready to admit that as long as confessionalism prevails no real progress towards ecclesial unity can be made. Taking the reality of the local Church and its theology more seriously than we have done so far may prove to be of extreme importance to the ecumenical movement.

List of Sources

The Introduction was first published in French as the Introduction to the book *L'être ecclésial,* (Labor et Fides, Geneva 1981), and translated into English by John Clarke and Elizabeth Templeton.

Chapter I was first published in Greek in *Charisterion,* volume in honor of Metropolitan Meliton of Chalcedon, Institute of Patristic Studies, Thessalonika, 1977. It was also published in French in *L'être ecclésial.* The present text is a translation from the original Greek by Norman Russell.

Chapter II was first published in French in *Irenikon* 50 (1977) as "Verité et Communion dans la perspective de la pensée patristique grecque." The present English text is a translation from the French by Dr. P. J. Bussey.

Chapter III appears for the first time in English here. It was given as a contribution to the Symposium organized jointly by the University of Louvain and the "Istituto per le scienze religiose" of Bologna on the perspectives of Ecclesiology after Vatican II, and was published first in Italian in *Cristianesimo nella Storia 2 (1981).*

Chapter IV was first published in French as "La communauté eacharistique et la catholicité de l'Eglise" in *Istina* 14 (1969) and then in German in W. Pannenberg *et al. Katholizität und Apostolizität* (Beiheft zu *Kerygma und Dogma* No 2 [1971]). In English it appeared first in *One in Christ* vol. 6, 1970.

Chapter V was originally given as a paper for the "Academie Internationale des Sciences religieuses" in 1974 and was published in the Proceedings of the Academy and in *Istina* 19 (1974) under the title "La continuité avec les origines apostoliques dans la conscience théologique des églises orthodoxes." In English it appeared first in *St Vladimir's Theological Quarterly* 19 (1975).

Chapter VI appears for the first time here in English. It was first published in German as a contribution to the series *Questiones Disputatae,* ed. by K. Rahner and H. Schlier, vol. 50, 1973 under the title "Priesteramt und Priesterweihe im Licht der östlich-orthodoxen Theologie."

Chapter VII was first published in English as a contribution to the volume *In Each Place,* a publication of the World Council of Churches (Faith and Order), Geneva, 1977.

Index*

Afanasiev, N.A., 23, 24, 25, 132, 133, 145n., 155n., 156n., 194n., 196n., 201n., 226n.
Agourides, S., 49n.
Alberigo, G., 239n.
Alivisatos, H., 98n., 233n., 245n.
Allmen, J. J. von, 145n., 158n., 163n., 203n., 213n., 221n., 245n.
Andresen, C. 70n.
Androutsos, Chr., 233n.
Aristophanes, 62n.
Aristotle, 17, 28, 29n., 31n., 38n., 71n., 79, 85n., 95n., 118, 154n.
Arnim, J. ab, 30n., 32n.
Athanasius of Alexandria, 16, 17, 36n., 38n., 83ff., 87, 89n., 94n., 100, 111n., 120n., 121n., 134, 190
Athanasius the Greek, 242n.
Audet, J. P., 144n.
Augustine, 25, 41n., 88, 95, 100, 101n., 104n., 144n., 182n., 200n., 214n., 220n., 235

Balthazar, H. U. von, 130n.
Bardy, G., 144n.
Barlaam, 212n.
Barr, J., 67n.
Barreau, H., 71n.
Barth, K., 45n.
Basil of Caesarea, 17, 40, 41, 88n., 94n., 111n., 134, 160n., 179n., 182n., 235, 254n.
Batiffol, P., 144n.
Benoit, A., 190n.
Berdyaev, N., 164n., 226n.
Bevenot, M., 144n.
Bobrinskoy, B., 125f.
Bonhoeffer, D., 110n., 212n.
Botte, B., 157n., 196n.

---

*With the kind co-operation of the Rev Father Stamatis Skliris and Mrs. Marina Skliris.

Bouyer, L., 127n.
Brown, R. E., 130n.
Buber, M., 17, 165n., 226n.
Bultmann, R., 181n.
Bussey, P. J., 120n.

Camelot, Th., 144n.
Canones Apostolorum, 135, 223n., 233n.
Casel, O., 145n., 213n.
Celsus, 70n.
Cerfaux, L., 174n.
Chadwick, H., 74n., 94n., 190n., 239n.
Chrysippus, 32n.
Chrysostom, John, 143n., 160n., 169n., 199n., 210n., 220n., 228, 230,
    233n., 237n., 240n., 254n.
Cicero, 34n.
Clayton, L. P., 38n., 85n.
Clement of Alexandria, 16, 69n. 72, 74f. 167n.
Clement of Rome, 146, 153n., 167n., 176f., 192, 194n., 195n., 196n.,
    199, 216n.
Clement, O., 161n.
Cochrane, C. N., 69n.
Colson, J., 173n., 202n.
Congar, Y., 111n., 123, 124n., 127, 171n., 174n., 178n., 179n., 189n.,
    194n., 197n., 200n., 202n., 209n., 211n., 215n., 220n., 233n.,
    242n., 246n.
Constitutiones Apostolorum, 113n., 177n., 195n., 204, 230
Cothenet, E., 215n.
Craig, C. T., 148n.
Cross, F. L., 28n., 83n.
Crouzel, H., 76n.
Cullmann, O., 98n., 230n.
Cyprian, 144n., 152n., 155, 156n., 165n., 168n., 200f., 203, 204n.
Cyril of Alexandria, 55, 94n., 109n., 111n., 130n., 190, 228f., 243n.
Cyril of Jerusalem, 113n., 144n., 161n., 214n., 235n., 236n.

Dalmais, I. H. 96n.
Daniélou, J., 74n., 75n.
Didache, 62n., 144n., 146, 155, 174n., 187n., 193
Didascalia Apostolorum, 155n., 177n., 195n., 204, 230
Dionysius the Areopagite, 44n., 86, 90n., 91, 92n., 210n., 214n., 217,
    223n., 234n.
Dionysius of Halicarnassus, 143n.
Dix, G., 128n., 145n., 167n., 198n., 213n.
Dodds, E. R., 30n.
Dositheus of Jerusalem, 233n.
Dostoevsky, F. M., 42, 43, 51n., 108n.